THE UNBEARABLE SAKI

THE UNBEARABLE SAKI

The Work of H. H. Munro

SANDIE BYRNE

OXFORD
UNIVERSITY PRESS

OXFORD
UNIVERSITY PRESS

Great Clarendon Street, Oxford OX2 6DP

Oxford University Press is a department of the University of Oxford.
It furthers the University's objective of excellence in research, scholarship,
and education by publishing worldwide in

Oxford New York

Auckland Cape Town Dar es Salaam Hong Kong Karachi
Kuala Lumpur Madrid Melbourne Mexico City Nairobi
New Delhi Shanghai Taipei Toronto

With offices in

Argentina Austria Brazil Chile Czech Republic France Greece
Guatemala Hungary Italy Japan Poland Portugal Singapore
South Korea Switzerland Thailand Turkey Ukraine Vietnam

Oxford is a registered trade mark of Oxford University Press
in the UK and in certain other countries

Published in the United States
by Oxford University Press Inc., New York

British Library Cataloguing in Publication Data
Data available

Library of Congress Cataloging in Publication Data
Data available

Typeset by Laserwords Private Limited, Chennai, India
Printed in Great Britain
on acid-free paper by
Biddles Ltd., King's Lynn, Norfolk

ISBN 978-0-19-922605-4

1 3 5 7 9 10 8 6 4 2

Hynn ydg drosti, Cariad

ACKNOWLEDGEMENTS

Anyone writing about Saki must acknowledge the achievement of journalist and biographer A.J. Langguth, the pathfinder in this area of study through his 1980 *Saki: A Life of Hector Hugh Munro: With Six Stories Never Before Collected*, a detailed, sympathetic, yet unblinkered account of the life of H. H. Munro which skilfully knits first-hand memories, memoirs, letters, and secondary sources into a readable narrative. More recently, Professor Langguth has encouraged this further work through undying, infectious enthusiasm, and has given me gracious permission to quote from his book. Publisher Adam Newell was ahead of me in the archives of the *Westminster Gazette* and *Morning Post*, his Sangrail Press has done a wonderful job in making some of Saki's less well-known work available to a new public, and he has recently published a new anthology of Saki stories, *A Shot in the Dark*, which includes the six collected by A. J. Langguth. I have very much enjoyed correspondence with this most knowledgeable of Saki readers and editors. Historian and playwright Michael Connor, whose *TLS* piece on the authorship of *Mrs Elmsley* stimulated further thought and discussion about that novel, has been more than generous in responding to emails and sharing his discoveries about the 'other' Hector Munro. Mrs Eleanor Munro kindly responded to enquiries about traces of any visit by H. H. Munro to Foulis Castle, in Ross-shire. Mr John Sharman, Secretary of the Old Bedfordians, painstakingly scrutinized the archives of the Old Bedfordians for a record of Munro's time at the school. I should also like to thank the Promotion of the History of Zoos and Natural History in India organization, who sent me a copy of their newsletter so that I could see how they have adapted 'The Death of Munrow' china

ACKNOWLEDGEMENTS

figure as a logo, and the Maine Antiques Digest for granting me permission to quote from their description of the 'Captains and Kilns' sale of antique British ceramics, which featured 'The Death of Munrow'.

I am grateful to everyone who provided or pointed me in the direction of information, answered letters, or offered opinions, especially Fred Bilson, John Dixon, and Katherine Duncan-Jones. My mistakes, of course, are mine and not theirs.

I should like to thank Andrew McNeillie, Jacqueline Baker, and Eva Nyika at Oxford University Press, and copy editor Sylvie Jaffrey, for their enthusiasm and professionalism.

Although every effort has been made to establish copyright and contact copyright holders prior to printing this has not always been possible. The publishers would be pleased to rectify any omissions or errors brought to their notice at the earliest opportunity.

S. B.

CONTENTS

ABBREVIATIONS

Russian Empire	*The Rise of the Russian Empire*. London: Grant Richards, 1900.
Alice	*The Westminster Alice*. London: The Westminster Gazette, 1902.
Reginald	*Reginald*. London: Methuen, 1904.
Reginald in Russia	*Reginald in Russia*. London: Methuen, 1910.
Clovis	*The Chronicles of Clovis*. London: John Lane, The Bodley Head, 1911.
Bassington	*The Unbearable Bassington*. London: John Lane, The Bodley Head 1912.
William	*When William Came: A Story of London under the Hohenzollerns*. London: John Lane, The Bodley Head, 1913.
Beasts	*Beasts and Super-Beasts*. London: John Lane, The Bodley Head, 1914.
Toys	*The Toys of Peace and Other Papers*. London: John Lane, The Bodley Head, 1919.
Square Egg	*The Square Egg and Other Sketches*. London: John Lane, The Bodley Head, 1924.
Gondola	Rothay Reynolds, *The Gondola*. London: John Lane, The Bodley Head, 1913.
Lambert	J. W. Lambert, Introduction, *The Bodley Head Saki*. London: Bodley Head, 1963.
Langguth	A. J. Langguth, *Saki*. London: Hamish Hamilton, 1981.

Munro   E. E. Munro, 'Biography of Saki', in Saki, *The Square Egg* London: The Bodley Head, 1924.

Morley   Christopher Morley, Introduction to *The Complete Short Stories of Saki*: London: John Lane, The Bodley Head, 1930.

Reynolds   Rothay Reynolds, 'A Memoir of H. H. Munro' in Saki, *The Toys of Peace and Other Papers*. London: John Lane, The Bodley Head, 1919.

NOTE ON EDITIONS

QUOTATIONS have been taken from the first editions of Saki's book-length publications and from the journals in which his short stories and other writing first appeared. Readers without access to the first editions and their reprints can find most of Saki's fiction in the anthologies and other works collected below.

The Penguin *Complete Saki* (Harmondsworth, Penguin, 1982) contains stories from *Reginald* (3–40), *Reginald in Russia* (41–98), *The Chronicles of Clovis* (99–232), *Beasts and Super-Beasts* (233–390), *The Toys of Peace* (391–536), and *The Square Egg* (537–66), the novels, *The Unbearable Bassington* (567–688), and *When William Came* (689–814), *The Westminster Alice* (815–42), and the plays *The Death-Trap* (843–50), *Karl-Ludwig's Window* (851–62), and *The Watched Pot* (863–944). Does not include 'Dogged', 'The Pond', 'The Holy War', 'The Almanack', 'The Housing Problem', 'A Sacrifice to Necessity', 'A Shot in the Dark', or 'The East Wing'.

A.J. Langguth, *Saki: A Life of Hector Hugh Munro: With Six Short Stories Never Before Collected* (London: Hamish Hamilton, 1981) includes 'The Pond' (281–6), 'The Holy War' (287–92), 'The Almanack' (293–8), 'The Housing Problem: The Solution of an Insoluble Dilemma' (299–303), 'A Sacrifice to Necessity' (304–9), and 'A Shot in the Dark' (310–15).

Saki Short Stories 2, Everyman Library, selected and introduced by Peter Haining (London: Dent, 1983) includes 'Dogged' (1–6).

'John Bull's Christmas' and 'The East Wing', selected and introduced by Adam Newell (London: The Sangrail Press, 2001) includes the political journalism piece 'John Bull's Christmas' and the story 'The East Wing'.

NOTE ON EDITIONS

Saki, A Shot in the Dark, selected and introduced by Adam Newell, foreword by Jeremy Dyson (London: Hesperus, 2006) includes the short stories 'Dogged', 'A Jungle Story', 'The Pond', 'The Holy War', 'The Almanack', 'A Sacrifice to Necessity', 'A Housing Problem', 'A Shot in the Dark', 'The East Wing', 'The Miracle Merchant', 'Tobermory', the autobiographical 'Travelling with Aunt Tom' and 'On Being Company Orderly Corporal', and the fragment 'The Garden of Eden'.

Introduction: Three Deaths

IN January 2003, a private collector paid $50,190 for a Stafford-shire pearlware group of *c*.1825 attributed to the potter Obadiah Sherratt.[1] The group comprises a large yellow tiger with improbable black squiggles whose mouth encloses part of the head of a young man dressed in breeches and boots. It stands on an ornate green rectangular table base decorated with moulded ribbon swags enclosing the words 'The Death of Munrow'. The design may be fanciful, but the death was real. Christie's catalogue notes explain that the group commemorates the fate of one Lieutenant Munro, who 'having occasion to retire into the surrounding undergrowth for a necessary moment, was pounced on by a tiger while his attention and natural caution were diverted'.[2] An extract from a letter describing the incident was printed in the Deaths section of the *Gentleman's Magazine* of July 1793[3] and in the 'Births, Marriages and Deaths' section of the *Scots Magazine* in the same month. The account is headed 'Extract of a letter from a Gentleman to his friend at Calcutta, dated on board the Ship Shaw Ardasier, off Saumur Island, Dec 23 1792.'

To describe the aweful [*sic*] horrid and lamentable accident I have been an eye-witness of, is impossible. Yesterday morning, Mr. Downey, of The Company's troops, Lieut. Pyefinch, poor Mr. Munro (son of Sir Hector) and myself, went on shore at Saugur island to shoot deer. We saw innumerable tracks of tiger and deer, but still we were induced to pursue our sport, and did the whole day. About half past three we sat down on the edge of the jungle, to eat some cold meat sent to us from the ship, and had just commenced our meal, when Mr. Pyefinch and a black servant told us there was a fine deer within six yards of us. Mr. Downey and myself immediately jumped up to take our guns; mine was the nearest, and I had just laid hold of it when I heard a roar, like thunder, and saw an immense royal tiger spring on the unfortunate Munro, who was sitting down. In a moment his head was in the beast's mouth and he rushed into the jungle with him, with as much ease as I could lift a kitten, tearing him through the thickest bushes and trees, every thing yielding to his monstrous strength. The agonies of horror, regret, and, I must say, fear (for there were two tigers, male and female) rushed on me at once. The only effort I could make was to fire at him, though the poor youth was still in his mouth. I relied partly on Providence, partly on my own aim, and fired a musket. I saw the tiger stagger and agitated, and cried out so immediately. Mr. Downey then fired two shots, and I one more. We retired from the jungle, and a few minutes after, Mr. Munro came up to us, all over blood, and fell. We took him on our backs in the boat, and got every medical assistance for him from the Valentine East India-man, which lay at anchor near the island, but in vain. He lived 24 hours in the extreme of torture; his head and skull were torn and broke to pieces, and he was wounded by the claws all over his neck and shoulders; but it was better to take him away, though irrecoverable, than leave him to be devoured limb by limb. We have just read the funeral service over the body, and committed it to the deep. He was an amiable and promising youth. I must observe, there was a large fire blazing close to us, composed of ten or a dozen trees; I made it myself, on purpose to keep tigers off, as I had always heard it would. There were eight or ten of the natives about us; many shots had been fired at the place, and much noise and laughing all the time; but this ferocious animal disregarded it all. The human mind cannot form an idea of the scene; it turned my very soul within me. The beast was about four and a half feet high, and nine long. His head appeared as large as an ox's, his eyes darting fire, and his roar, when he first seized his prey, will never be out of my recollection. We had scarcely pushed our boats from that cursed shore when the tigress made her appearance, raging mad almost, and remained on the sand as long as the distance would allow me to see her.[4]

The unfortunate lieutenant was the son of a General Munro, the great uncle of a Lieutenant Colonel Munro and the great-great uncle of a Lance-Sergeant Munro.

The second death was almost a hundred years later, in 1872. Mary Frances Mercer returned to the safety of England and her husband's family for the birth of her fourth child. The pregnancy may have been difficult, since she had stayed with her husband in India and Burma for the births of her other three children, the youngest of whom was less than 2 years old when she left him. Walking in a country lane in Devon, she was charged by a runaway cow, the shock caused her to miscarry, and she died.[5]

The husband of Mary Mercer, Charles Augustus Munro, had been a major in the Bengal Staff Corps but was seconded to the Burma Police in which he was to be promoted to lieutenant colonel and later made inspector-general. A career officer, he had been at the appalling siege of Lucknow in 1857–8. After the death of his wife, he decided to send his children, Charles Arthur, Ethel Mary, and Hector Hugh Munro, then 4, 3, and 2 years old, to the care of his mother and sisters in England. He took a house, Broadgate Villa, for them in Pilton, near Barnstaple, North Devon. Received wisdom deemed it dangerous for white children to grow up in a tropical climate, especially without a mother. Their father was sending them away from fevers, diseases, a trying climate, and a lack of 'suitable' companions and 'decent' schools. He sent them to hell.

The third death happened near Beaumont-Hamel on the Somme in November 1916. A group of infantrymen was resting on the lip of a crater between bombardments. One of them heard the Lance-Sergeant speak sharply: 'Put that bloody cigarette out', then the crack of a rifle shot. Later, he learned that the man who had spoken had been shot through the head, by a sniper presumably aiming for the glowing tip of the cigarette. He was Hector Hugh Munro, also known as Saki (Munro, p. 119).

Munro almost certainly encountered the first death, represented in china on mantelpieces and in cupboards around the country during the 1870s and after. So many copies of the Staffordshire group were sold throughout the century that it is hard to imagine his not having seen one. He might have been amused; he would almost certainly have professed himself amused. The bizarre afterlife as ornament of the lieutenant's death persisted into an even more bizarre afterlife as a decorative motif. Joseph Crawhall painted the scene as a watercolour, and it may have been the inspiration for a tiger-shaped wooden carcass made to contain an organ in Tippoo's Palace in 1795. In the twentieth century, Robert Michell and Danka Napiorkowska rearranged the pose for a lustreware tureen which they inscribed 'A memento of the demise of a Young Man called Munro in 1792 . . . and a reminder of the "Man Tyger Organ" taken from Tippoo's Palace at Seringapatam and now resting in the Victoria and Albert Museum, London'. In 1997, the pearlware group was proposed as the logo for the Promotion of the History of Zoos and Natural History in India organization, and appeared on the front page of the Society's Newsletter (vol. 2) in August 1997.

Custom permits, and even encourages, observers of representations such as 'The Death of Munrow' to objectify the suffering of subjects unknown to them or distanced by time and space, and such pieces are conventionally acceptable as amusing ornaments. Rendered in clay, the young man's pain becomes folk art; rendered in print, the horrific can become humour. Readers might be faintly amused by the notion of a man being pounced on by a tiger while retiring behind a bush for 'a necessary moment', presumably to urinate. The little figure with its pink coat, blue sash, neat black hair and formal pose (looking as though it had been taken from a standing group, and laid sideways) is droll. Gruesome fiction in which the unfeasibly wicked suffer unfeasibly horrible and preferably ironic fates, and the unfeasibly good suffer even worse ones, is considered appropriate in black comedy and even children's literature. If the observer knows the subject, however, or can readily identify with him or her, the representation becomes too personal to be objectified, and the same piece can be tasteless or distasteful. Having suffered from the convention which dictates that art can turn something too horrible to contemplate into something acceptably comedic, Saki exploited it, and constantly tested, and transgressed, the boundaries of acceptability and taste.

It is tempting to look to the deaths of the two earlier Munros, the young man killed while serving his country and the mother killed in a way both random and bizarre, for an explanation of the later, which otherwise might seem like an episode from the wrong biography. When Saki is mentioned in critical works it is usually as a master of the macabre. His work is most often remembered from adaptations in the *Tales of the Unexpected* television series or from anthologies of black comedy, and it is anachronistically taken to be archetypal of *fin de siècle* decadence. Those who associated Saki with his protagonists, Reginald, Clovis, Comus, Bertie, and the others, who drawl monologues about oysters, champagne, waistcoats, and duchesses, would hardly have predicted for him a death in the trenches, toothless, among Other Ranks, after having lied himself back from hospital at Base (Munro, p. 118).

Because Saki's Clovis, like Nancy Mitford's Cedric, could have said with conviction: 'Darling, you can't really imagine ONE going over the top?',[6] it does not follow that we cannot imagine that his creator did. Munro was not Comus, Clovis, or Reginald, and neither was he entirely Saki. Nonetheless, the way in which Munro embraced a soldier's life (it was reported that he put on his khaki tunic with the reverence of a nun taking the habit), and death, does come as a surprise. The snapshots from which we might try to piece together an account of Hector Munro's life and character seem to record a progress towards something that was not the Saki-persona, but not Lance-Sergeant Munro either. Whichever way the facts are mustered, there is always another, contradictory, reading: a different Munro.

He was born in Akyab, in north-west Burma, on 18 December 1870, to a family with strong military and imperial connections on both sides.[7] After school and a period abroad, he followed his father and brother into service in Burma. Invalided home, he wrote a history of the Russian Empire before becoming a foreign correspondent of the Tory *Morning Post*, based in the Balkans and later Russia. Back in England, he took up the life of letters. As a young man he dutifully upheld the family tradition and imperialist values in colonial service before becoming the chronicler of another empire; he then became a foreign correspondent for a High Tory journal, who watched slaughter and narrowly escaped death with cool detachment; in early middle age he transmuted into a merciless but humorous political satirist, and ended as anthemist of all things conservative and Conservative. He was a popular guest and host, known for his equally impeccable manners and tailoring. He was a friend of artists, writers, aristocrats, and minor gentry; London 'society' of the day, which was astounded to find him in the trenches soon after being at their dinner tables.

Or: after an extended adolescence during which he was fond of immature and sometimes cruel practical jokes, an artistic but rather directionless young man joined the Burmese Police to earn a living and avoid disappointing his father. His frail constitution suffered from the climate, and, having hated the life, he was glad to be sent home after several bouts of fever. Barely surviving the journey back, he pursued no gainful employment for an extended period before moving to London where, still supported by his father, he spent three years researching a book on Russian history but did not visit Russia. Family interest got him an introduction to Francis Carruthers Gould, a well-known political cartoonist, whose name secured publication of a series of skits on parliamentary figures of the day. This led to political commentary but not political activism or office, a post as foreign correspondent of a High Tory newspaper, and financial independence. At 40, settled in London, he was best known as a well-dressed bridge player at the Cocoa Tree club, but still given to childish pranks and extreme prejudices. By then he had an established reputation as a writer of polished black comedy in upper-class settings.

Neither of these is the whole story. Somewhere there developed the man whom 'wolves have sniffed at', calmly mocking those about to shoot him as a suspected *Komitniki* saboteur; the enlisted man carrying slop buckets for his hut, and longing to 'get at the Bosch', the devoted and dogged NCO; and the author of the astonishing *When William Came* (hereafter *William*) which seems to renounce his earlier work and to denounce his characters.

His friend A. Rothay (Roy) Reynolds suggested that the war had brought about a metamorphosis.[8] Fighting for his country had purged Munro of the habits of adult life and re-established his true nature, so that he again experienced the love of 'the woodlands and the wild things in them, that he had felt as a child, returning'.[9] Reynolds said that the 'dross had been burnt up in the flames of war' and Munro had turned away from the city back to the wild (Reynolds, p. xxiii). 'The dross' seems to refer to Munro's adult life, journalism, and blackly comic stories, and to imply an opposition of the city, which is associated with dross, adulthood, and impurity, and the wild, which is associated with childhood, truth, and purity. That opposition is important in any reading of Saki's work, and will be crucial in this study, but not necessarily in the way Reynolds suggested.

On leave in June 1916, Munro stayed with his brother and sister in the Richelieu (later Dean) Hotel in London. According to Ethel Munro, Hector spoke of his plan to buy some land in Siberia after the war. ' "I could never settle down again to the tameness of London life," he told me.' She seems to have assumed that she was included in the plans: 'It would have been a remarkable life, wild animals beyond the dreams of avarice, at our very doors, and, before long, inside them' (Munro, pp. 108–9). While it is more than likely that in the mud of the trenches, just as on the streets of the West End, Munro had dreamed of Siberian forests, when he was living in the swamps of Burma, crossing the Macedonian plains, or enduring a Russian winter he had not written, lived, or, as far as we can tell, thought in ways remarkably different from those of his London life. There is no evidence for a burning away of dross; no obvious evidence for a road to Damascus, radical change of heart or volte-face of personality, politics, or assumed personae. The rejection of the urban does not necessarily entail a refutation of a whole way of life, or any kind of moral reformation. Munro may have been complex, but he was consistent. The only dramatic change evident in the writing is the complete reversal in the narrators' and central protagonists' attitudes to 'manliness' (i.e. pugilistic patriotism). His second and last novel, *William*, published in 1913, has a strong, reticent, stiff-upper-lipped hero, and a number of his pieces of journalism deplore the moral laxity of modern life, the corruptive influence of 'effete' or 'degenerate' aesthetes, and the concomitant softness of male youth that leaves the country open to foreign invasions of one kind or another. Saki's characteristic short stories with their languid dandies and demonization of women, and the first novel, *The Unbearable Bassington* (hereafter *Bassington*), whose anti-hero is the quintessence of Saki *kouroi* or ephebe, are followed by works whose principal voices appear to despise and fear those corruptive influences.

Saki's narrators appear to move from an entirely self-centred focus on immediate sensual gratification to an entirely altruistic acceptance of self-sacrifice. Of course, authors write in different voices, and the narrators of the jingoistic *William* or the martial 'An Old Love' (*The Toys of Peace*, hereafter *Toys*, pp. xvii–xxi) are no more Hector Hugh Munro than the anonymous narrator of *Bassington*, or Clovis Sangreal, central protagonist of many characteristic stories, but the differences of tone, subject, and style are so very marked that they invite examination. Was there a sea-change? Did 'Saki' find something to believe in?

The transformation of pathos to bathos and seriousness to farce in the stories could give the impression of an art to which nothing is sacred and all is fair game. Saki can force a guilty laugh out of readers even when the humour is directed against a serious and worthy cause. In 'The Gala Programme: An Unrecorded Episode in Roman History', the 'Suffragetæ' disrupt the chariot race of the imperial games, which is to precede a 'grand combat of wild beasts', rather as the Suffragettes drew attention to their cause by disrupting the Derby. Women are lowered into the arena and run across the race track. The Master of Ceremonies is hysterical with rage and mortification, but the 'popular and gifted young Emperor Placidus Superbus' remains calm and unruffled, and arranges what appears to be Saki's answer to the demonstrations: the stable gates are closed and the menagerie dens opened, so that the second portion of the programme happens first (*The Square Egg*, pp. 140–2.)

Saki's narrators appear to allow their protagonists considerable leeway in the matters of eating children, disrupting garden parties, and playing nasty practical jokes, but they are not amoral; they do represent certain codes. Meanness and cruelty to children are both deplored and punished. That the Saki youths take on themselves the role of Nemesis, meting out poetic justice in a number of stories, shows that they are not amoral. They do have a value-system. Both the novels and short stories imply that there were some things Saki held sacred, and one in particular. However disruptive and subversive the characters in the fiction, this is no postmodern universe of sliding surfaces and destabilization. There is a centre, a fixed point around which reality and morality revolve for Saki characters and narrators: England.

Ethel Munro ranked pride in being a Highlander first among — her brother's strongest characteristics (the others are whimsicality, keen sense of humour, and love of animals: see Munro, pp. 57–8). In spite of Scots ancestry on both sides of the family (his maternal ancestors were McNabs),[10] however, Munro was an English patriot, England here meaning not English society in its entirety, but the land and a mystical nationhood.[11] He was a product of a system that generated a sense of England's superiority and superior

9

rights, with concomitant patronization (at best) and demonization (at worst) of those deemed not English. It is important to distinguish between the two traits. Having been on the inferior side of one of the hierarchized oppositions which articulated British society in the late nineteenth century (white/black, male/female, upper class/lower class, adult/child), Munro made the most of his position as superior (an *adult*, white, English, upper middle-class male). This is not to say that he necessarily saw himself as fighting for English or British superiority or against the alleged inferiority of other races. What he did perceive, and warn against in much of his writing, was a threat to England, English independence, and English culture, and it was for those that he fought, and died.

In his introduction to an anthology of Saki stories, the writer Will Self singles out Saki's 'distinctly English capacity for irony' and his very English settings of 'country house parties, gentlemen's clubs and all the long twilights of Victorian imperialism', yet also describes his introduction of 'a most un-English quality of the sleek and the soigné',[12] This juxtaposition of the conventional and the dissident is characteristic of the stories' incident and their burden. In some ways, Saki's fiction as much as his journalism upholds the English, Establishment mores of High Toryism, nationalism, and imperialism, but two strands collide with them, the sleek and soigné and the feral, both of which entail a solipsistic rejection of the virtues which foster the greater good. The two sometimes coalesce in the form of the Saki youths, human or otherwise. Rather than embodying imperialist ideals taken from the Romans such as *industria, gravitas*, and *pieta*, Reginald, Clovis, Comus, and the others subvert them, putting great effort into their personal appearance, manifesting seriousness and single-mindedness of purpose in their pursuit of the right food and ignoring distracting trivialities such as lost babies or lack of funds en route to it, and asserting that they as works of art constitute a magnificent contribution to the greater good. For the narrative voice of both the fiction and the journalism, however, one Roman virtue is indispensable. *Virtus*, physical and intellectual courage and the ability to maintain self-control in the face of danger, is as much lauded by Saki as by Kipling. In Saki's writing, a male may be languid, flaunt his nice eyelashes, or be obsessed by his hair-parting, and be attractive. Similarly, he can consume human flesh, incite a stag to rip apart a woman, or plot a painful death for a mildly irritating character, and not be unattractive. He cannot, however, be weak-willed or cowardly. This possession of *virtus* and the love of England combine to make it not implausible that the Saki youths would put aside the pleasures of wardrobe and palate to fight for their country, and not impossible that the pipe-playing, goat-hoofed spirit of the countryside would also features in the stories would do the same.

One of the most refreshing things about Saki's writing is its lack of sentimentality about children, animals, or anything else. Characters who feign or exaggerate feeling or apply it to the wrong object (such as a lapdog) as well as those who withhold it from its correct object (usually a child) are mercilessly punished. The deadpan narration of the terrible fates met by such characters adds to the judicial tone of the stories. One of the most unpleasant things is the appalling anti-Semitism, expressed both in the narrative voice and that of the central protagonists, and echoing that of contemporaries such as Kipling. There are also a number of fairly narrow-minded stereotypes of Americans (pretentious and philistine), Germans (sentimental, crude, and greedy), and working-class English (ponderous, slow, and comic, apart from the children, who are sometimes sharp in face and wits). The assorted prejudices and stereotypes of the stories might lead readers to expect that Saki would declare, like Nancy Mitford's Uncle Matthew, that 'Abroad is unutterably bloody, and all foreigners are fiends,'[13] but he neither hated nor feared cultures foreign to him.

Munro lived in the Balkans, Russia, and France, and, as his sister and friend suggested, may have planned to buy land in Siberia after the war. He was cosmopolitan, spoke several languages, and had friends of many nationalities. The threat to England contracted his world and his ambitions to single-mindedness to the extent that in his later stories he struggled to retain the form and tone of his earlier writing whilst abandoning its best mouthpieces. They did not entirely vanish from his repertoire after the war began; a short Clovis monologue, 'Clovis on the Alleged Romance of Business', was published posthumously in *Square Egg* in 1924 (pp. 159–69), but they do appear less frequently than before.

It is important to remember, however, that the protagonists of Saki's earlier stories never speak against war. Reginald, Clovis, Bertie, and Comus may be languid and affected, but they do not deplore action or even violence in an approved cause, which can include retribution, defence of possessions, and establishing the pecking order. Only Comus, who is not a hero, enjoys the physical act of hurting others (younger schoolboys) for its own sake, but other Saki characters rejoice in physical manifestations of triumph or superiority. Even so, violent encounters in Saki's writing are rarely described in literal detail. Often they happen offstage. Beatings in school studies and fights in nurseries are described in oblique, sometimes arch language; warfare is described in romanticized and mythical terms. Though sometimes he stage-dresses his scenes with a plethora of significant material objects, Saki also employs the full gamut of rhetoric of the ideal in the cause of nationalism.

Munro publicly demanded that English people fight to defend England, but Saki's writing invokes an ideal ('England') which is at odds with the portions of it represented in his satire. The sum of its parts, he seems to suggest, is far greater than the whole. In the stories of Rudyard Kipling and others, school is where boys receive a classical education both in the sense of learning classical languages and philosophy, and in being inculcated with the classical codes of patriotism, duty, responsibility, discipline, and honour.

Education tames the chaos of childhood and produces the rational adult who will be a product of Enlightenment thinking, a future ruler and servant of Empire. As late as the 1950s, William Golding represented boys who, left to their own devices, would revert to the barbaric, unless among their number are some youths further along the socialization process who ventriloquize the voice of the adult world. In *The Lord of the Flies*, it is necessary for adults to rescue the children and restore them to civilization and enlightenment. In Saki's stories, the triumphal moments are not those in which boys demonstrate that they have interiorized classical and imperial values, but the moments in which natural law overthrows the law of the nursery, the classroom, or the barracks. Boys take on animal characteristics, and huge, mythic animals, the quintessence of the wild, are called into being to avenge children abused by the adult, 'civilized' world. In Kipling's stories, aggression is channelled into sports and other 'manly' team activities which prepare the boys to fight and die for their country or an abstract notion of it. In his later writing, Saki manages to retain his distaste for school, team sports, and imperial, classical values, yet to suggest that war, in the service of one's country, is the natural condition of young manhood. He also makes latent violence and the scent of danger erotic, anticipating Ted Hughes in his admiration for the terrifying attent, sleek killer.

Saki's work influenced Noël Coward, P.G. Wodehouse, and Evelyn Waugh, among others, and its devotees include Graham Greene, A. A. Milne, and Will Self, but the readership has expanded largely through personal recommendation rather than fame, and the fame tends to be restricted to the short stories. These are varied in theme, setting, tone, and structure, as befits the genre.

The short story, like any other literary form, varies according to the period in which it is being written, but it has a unique ability to preserve and at any time recall its mixed origins in fable, anecdote, fairy-story and numerous other forms. Because individual short stories keep revealing affinities with their forerunners, it is almost impossible to stabilize a definition of the genre; no summary phrase can encapsulate the diversity of possible story types, lengths, and approaches.[14]

The stories written for publication in newspapers and journals are bound by constraints of space, and Saki frequently employs favourite devices and tropes such as the revenge-plot, the practical joke, the metamorphosis, the knowing child, and the twist in the tale, but nonetheless, his stories are varied in form, subject, theme, and dramatis personae, and range from the comic to the satirical to the supernatural to the didactic.

Saki's writing is elegant, economical, and witty. The dominant tone is worldly, flippant irreverence delivered in astringent exchanges and epigrams more neat, pointed, and poised even than Wilde's. The deadpan narrative voice allows for the recitation of horrors and grotesquerie, and the punchlines are masterpieces of understatement. Introducing the 1930 omnibus edition of stories, Christopher Morley sums up Saki's gifts.

Delicate, airy, lucid, precise, with the inconspicuous agility of perfect style, he can pass into the uncanny, the tragic, into mocking fairy-tales grimmer than Grimm. His phrases are always urbane and usually final [...] Saki writes so lightly that you might hardly notice how beautifully also [...] Let me repeat what I once put into the mouth of the 'Old Mandarin' in a pseudo-Chinese translation:

> There is something specially Chinese
> In Saki's Tory humour,
> He has the claw of the demon-cat
> Beneath his brilliant robe.
> Suavest comedian, silkiest satirist,
> Smooth as a shave,
> With a new razor-blade.[15]

The style, at once suavely smooth and razor-sharp, can be deceptive. It is all too easy to miss the skill with which words and phrases are pared-down and placed. In his introduction to the Penguin

Complete Saki, Noel Coward praises Saki's stories for an Edwardian
'evanescent charm'.

> His stories and novels appear as delightful and, to use a much abused
> word, sophisticated as they did when he first published them. They are
> dated only by the fact that they evoke an atmosphere and describe a
> society which vanished in the baleful summer of 1914. The Edwardian era,
> in spite of its political idiocies and a sinister sense of foreboding which,
> to intelligent observers, underlay the latter part of it, must have been,
> socially at least, very charming. It is this evanescent charm that Saki so
> effortlessly evoked.[16]

Charm is not a word that leaps to mind in relation to Saki's
descriptions of country-house life, where animals may mock, gore,
or eat the guests, and the guests are worse, with less excuse. In
associating Saki's work with froth, Coward and others have done
him a disservice. Even Morley compares the writing to a fragile
crystal champagne flute, and refers to Saki's sparkling and fuming
with 'incessant bubbles of wit' (Morley, p. v). Like Virginia Woolf
finding Jane Austen difficult to catch in the art of being great,
Morley effectively devalues Saki whilst praising him: 'The fact is
that there are few writers less profitable to write *about*. Saki exists
only to be read. The exquisite lightness of his work offers no grasp
for the solemnities of earnest criticism. He is of those brilliant and
lucky volatiles who are to be enjoyed, not critic-handled' (pp. v–vi).
This study attempts to write about Saki's work, to set it in the
context of English culture and English preoccupations of the late
nineteenth and early twentieth centuries, and, without recreating
Munro from Saki or Saki from Munro, to look at Saki's writing
in the context of Munro's life. The argument of the study is that
Saki's writing is centred on three significant things: England, in an
idealized form; the British Empire, as a symbol of an idealized code
of behaviour and beliefs; and the feral ephebe, the sleek young
male killer in his several forms.

Alan Sinfield offers a warning that might be salutary to any reader of Saki's work: 'Many commentators assume that queerness, like murder, will out, so there must be a gay scenario lurking somewhere in the depths of *The Importance of Being Earnest*.'[17] This book will not be searching for gay scenarios in Saki's work, and will consider Munro's sexuality, like other aspects of his life, as something we have access to only as text, not fact, and as something which neither reflects his life nor is necessarily transcribed in his writing.

The first three and last chapters of this study look at Munro's early life and artistic influences, and his life as a soldier, and are largely descriptive. Other chapters each take as a starting point a phase in Munro's life and career but focus on a theme or other aspect of the writing such as youths, boys, women, war, the countryside... and are therefore less strictly chronological and more analytical.

As a prelude to a brief summary of some of the known accounts of the life of Munro, I give an account of his death from the letters of Christopher Stone, then an officer in the Royal Fusiliers.

You will see in the papers that Sgt. Munro, Hector Munro, 'Saki' the writer was killed, one of the men that I really and honestly admire and revere in this War. He steadfastly refused a commission, and loved his friends in A. Coy.

From being a very smart man about town he became the dirtiest looking old ruffian you ever saw; and when he got really ill two months ago instead of going home and making the most of it as those other blighters do, he managed to get back to us about a week ago. He was sitting in a shell-hole talking to two men and was actually in the middle of a sentence when he was shot clean through the back of the head.

He did very finely for us all.[18]

I

Early Life and Influences

OF course many people were worse off. Children were being abused, starved, or killed by poverty, disease, neglect, overwork, ignorance, or all five. It could be both melodramatic and insensitive to call life in an upper middle-class, middle-England villa with adequate food and fewer beatings than inflicted on most Victorian minors hell, but if hell is subjective, the opposite of what any individual needs to remain reasonably content, then the Munro children were in it. Charlie, Ethel, and Hector were powerless in the power of people who did their duty by but did not care for them. They were confined in unrelenting, unrelieved monotony. That surely is hell, and they were in it for ten years, which must have seemed like eternity.

The nominal head of the Pilton household was Mrs Lucy Munro (née Jones), the children's grandmother. She was 65 when Charles, Ethel and Hector were brought to England, a product of the Regency era, and apart from a rigorous insistence on Sunday observance, gentle with the children. The real rulers of the house were The Aunts. Aunt Charlotte, known as Aunt Tom, 42 when the children arrived, and Aunt Augusta, eleven years younger but the more domineering, imposed a regime of seclusion, restraint, and arbitrary rules enforced in the case of Charlie by corporal punishment and in the case of Hector and Ethel by coldness, removal of privileges, and guilt.[1] What made it worse was that each aunt imposed a set of inflexible and conflicting rules. The aunts hated each other 'with a ferocity and intensity worthy of a bigger cause' (Munro, p. 6).

Ethel Munro judged Aunt Tom 'a colossal humbug' who was blithely unaware of the way she hurt people's feelings, but the less intimidating of the two. Aunt Augusta features in the memoir as 'the autocrat of Broadgate—a woman of ungovernable temper, of fierce likes and dislikes, imperious, a moral coward, possessing no brains worth speaking of, and a primitive disposition' (ibid. 7). Her niece continues:

I think Aunt Augusta must have mesmerised us—the look in her dark eyes, added to the fury in her voice, and the uncertainty as to the punishment, used to make me shiver. She had the strange characteristic of being unable to be just annoyed at anything, she had to be so angry that she would work herself into a passion.   (ibid. 19)

The family doctor declared that the children would never live to grow up, and doctors to middle-aged, middle-class Victorian ladies, when they 'counted', as Saki was to note, didn't just predict, they decreed. 'Conradin was ten years old, and the doctor had pronounced his professional opinion that the boy would not live another five years. The doctor was silky and effete, and counted for little, but his opinion was endorsed by Mrs. De Ropp, who counted for nearly everything' ('Sredni Vashtar', *Clovis*, p. 93). All three children lived to adulthood, however, and both Charlie and Ethel outlived their younger brother by many years.

If Hector was a delicate child, as Ethel reports in her memoir of her brother, it was not in a languid, drooping way (Munro, 4). He was highly strung, excitable, and volatile. Metaphorically, Broadgate Villa might have been to the Munro children what Gateshead was to Jane Eyre, the gate to their futures, but it was also, like Gateshead, a place of misery, and while they were inside the gates were firmly locked and bolted. Ethel Munro describes the house as 'too dark, verandas kept much of the sunlight out, the flower and vegetable gardens were surrounded by high walls and a hedge' (p. 4). The kitchen and back flower gardens and the upper storey were out of bounds, on rainy days they were kept inside, and as for the garden, Ethel Munro recollected: 'it was, "Don't play on the grass," from one aunt, and "Children, you're not to play on the gravel" from the other' (p. 5). On Sundays there were '[n]o toys, no books except Sunday books, Dr Watts's ghastly catechism, a collect and a piece of a hymn to be learnt and repeated to [their grandmother . . .]' (p. 13). The house was surrounded by fields, but walks were hardly allowed. Ethel Munro remarks, apparently without any sense of the possible cause, that Aunt Augusta was afraid of cows (p. 4). The village was 'a sort of Cranford' with few children, and fewer diversions (p. 14). 'We went much too seldom to visit my mother's people in Kent. They were much more our sort of people than the home aunts. My grandfather, Rear-Admiral Mercer, was full of fun, and his daughters were young and lively, and they let us do lots of things we could never do at home' (pp. 20–1). A wistful remark sums up the lives of the Munros with both pathos and comedy. 'With the best will in the world we could not be really naughty, for there simply was not the scope. Three children with three grown-ups to manage them are really handicapped from the outset' (pp. 12–13). The Aunts seem to have subscribed to Reginald's opinion of children: ' "[p]eople talk vaguely about the innocence of a little child, but they take mighty good care not to let it out of their sight for twenty minutes. The watched pot never boils over" ' ('The Innocence of Reginald', *Reginald*, 8). Reginald also makes a characteristically metaphysical comparison, yoking together hors d'oeuvres and his childhood in a way that is not quite a joke. ' "Hors d'oeuvres have always a pathetic interest for me," said Reginald: "they remind me of one's childhood that one goes through, wondering what the next course is going to be like—and during the rest of the menu one wishes one had eaten more of the hors d'oeuvres" ' ('Reginald at the Carlton', *Reginald*, pp. 63–4). That he uses the word 'pathetic', and immediately rushes into another topic: 'Don't you love watching the different ways people have of entering a restaurant?' (ibid. p. 64) suggests that the subject has raised more painful memories than the flippancy would suggest.

Hector did his best to get what he could out of the meagre hors d'oeuvres, and the children did manage to bypass the aunts' surveillance occasionally to effect some minor infringements. Once, the boys took a jar of tamarinds from the store-room and, having eaten as much as they could of the contents, hid it in a trunk containing Aunt Augusta's spare clothes. 'Broadgate resounded to her bellowings, and the row was frightful. In a former life she must have been a dragon. No toys allowed for two days, disgrace for all of us, and, of course, nothing to do. But mercifully we had fertile brains, and Hector was never nonplussed for occupation' (Munro, p. 14). Hector was considered too sickly to attend school and would have spent a lot of time 'resting', being 'seen but not heard', or being neither seen nor heard. Far worse than those restrictions on his life would have been the lack of affection. The story 'Sredni Vashtar' depicts the effect on a small boy of a loveless upbringing, the development of an ability to blame and to hate that even now shocks in its power and ferocity.

One of these days Conradin supposed he would succumb to the mastering pressure of wearisome necessary things—such as illnesses and coddling restrictions and drawn-out dullness. Without his imagination, which was rampant under the spur of loneliness, he would have succumbed long ago.

Mrs de Ropp would never, in her honestest moments, have confessed to herself that she disliked Conradin, though she might have been dimly aware that thwarting him 'for his good' was a duty which she did not find particularly irksome. Conradin hated her with a desperate sincerity which he was perfectly able to mask [. . .] from the realm of his imagination she was locked out—an unclean thing which should find no entrance.   (*Clovis*, pp. 93–4)

Woman, particularly the 'managing woman', is demonized in Saki's work from the first.[2] Ethel's assertion that Aunt Augusta was the model for Mrs Van De Ropp in 'Sredni Vashtar' and the aunt in 'The Lumber Room' (Munro, p. 7) cannot be proved, but if she was like those two monsters, or if the children believed her to be like that, then we should not be surprised that their emotional development was retarded. They learned early to grow a carapace around their feelings, and to rejoice in the misfortunes of enemies. As a small boy, Hector was very fond of a Houdan cock which followed him about like a shadow.

Unhappily he got something wrong with one leg, and had to be destroyed. I believe a 'Vet.' would have cured him, but this would have been considered a sinful extravagance. No one but myself knew what Hector felt at the loss of the bird. We had early learned to hide our feelings—to show enthusiasm or emotion were sure to bring an amused smile to Aunt Augusta's face. It was a hateful smile, and I cannot imagine why it hurt, but it did.   (Ibid. 10)

When Saki fictionalizes the episode, he gives the betrayal and cruelty its full subjective weight. In 'Sredni Vashtar', Conradin has two sources of solace in a cheerless life presided over by his guardian, Mrs De Ropp: a ragged Houdan hen, and a polecat-ferret, whose hidden presence in a toolshed is 'a secret and fearful joy, to be kept scrupulously from the knowledge of the Woman, as he privately dubbed his cousin'. Mrs De Ropp finds the hen and has it taken away. When she attempts to remove the ferret a terrible force is unleashed; the anger and pain of the child manifest; and Mrs De Ropp dies for her cruelty (see below).

The children's happiest time was 'during some pitched battle in their internecine warfare, "with Aunt calling to Aunt like masto-dons bellowing across primeval swamps"[3]; we lived our little lives, criticized our "elders and betters" and rejoiced exceedingly when Aunt Augusta went to bed for a whole day with a headache' (Munro, 8). Headaches were perhaps frequent. Clovis was later to recite a catalogue of aunts' opportunities to be indisposed: ' "measles and influenza and nervous headache and hysteria, and other things that aunts do have [. . .] Aunts that have never known a day's illness are very rare; in fact, I don't personally know of any" ' ('Clovis on Parental Responsibilities', *Beasts and Super-Beasts*, p. 209).

Headaches, real and feigned, become both defences and weapons in stories such as 'The Holy War' (*Morning Post*, 5 May 1913, p. 5) and 'The Unrest Cure' (*Clovis*, pp. 73–85) and are always wielded by older women.

Ethel casually remarks that '[b]oth aunts were guilty of mental cruelty' without elaborating (Munro, p. 10), and continues: 'we often longed for revenge with an intensity I suspect we inherited from our Highland ancestry'. Later in life, however, Ethel seems to have rewritten their early history. In response to a review of *The Best of Saki* in the *Spectator*, she wrote:

In Mr Hudson's comments in the *Spectator* on the book *The Best of Saki*, selected and with an introduction by Graham Greene, he mentions the extraordinary delusion that some writers on Saki have had, that he had 'a miserable childhood'. He had nothing of the sort. He and my other brother and myself (his sister) enjoyed our childhood in our grandmother's house, and, being blessed with amazing vitality and love of mischief, rode over all storms with an appetite for the next! When forbidden visits were paid to the lumber-room, with knowledge of the punishment that would follow if found out, those visits were naturally intensely exciting, and exciting events were continually happening in that house. I should say that the stern discipline he had in early life, far from causing a 'cruel element' in him, was enough to make him detest cruelty in any form but not enough to stop him from writing about it. He once said to me that, in spite of our strict upbringing and having no other children to play with, he was glad of it, as otherwise we should never have been original.[4]

Graham Greene replied the next week, reminding her that the stories of her brother's miserable childhood came from her own memoir.

Miss Munro speaks of 'the extraordinary delusion that some writers on Saki have had, that he had "a miserable childhood".' Miss Munro seems to look now through far more rosy spectacles at her brother's childhood and her own than she did when she wrote the short biography of Saki which was included in the collected short stories. If writers on Saki suffer from delusions, the delusions are all based on her own writing.[5]

Greene quotes eight examples from the memoir and leaves his letter at that, but Ethel Munro was not a woman who could leave anything at that. The following week she wrote again, ignoring her own recollections of the aunts' cruelties, or asserting that they did not affect her brother.

Mr Graham Greene seems to think from my remark (that some writers on Saki had the extraordinary delusion that he had 'a miserable childhood') that such delusions are all based on my own writing. It is rather strange that only in the last two or three years has the theory of 'miserable childhood' cropped up. My memory of that childhood is extremely fresh. Saki 'was a Puck to the end of his life'—I cannot imagine a miserable Puck. 'Aunt Augusta being such an unlovable character, we extended only a lukewarm sort of liking to her.' But a miserable boy would have had no liking at all for her. 'We lived a life of our own, in which the grown-ups had no part.' 'We lived our little lives, criticised our elders and betters, and rejoiced exceedingly when Aunt Augusta went to bed for a whole day with a headache.' Those are all quotations from my biography of Saki. Mr Greene quotes from that biography 'that we slept in rooms with windows shut and shuttered'—though unhygienic, this did not constitute a misery—and 'our grandmother was entirely over-ruled by her turbulent daughters'—this was also no misery to us.

A friend who had read the biography said she never noticed anything suggesting misery in it. Moreover Saki's remark to me (and his memory of our childhood was as distinct as mine), that in spite of a strict upbringing, and having no other children to play with, he was glad of it, as otherwise we should never have been original, is not what he would have said if he had had a miserable childhood—[6]

After this, Greene seems, probably wisely, to have declined to continue the exchange. Restraint, ill-health, and loneliness did not produce languor and apathy, but, as with Conradin, were 'a spur' to make the imagination and the personality 'rampant'. Among the reminiscences of Hector Munro passed from Charlie Munro to his younger daughter Juniper, later Mrs P. A. G. Bryan, and told to A. J. Langguth, was the story that the aunts knew that one board in the boys' bedroom squeaked, and counted on it to alert them to nocturnal activity. The children were one step ahead, however, and had learned to skip over the loose board without a sound (Langguth, p. 13). The first glimpse we have of Hector Munro himself is Ethel's first memory of him in the nursery, chasing her and Charlie around a table with a flaming hearth brush, shouting ' "I'm God! I'm going to destroy the world!" ' (Munro, p. 3.) When the lid came off, the watched pot boiled over.

The other inhabitant of Broadgate was Leah Hepper, a local woman who worked as a servant there and was 27 at the time of the census which fell before Hector's eleventh birthday in 1881. She is not mentioned in either the published letters or the memoir. None of the servants seems to have helped to alleviate the children's monotonous regime, which was enlivened only by their father's four-yearly leave, the annual visit of Charles Munro's brother, Uncle Wellesley, and one Christmas party at which they were not allowed to eat the food (ibid. pp. 14–18). In their father's six-week vacations, Ethel Munro reports: he 'took us for picnics, and to the houses of friends who had farmyards, where Hector rode the pigs, climbed haystacks with Charlie and arrived home rakish and buttonless, but in unquenchable spirits, snapping his fingers (figuratively, of course) at Aunt Augusta' (Munro, p. 18). She adds, '[w]e did not fear her when Papa was about.' In spite of the obligatory Sunday services, improving books, collects, and hymns, '[t]he wonder was we did not fear God with every inducement to do so. It was patent that our characters were fatally attractive to Him, and when we went a bit too far we were told that He sent a thunderstorm as a warning that we had better be careful.' The Old Testament focus on vengeance and punishment was instilled in all three children. Charlie, kept out of the army by poor eyesight, joined the Burma Police and later the prison service (becoming Governor of Mountjoy Gaol during the Troubles). Ethel seems entirely to have concurred with the doctrine of smiting one's (and one's country's) enemies; seeing Hector off from Victoria Station at the end of his leave in July 1916, and allowed no closer to the troop train than the outside edge of the platform, she shouted 'Kill a good few for me!' She was in no doubt that he did, but regretted that 'he was never, though, to have the satisfaction of a bayonet charge' (p. 109). Hector produced macabre poetic justice, in romances, at short notice. Saki characters' predilection for vindictiveness and relish for humiliating and painful reparation suggests that their world-view was similarly untroubled by notions of Christian altruism, or perhaps overly steeped in Christian Old Testament morality. Clovis fondly imagines consecrating thirst for revenge as a festival in 'The Feast of Nemesis' (*Beasts*, p. 319).

Before the stories provided opportunities for him to play a vengeful god, Hector found other outlets for violent energies. At the annual children's parties, Ethel recalled, should Aunt Augusta break off her surveillance to gossip with the grown-ups: 'Hector leapt at the opportunity and the nearest boy, and was soon in the ecstasies of a fight. Then Aunt Augusta would look in and in a restrained fury drag him off to be tidied. But his blood was up and any threat as to subsequent punishment was ignored' (Munro, pp. 15–16). Ethel clearly does not count this as being 'really naughty', and represents it as another instance of the pot boiling over. 'It was not that he was pugnacious—he was a very sweet-tempered child, but his high spirits had to have some outlet, and life at Broadgate was very monotonous' (p. 16). She seems to have had no difficulty in reconciling a sweet-natured child with one who threw himself into a fight (evidently unprovoked) at the first opportunity, nor does she consider for an instant the damage inflicted on the child on the receiving end of the launch. He is the means to relieve monotony and a valve for Hector's high-spirit-letting, with no existence beyond.

Their repressed upbringing did not make the young Munros overly introspective, empathic, or humble; they emerged from it solipsistic, arrogant, and, though sensitive in some ways, given to *schadenfreude* and curiously immune to the feelings or even three-dimensionality of those (most of the world) whom they dubbed 'fools' or 'types', and whom they viewed with all the prejudices of nineteenth-century imperialists, or cast as extras on the fringes of their dramas. As an adult, Munro was a self-effacing, watchful outsider, but if in company he was a spectator, in private he was not an open-minded or impartial one. Reginald's remark in 'Reginald on Christmas Presents': 'No boy who had brought himself up properly could fail to appreciate one of those decorative bottles of liqueurs that are so reverently staged in Morel's window' (*Reginald*, p. 15) is flippant and throwaway, but that upbringing is generally neglected or perverted by adults is repeatedly endorsed by other young male characters. The Saki youth characteristically has indifferent parents; even those possessed of a mother or father (as in Jane Austen's works, there is rarely a full or fully functioning complement) have remained profoundly detached from them; and have therefore attended to their own character formation. Mrs Eggelby asserts that her children have been most carefully brought up.

'That shows that you were nervous as to how they would turn out,' said Clovis. 'Now, my mother never bothered about bringing me up. She just saw to it that I got whacked at decent intervals and was taught the difference between right and wrong; there is some difference, you know, but I've forgotten what it is.' ('Clovis on Parental Responsibilities', *Beasts*, 207).

Like many Saki characters, Clovis describes parenting at a remove, or by proxy, and associates (ineffectual) moral education with corporal punishment and teaching but not learning. Other adults in guardian roles make equally little impact. 'To my mind, education is an absurdly overrated affair. At least, one never took it very seriously at school, where everything was done to bring it prominently under one's notice. Anything that is worth knowing one practically teaches oneself, and the rest obtrudes itself sooner or later' ('Reginald on Worries', *Reginald*, pp. 51–2). Reginald and the other effectively orphaned Saki youths are social autodidacts who become both prematurely aged, or precociously knowing, and obsessed with staying young.

Some Saki mothers need children because they need someone to beat, at least, Saki suggests that a childless woman is deprived of a whipping-boy.

And the page-boy stood there, with his sleekly brushed and parted hair, and his air of chaste and callous indifference to the desires and passions of the world. Eleanor hated boys, and she would have liked to have whipped this one long and often. It was perhaps the yearning of a woman who had no children of her own.   ('The Jesting of Arlington Stringham', *Beasts*, 89)

Hector compensated for the narrowness of the children's daily lives with highly developed imaginative powers, and led Charlie and Ethel in every form of mischief that might escape detection or from which his cunning might extricate them. When their toys were taken away or they were ordered to be quiet, reading was a sanctuary. Hector was not a literary infant prodigy. Most of his contributions to 'The Broadgate Paper', the children's newspaper, were drawings, but he was an avid reader. Whilst remaining seen and not heard, as he would have been told a good child should, he could escape life in which every day was the same and every floorboard, every overstuffed sofa, every cushion, every cretonne, every anti-macassar, every ornament too well known, and encounter the Other. Their father sent books. Ethel Munro records that Hector's early favourites included *Robinson Crusoe* (1719), *Alice's Adventures in Wonderland* (1865), *Through the Looking Glass and What Alice Found There* (1871), which was a present to Ethel, and Charles G. Leland's *Johnnykin and the Goblin* (1877). Ethel Munro says that the latter had always fascinated Hector. 'Being a Celt, I suppose it was natural he should be fond of goblins and nature spirits' (Munro, p. 14). The book is a dream-vision fantasy interspersed with verse and riddles, in which a good boy defends a stone goblin from some nasty rough boys, and is rewarded by the goblin's coming to life and taking him into fairyland.[7] The incidents are imaginatively varied, and the characters range from anthropomorphic creatures, nursery-rhyme favourites, and the 'flower-fairy' type of Victorian fancy, to the equally typical comic grotesque. The humour, whimsical, knowing, based on cod-logic and the subversion of contemporary adages, aphorisms, and nursery rules, has much in common with Lewis Carroll's *Alice* books. It also has much in common with Saki's stories. Though most of the discussion of the fiction follows in subsequent chapters, it seems worth interrupting the chronological order of this biographical section in order to examine the enduring influence of these oases of imaginative vistas in a narrowly confined (Saki was to use the word 'Mappined'[8]) existence.

Johnnykin opens with Johnnykin sketching a stone goblin in a graveyard. In spite of his priggishness, he is immediately recognizable as a Saki-esque hero, a lonely and unwanted child bullied by bigger, less artistic, and less sensitive boys, but in this case persecuted by an uncle rather than aunt. Where Munro became much addicted to doggerel verse written to accompany sketches, Johnnykin 'can't help' repeating verse, usually execrable. Some 'wild children, intent on mischief' arrive to throw stones at the statue, but Johnnykin saves it by giving them his apples.[9] The grateful Goblin comes to life, whisks Johnnykin away and, so that he won't be missed, charms a donkey to take his place. The uncle is delighted with the impostor. The fey, dreamy nephew with 'unnatural fancies' about drawing and poetry (p. 205) who set out that morning has returned like other boys. 'He was not nice at all, and there was No Nonsense about him.'[10] The artistic, imaginative character is immediately confirmed in its superiority over the 'donkeys' who regard him as weakly effeminate (also the middle-class character, since Johnnykin speaks Victorian Standard English and the rough boys with a kind of generic working-class accent).

'Hullo' roared Bill, 'here's old Johnnykin a-drawin' a pictur'. Let's give him a rollin'!'
'Let's smash his figure for him,' cried Sam Slapps [. . .]
'Oh fy!' said Johnnykin. 'This is very unkind and cruel. Remember what Milton says:—
"He that would knock a statue's nose off, Ought to be whipped with all his clothes off."

'Milton ain't the Stilton,' replied the vulgar Sam. 'Hurrah boys! let's
pelt the graven immidge! That'll break Miss Johnnykin's heart' [...]
   'Oh please cease!'[11]

In contrast to Johnnykin's hyper-polite speech, the Goblin is
knowing, witty, and slightly acerbic; like a Saki narrator.

'So you would like to have a different sort of life, Johnnykin,' said the
Goblin. 'Well, why shouldn't you? I don't think you're of much use to
anybody in that home of yours,—and, what's of far more consequence,
there is nobody in it of the slightest use to you. I dare say they'd like to be
rid of you altogether, and I shouldn't wonder if they thought you were
out of your mind—*non compos mentis*, you know.'[12]

Hearing that Johnnykin's uncle has wished that his artistic, poetic
nephew would never darken his door again, the Goblin prophesies
a future that the young Hector Munro must have longed for.

'I hope, Sir', he continued, 'that you won't consider me a stupid boy.'
'No, Johnnykin, I don't. Some day you may live among people who
will be astonished to know that you were once supposed to be troubled
with such a disorder [...]'[13]

Johnnykin enters fairyland, a magical place from which grown-ups
are excluded and where wishes can come true. Saki's boys are
generally excluded by fierce adult guardians from more earthly
and confined paradises such as gardens, attics, and pantries, but
in their turn exclude adults from their own closely guarded inner
worlds. Johnnykin's fairyland could stand for the imagination but,
populated with stock nursery-rhyme characters and situations, and
an ethos of king, country, and honour, it is an imaginary world
firmly shaped by prevailing convention.

Some of the humour of *Johnnykin* is archly knowing and aimed
at adults, as when the Goblin says of the metamorphosed donkey,
'It would be lucky, Johnnykin [...] if a great many people
were even as well represented as you are. Donkeys are nice
enough in their places on the Commons—and sometimes *in* the
Commons—under a good Whip [...]'[14] If Saki learned from
Leland that adults could be addressed in genres associated with

children's literature, such as animal stories and fantasies, he took the lesson beyond the teacher, using the forms of children's literature for political satire (in *The Westminster Alice*, articles which were collected in book form, and *The Political Jungle Book* articles, later *The Not-So Stories*, which were not collected) and black humour (*Beasts*) for an exclusively adult audience.

Like Carroll, Leland creates humour from the literalizing of the abstract or metaphorical, and the twisting of symbolic relations. The Goblin insists that 'charitable' should be spelled 'haT' because the 'h' looks like a chair and the 'T' a table: 'chair—a—table', while 'bed' is an 'H' stretched out to look like a bed.[15] He insists that there are only twelve letters in the alphabet, because so many of them can be used for different sounds. Linguistics, logic, and mathematics provide most of the jokes. There is also both ironic and absurd humour. Johnnykin hears one of the fairies' favourite kind of stories: 'probable stories about real children', in which a child gets up, gets dressed, and has breakfast. The story becomes a multiplication table, which is delightful to the fairies because it is so predictable and stable.[16] He also meets characters who personify abstractions, such as The Absurd,[17] The Stupids,[18] and The Old Bogey.[19]

If *Johnnykin* seeded some ideas for future writing, its hero did not provide a model for present behaviour. In fairyland, Johnnykin learns that toys can be brought to life. 'Whenever a girl or boy— particularly a boy—has been *perfectly good* all day long, and teased nobody, and been very polite and used only the best language, and not listened to other people's conversation, it may be done; for such magic deeds can only be worked by very pure people'[20] (pp. 52–4). We know from his sister what the young Hector Munro thought of perfectly good little boys. The Munro children were required to play with one during the annual visit of a friend of the aunts.

'So good a boy,' we would be told, 'he always does what he is bid.'
From that moment a look of deep purpose settled on Hector's face, and on the day when the good Claud arrived an entirely busy and happy time for Hector was the result.

He saw to it that Claud did all the things we must never do, the easier to accomplish since his mother would be indoors tongue-wagging with Granny and the aunts. Poor Claud really was a good child, with no inclination to be anything else, but under Hector's ruthless tuition, backed up by Charlie, he put in a breathless day of bad deeds.

And when Aunt Tom [. . .], after the visitors' departure, remarked, 'Claud is not the good child I imagined him to be,' Hector felt it was the end of a perfect day. (Munro, 5)

Claud's feelings and the consequences to him are of little importance. Hector had a happy, busy day, which is the important thing. He seems to have remembered it. A Claude with an 'e' appears in 'The Boar-Pig' and is suitably chastised. The story's heroine, Matilda, has been ordered to be particularly good during a garden party and to imitate her cousin Claude, 'who never does anything wrong except by accident, and then is always apologetic about it' (*Beasts*, p. 25). Matilda has been told that she takes too much raspberry trifle, unlike Claude, who would never eat too much, so, with the unanswerable logic of the Saki child, she explains:

'Claude always goes to sleep for half an hour after lunch, because he's told to, and I waited till he was asleep, and tied his hands and started forcible feeding with a whole bucketful of raspberry trifle that they were keeping for the garden party. Lots of it went on to his sailor-suit and some of it on to the bed, but a good deal went down Claude's throat, and they can't say again that he has never been known to eat too much raspberry trifle' (ibid. 26)

In 'The Story-Teller' (ibid. 229–38), the good Claud/Claude becomes the horribly good Mabel, and turns the moral of *Johnnykin and the Goblin* upside down. Like Johnnykin, Mabel's reward is a magical excursion, but instead of fairyland she gets the Prince's exotic garden, and instead of live toys she gets medals for good conduct, punctuality, and cleanliness. Johnnykin, pure in thought and deed, is granted his dearest wish, Mabel gets her come-uppance. Her spotless pinafore attracts the attention of a wolf and the medals clash together and give away her hiding place. The wolf eats her.

At a magical banquet, Johnnykin and the fairies feast on oysters, something some readers would find disgusting but less revolting than Lewis Carroll's take on the consumption of living food in *Alice's Adventures Through the Looking-Glass*, in which the food is sentient, and talking. Alice is introduced to a leg of mutton which bows to her, and to a pudding, which speaks in a 'thick, suety sort of voice'.[21] Saki takes this to another level. Oysters are Reginald's food of choice. Unlike the Red Queen, he does not consider it a breach of etiquette to eat something to which he has been introduced. "They not only forgive our unkindness to them; they justify it, they incite us to go on being perfectly horrid to them. Once they arrive at the supper-table they seem to enter thoroughly into the spirit of the thing. There's nothing in Christianity or Buddhism that quite matches the sympathetic unselfishness of an oyster" (*Clovis*, pp. 24–5).

More inspiration for Saki's protean and anthropomorphic characters may have come from Leland's 'Chesmé the cat-girl', who shape-shifts from a Persian cat with a girl's face to other animals and 'a very wild gypsy girl' (*Johnnykin*, pp. 62–3). Cat-girls, Johnnykin learns, smile all the time, so that Chesmé is reminiscent both of Carroll's Cheshire Cat and Saki's Esmé, the hyena passed off as a dog in *Clovis*.

A curious passage follows Johnnykin's inconsequentially asking to be told about the nursery-rhyme character Little Boy Blue, who has not appeared in the story. The answer evokes, through synecdochal hayfields and blue sea, an image of pastoral England which is then associated with a woman who stands for an ideal of purity, Englishness, and freedom. The heading for this page is 'TRUE BLUE'.

'Whenever there are blue eyes and blue skies in dear old England, and while the blue sea surrounds it. And while there are hay-fields, and while people think with love of quiet days of the olden time, and while fairy tales are written for children—there will be Little Boy Blue.'

As she said this, Johnnykin looked into *her* blue eyes and saw in them the same sweet look as in the little boy's, and felt that she was to him what the Little Boy Blue is to all children 'in Summer when the days are long'.[22]

The same image of England and Englishness embodied in one woman was to be evoked, more elaborately, and the same association made, more than thirty years later in Lady Greymarten, a true blue (Tory) Englishwoman and Mrs Kerrick, frequently signified by 'the Englishwoman', who becomes emblematic of her country in *William* (pp. 273–4).[23]

Johnnykin is returned to reality having been granted the dearest wish of the powerless and unhappy fictional child outside the work of Saki and Barrie; he is magically made grown-up. He remains a model of virtue, but the last line of his story fortunately abandons moralizing and sentiment, and ends in a manner closer to that of Saki: 'But it is very difficult for some little Goblins to become good.'[24] The mischievous character is the catalyst who might bring about a moral equilibrium but remains mischievous.

A goblin features in one of the *Reginald in Russia* stories, 'The Saint and the Goblin'. Wilde's stories set in cathedrals or gardens and about stone saints, or princes, and birds are invariably sentimental, but Saki's are emphatically not. 'The Saint and the Goblin' is not one of his best, and the stone goblin, unlike Leland's, has only a few lines, but the characterization is effective, and characteristically Saki, as is the delineation of social hierarchies among stone carvings (the Goblin, with his connections among 'queer carvings' and gargoyles, is a 'person of recognized importance in the cathedral world' (*Reginald in Russia*, p. 60)). The Goblin is a Sakian, Mephistophelian, influence on the unworldly Saint. The Saint worries about the church mice, who are so very poor. The Goblin says it is their function to be poor. When a jackdaw drops a silver coin at his feet, the Saint resolves to use it to dispense charity to the mice. He will appear to the vergeress in a vision and tell her to buy corn to lay on his shrine, the mice will then have food for the winter.

'Of course *you* can do that,' observed the Goblin. 'Now, I can only appear to people after they have had a heavy supper of indigestible things. My opportunities with the vergeress would be limited. There is some advantage in being a saint after all.' (ibid. 62–3)

Then follows the moment in which the Saint succumbs to the Goblin's temptation.

All this while the coin was lying at the Saint's feet. It was clean and glittering and had the Elector's arms beautifully stamped upon it. The Saint began to reflect that such an opportunity was too rare to be hastily disposed of. Perhaps indiscriminate charity might be harmful to the church mice. After all, it was their function to be poor; the Goblin had said so, and the Goblin was generally right.

'I've been thinking,' he said to that personage [. . .]

The Saint decides to tell the vergeress to buy candles for his altar instead. She remembers her dream, finds the coin, bites it, and ties it around the Saint's neck. ' "The only possible explanation," said the Goblin, "is that it's a bad one" ' (p. 64). The professedly honest and charitable Saint's venality and hypocrisy is advertised to the whole cathedral, but the professedly unaltruistic Goblin spares his feelings with a lie.

'What is that decoration your neighbour is wearing?' asked a wyvern that was wrought into the capital of an adjacent pillar.

The Saint was ready to cry with mortification, only, being of stone, he couldn't.

'It's a coin of—ahem!—fabulous value,' replied the Goblin tactfully. (ibid. 65)

Other childhood reading provided source material for Saki's fiction and forms for his political satires, as well as the names of characters in his first novel, though Saki gave his own particular spin to any source material he appropriated. The appearance in *Mrs Elmsley* (published by Hector Munro) of an Alice and a 'Liddel' could even offer grounds for attributing the novel to Saki, but the style and content suggest otherwise. Whereas Lewis Carroll follows the archetype in allowing Alice to find a key which unlocks a door to a land of wonders, Saki's boys have to steal the keys to lumber rooms and store cupboards whose forbidden wonders (jam, toys) would be commonplace to most children. In the *Alice* stories the pointless rules of games and rituals (croquet, tea, and court, in *Wonderland*, and chess, fighting, and parlour-games in *Looking-Glass*) represent the (female) child's-eye view of the seemingly unpredictable and incomprehensible rules imposed by large, loud, all-powerful, and capricious rulers (adults), and the penalties incurred by those who break the rules, or lose the games, represent the apparently causeless and inconsistent slaps and other punishments the adults deal out. The Wonderland Duchess and Queen both peremptorily order ' "Off with his/her head!" ' The Queen 'had only one way of settling difficulties, great or small. "Off with his head!" she said, without even looking round' (p. 125). Characters in the story also make baffling pronouncements based on cod-logic, and subject the child to a constant barrage of interrogation, admonition, and instruction. Carroll makes nonsense of the rules, the orders, and the punishments, which never seem likely to be visited on anyone, but in the world of Saki's boy-children, the rules have cruel and repressive intent and adults are indifferent, menacing, or positively sadistic.

When Alice finds the bottle marked 'Drink Me' she rehearses her knowledge of the kind of cautionary tales we still parrot today, of children who fall prey to various hideous fates through their folly or disobedience, and who are 'eaten up by wild beasts and other unpleasant things, all because they would not remember the simple rules their friends had taught them'.[25] Carroll refuses to collude in exaggerating the consequences of children's natural desire to test the properties of, for example, fire or sharp knives, and by comically downplaying them suggests that children who have these conventional lessons on safety forced on them by repetition cannot relate them to the real world. Alice recalls maxims 'Such as that a red-hot poker will burn you if you hold it too long; and that if you cut your finger *very* deeply with a knife, it usually bleeds;

and she [Alice] had never forgotten that, if you drink much from a bottle marked "Poison", it is almost certain to disagree with you, sooner or later' (p. 10). Alice has learned from 'nice little stories'. Carroll's 'nice' is of course ironic (he is presumably thinking of the kind transcribed by the Brothers Grimm) and he did away with the insistence that such stories should be cautionary or morally improving. Saki does not do away with the morality, though he sometimes inverts it. His boy-children and youths have probably heard the same cautionary tales, but they are unlikely to follow their precepts, even as notionally or misguidedly as Alice, and are far more likely to take the first opportunity of throwing caution to the winds. Those who obey the rules and take heed of the tales, such as Mabel (and Claud), are much more likely to be eaten by wild beasts, or, like the stolidly obedient child in 'The Easter Egg' (*Clovis*, pp. 135–42), blown up by a bomb.

Alice has internalized the rules and cautions to the extent that she is largely self-policing, and the voices of her conscience and her loin-girding have a ring of the Aunt or the Duchess in Saki's work.

'Come, there's no use crying like that!' said Alice to herself, rather sharply; 'I advise you to leave off this minute!' She generally gave herself good advice, (though she very seldom followed it,) and sometimes she scolded herself so severely as to brings tears into her eyes; and once she remembered trying to box her own ears for having cheated herself in a game of croquet she was playing against herself.[26]

Like *Johnnykin*, *Alice in Wonderland* contains the transformation of an unappealing child (a noisy baby) into an animal, a pig rather than a donkey, and as in *Johnnykin*, the child is male and the metaphorical insult becomes the literal metamorphosis. ' "It would have made a dreadfully ugly child: but it makes a rather handsome pig, I think." And she began thinking over other children she knew, who might do very well as pigs, and was just saying to herself, "if one only knew the right way to change them—" '.[27] Saki's version of this is Adrian's kidnapping of the Grobmayer child, 'a particularly loathsome five-year-old' who had appeared as 'Bubbles' during the early part of an evening's entertainment, and introduction of it 'thinly disguised as a performing pig'.

'[He] certainly *looked* very like a pig, and grunted and slobbered just like the real article; no one knew exactly what it was, but every one said it was awfully clever, especially the Grobmayers. At the third curtain Adrian pinched it too hard, and it yelled Marmar! I am supposed to be good at descriptions, but don't ask me to describe the sayings and doings of the Grobmayers at that moment; it was like one of the angrier Psalms set to music.'(*Clovis*, 107–8)

There is no record of Munro's having read *Sylvie and Bruno*, in which Uggug, a hideous fat boy with an expression like a prize pig, is turned into a porcupine, but it is certainly possible that he did.[28] Whether his transformations are derived from Carroll's, or school reading such as Ovid's *Metamorphoses*, or were his own invention, they became something of a speciality. His boy-to-beast transformation is not punishment but blessing, and his animal persona does not have connotations of stupidity, stubbornness, ugliness, dirt, or inferiority, but it does have the same kind of like-for-like logic as Leland's and Carroll's. Gabriel-Ernest is beautiful, desirable, coolly ruthless, and uncanny as a boy, and beautiful, predatory, and terrible as a wolf ('Gabriel Ernest', *Reginald in Russia*, pp. 47–59).[29] Adult metamorphoses are a different matter, and usually both forced on the transformed person and either bogus, as when Clovis pretends to have transformed Mary Hampton into a wolf in 'The She-Wolf' (*Beasts*, pp. 1–12) or an act of containment, as when the highly religious Duke of Scaw turns cabinet members into animals while angels take their place in parliament in 'Ministers of Grace' (*Clovis*, pp. 266–85). Extraordinarily, a woman is allowed to have an enjoyable time as an otter in 'Laura' (*Beasts*, pp. 13–21), but Laura has the redeeming features of vindictiveness and mischievousness, and in her self-centred approach to life is better fitted than most to her animal persona.

Alice's own (imaginary) transformation may have inspired Saki's hyena motif, second only to the wolf in his stories. In *Looking Glass*,

Alice's favourite phrase is 'Let's pretend': 'And once she had really frightened her old nurse by shouting suddenly in her ear, "Nurse! Do let's pretend that I'm a hungry hyaena, and you're a bone!" '[30] Saki's animal-children are equally callous and carnivorous, but far less cutesy, and they are not pretending.

Like a number of Saki's characters, Lewis Carroll's Alice seems heartless to a modern reader, but she merely wholeheartedly endorses the scheme of crime and punishment instilled in her by the grown-ups. In *Through the Looking Glass*, she considers punishments, detachedly and unquestioningly aware that they will be inflicted on her in some regular but unpredictable pattern, and applies to them the same illogical logic as the Duchess-adult and Queen-adult who inflict them:

'Suppose they had saved up all *my* punishments!' she went on, talking more to herself than the kitten. 'What would they do at the end of a year? I should be sent to prison, I suppose, when the day came. Or—let me see—suppose each punishment was to be going without a dinner; then, when the miserable day came, I should have to go without fifty dinners at once! Well, I shouldn't mind *that* much!'[31]

She might well have minded missing two or more consecutive meals, but missing fifty would be tantamount to starvation. The withholding of food or of favourite food was a common sanction in Victorian and Edwardian times. As the White Queen says in *Looking-Glass*: ' "The rule is, jam tomorrow and jam yesterday, but never jam today." '[32] This explains the greed of Bertie, Reginald, and Comus, celebrating their liberation from boyhood restriction into the haven of meals bought for them at the Ritz and Savoy, and the smaller boys' avid interest in the acquisition of any stray peach or chocolate ('The Strategist', *Reginald in Russia*, pp. 85–94; 'The Lumber Room' *Beasts*, pp. 274–84).

Like Saki's coolly indifferent boy-beasts, Alice feels no pity for the terrified gardener cards who are threatened with a worse punishment than hunger, and like his vengeful boys, reflects that the Duchess deserves her sentence of death.[33] Her indifference to the flamingos used as croquet mallets and the hedgehogs used as balls is another matter.[34] Saki is pleased to visit poetic justice on miscreant humans, but animals' deaths are to be deplored, and are usually accidental and unrelated, even if the animals have recently been eating gypsy children ('Esmé', *Clovis*, pp. 12–22) or embarrassing a whole house-party ('Tobermory', *Clovis*, pp. 29–44).

If Alice is callous about the punishment and death of others, she is also quite cavalier about her own. William Empson notes the number of 'death jokes' in the Alice books[35] and Martin Gardner identifies more in *The Annotated Alice*.[36] Saki's stories, of course, contain numerous deaths, few of them natural or lamented, as well as deaths which have not taken place but which are fondly imagined. 'Waldo is one of those people who would be enormously improved by death,' said Clovis ('The Feast of Nemesis', *Beasts and Super-Beasts*, p. 174).

At 9, Hector was ill with something then diagnosed as 'brain-fever', possibly meningitis. The aunts' severity was immediately relaxed, and they nursed Hector devotedly. Confounding medical opinion, he survived the illness and apparently outgrew his alleged sickliness.

During one of his home leaves Charles Munro engaged a governess to teach the two younger children until Hector was old and strong enough to follow Charlie to school. The governess was popular with both. Ethel describes her as 'a real companion', and adds that she 'took us for the walks we loved and explored the whole country-side. She, like Uncle Wellesley, never found us naughty, because she took the trouble to amuse us' (Munro, p. 22). Aunt Augusta, however, took against her, perhaps because she was not of her own choosing; 'she thought Miss J.'s dark eyes were trying to mesmerize her', and had her dismissed. The children had to go without lessons for a term until their aunt found someone to her liking. During that time their grandmother died. Ethel remarks only they 'had a very sad time' (p. 22), but it is not difficult to imagine the real effect of their being returned to their state of imprisonment after a glimpse of the world beyond.

2

School and the European Tour

ROY REYNOLDS, who perhaps knew Munro as well as anyone, said that his friend 'professed violent Tory opinions' throughout his childhood, and from an early age 'began to take an interest in politics and to read any books or papers dealing with them that came his way', but that he loved 'above all, the woodlands and the wild things in them, especially the birds' (Reynolds, p. xii). Hector did not have much opportunity to study the wild things of Devon while he lived in Broadgates Villa, and in 1882, at 12, was released from one Mappin Terrace only into another. Having outwitted the oracular doctor who had declared that he was not to live to grow up (Munro, p. 4) and survived the 'brain fever' contracted when he was 9 (p. 20), he was considered strong enough to follow his brother to Pencarwick School in Exmouth, a prep school for boys which closed in 1908 (its two houses are now both hotels). Here, as at Broadgates, he was enclosed by high walls, though his sister reports that he was very happy there (p. 24). During his first holiday back in Pilton, he was detected in a minor misdeed and sent back to school with no pocket money. If not absolutely cruel, this was a particularly insensitive punishment, since being unable to buy his share of tuck would have made him both singular and unpopular, and having to tell the master who looked after the boys' money would have been humiliating. The children were always quick to close ranks when one of them was in need. Charlie and Ethel sold the books they had been given as Christmas and birthday presents, and sent the proceeds to their brother. Charlie also wrote to their father, who wrote to Aunt Augusta, which provoked a row (ibid.). According to his daughter, Charlie suffered a similar privation at Charterhouse (Langguth, p. 24). Though his father sent a regular allowance from India, none was sent on to Charlie, so that he was one of only two boys in the whole school who had no money for treats. Ethel does not record whether she and Hector did for Charlie what she and Charlie had done for Hector.

Among the books that Hector and his brother would probably have been sent by their father or Uncle Wellesley, or even to have chosen, when they had the money, were typical Victorian adventure and 'improving', didactic tales. The Reverend Frederick William Farrar's *Eric, or Little by Little: A Tale of Roslyn School* (1858), might even have slipped past their grandmother's interdict on fiction on Sundays, so overt is its moral. R. M. Ballantyne's *The Coral Island* (1858) promoted the imperialist agenda, as did the prolific output of ex-soldier and war correspondent G. A. Henty, the boy heroes of whose historical adventure stories would have appealed to Hector, as would Robert Louis Stevenson's *Treasure Island*, which first appeared in book form in 1883, when Hector was coming up to 13. Since history was Hector's favourite study, and he was a passionate Royalist (Munro, p. 20), it is easy to imagine that he would have liked Henty's *Friends Though Divided, a Tale of the Civil War* (1883).

At 14, Hector left Pencarwick, but was not allowed to follow Charlie to Charterhouse School, and instead entered Bedford Grammar School (now Bedford School) three months before his fifteenth birthday, in September 1885. He did not shine there. According to Ethel Munro, his masters reported that he had 'plenty of ability but no application' (ibid. p. 24). His career at Bedford seems to have been quiet, and he left no discernible mark beyond the record of his entry and departure, until his name was added to the roll of honour after he was killed. He won no prizes and did not become a member of the Old Bedfordians.[1] He was a pupil at the school for less than two years, and there is no evidence of his having been miserable, but neither is there any of his having had a good time. In his writing, school-aged boys, whether away at school or not, inhabit a world impenetrable to feminine or adult influence, and are far more vicious than the animals he depicts. Abandoning a young boy to this world is tantamount to exposing him in the jungle. He will become either predator or prey. None of the heroes of the short stories is physically cruel, but a number of minor characters are. In 'The Strategist' (*Reginald in Russia*, pp. 85–93) a group of schoolboys at a party (the Wrotsleys—presumably rotters) indulge in ritualized infliction of maximum pain on a boy, Rollo, stranded at a party without his own faction. It is made clear that he would have done the same thing had the positions been reversed. No metaphors or similes of animals are used for the boys who inflict pain purely for temporary dominance in a long-standing power struggle, but the boy who outwits them and escapes further beatings is described in animal terms: 'Rollo sank into a chair and smiled ever so faintly at the Wrotsleys, just a momentary baring of the teeth; an otter, escaping from the fangs of the hounds into the safety of a deep pool, might have given a similar demonstration of its feelings' (ibid. p. 93). A more fully developed, because older and even less defenceless, otter/wolf youth appears in 'Gabriel-Ernest' in the same collection. This youth hunts to kill, but to eat, and inflicts nothing worse than embarrassment and barbed comments on those he does not consider legitimate prey.

An exchange in the 'playlet' 'The Baker's Dozen' contains a line which might well get a laugh, but also has a painful resonance.

Em[ily Carewe].: There's always a chance that one of them might turn out depraved and vicious, and then you could disown him. I've heard of that being done.

Maj[or Richard Dumbarton].: But, good gracious, you've got to educate him first. You can't expect a boy to be vicious till he's been to a good school.　(ibid. 109–10)

It is at school that Saki males learn to take and inflict punishment physically, a lesson they evidently learn well, since a number of the practical jokes and cuttings-down-to-size they arrange have a physical dimension, but only Comus Bassington, central protagonist of *The Unbearable Bassington*, is shown as enjoying the infliction of pain for its own sake.

> 'I missed a footer practice,' said Lancelot.
> 'Six,' said Comus briefly, picking up his cane.
> 'I didn't see the notice on the board,' hazarded Lancelot as a forlorn hope.
> 'We are always pleased to listen to excuses, and our charge is two extra cuts. That will be eight. Get over.'　(*Bassington*, 37).

He draws a chalk line across the boy's buttocks to be sure of hitting him on the same spot each time.

> 'Bend a little more forward,' he said to the victim, 'and much tighter. Don't trouble to look pleasant, because I can't see your face anyway. It may sound unorthodox to say so, but this is going to hurt you much more than it will hurt me.'
> There was a carefully measured pause, and then Lancelot was made vividly aware of what a good cane can be made to do in really efficient hands. At the second cut he projected himself hurriedly off the chair.
> 'Now I've lost count,' said Comus; 'we shall have to begin all over again. Kindly get back into the same position. If you get down again before I've finished, Rutley will hold you over and you'll get a dozen.'
> Lancelot got back on to the chair, and was re-arranged to the satisfaction of his executioner. He stayed there somehow or other while Comus made eight accurate and agonizingly effective shots at the chalk line.　(ibid. 38)

The boy's posture and the sharp down-stroke of the cane make the metaphor 'executioner' apt. Saki does not labour the point that the beatings integral to the school system (they are so commonplace that receiving them can be described as going through the mill) breed a vicious line of surrogate reprisals (against those who become available as the victim rises in the pecking order rather than the original perpetrators); the narrative voice simply lets us know that:

Comus had gone through the mill of many scorching castigations in his earlier schooldays, and was able to appreciate to the last ounce the panic that must be now possessing his foredoomed victim, probably at this moment hovering miserably outside the door. After all, that was part of the fun of the thing, and most things had their amusing side if one knows where to look for it. (ibid. 36)

Saki depicts the youth now old enough to inflict rather than be the victim as retaining a vivid memory of the ordeal of caning but nonetheless unaffected in his enjoyment of inflicting it. Most of Saki's youthful protagonists know where to find the fun of things, but only Comus finds it in caning small boys.

Comus indicated the chair that stood in sinister isolation in the middle of the room. Never had an article of furniture seemed more hateful in Lancelot's eyes. Comus could well remember the time when a chair stuck in the middle of a room had seemed to him the most horrible of manufactured things. (ibid. 37)

Clovis Sangrail remembers, perhaps fondly, chastising smaller boys at school, but unlike Comus he had not purchased the pleasure from another boy in exchange for chocolate. The beatings he inflicts seem to be much more part of an inescapable system in which they are passed down from one generation to another. He remembers a day

'consecrated to the settlement of feuds and grudges; of course we did not appreciate it as much as it deserved, because after all, any day of the term could be used for that purpose. Still, if one had chastised a smaller boy for being cheeky weeks before, one was always permitted on that day to recall the episode to his memory by chastising him again. That is what the French call reconstructing the crime.'

'I should call it reconstructing the punishment,' said Mrs Thackenbury; 'and, anyhow, I don't see how you could introduce a system of primitive schoolboy vengeance into civilized adult life.' ('The Feast of St Nemesis', *Clovis*, 170)

Of course, that is exactly what some of Saki's characters do.

If readers are expected to disapprove of Comus' sadism, or the four-against-one tactics of the boys in 'The Strategist', they are clearly not being prompted to disapprove of boys' violence in general, since Saki depicts bellicosity as normal and natural, and any attempt to curb it as ridiculous and doomed. The title story of *Toys* satirizes a real article published in a London paper in March 1914 reporting the recommendations of the National Peace Council about the provision of 'peace toys' for children. Whilst acknowledging that boys 'naturally love fighting and all the panoply of war', the council finds that there is no reason for adults to encourage those 'primitive instincts', and draws the attention of toy manufacturers to a forthcoming exhibition of peace toys 'not miniature soldiers but miniature civilians, not guns but ploughs and the tools of industry' ('The Toys of Peace', *Toys*, p. 3). A mother persuades her brother to bring some of these new toys to his nephews, Eric and Bertie, and they are duly presented with models of a municipal dust-bin, municipal wash-house, public library, school of art, and Manchester branch of the Young Women's Christian Association; miniature figures representing John Stuart Mill, Mrs Hemans, Robert Raikes (the founder of Sunday schools), Rowland Hill, Sir John Herschel, a sanitary inspector, a district councillor, and an official of the Local Government Board; and miniature hop poles, wheelbarrow, hoe, ventilator, and beehive.

The boys, having hoped for toy soldiers, are disappointed, and actually try to get out of playing by pleading a holiday task, but are told that they must play with their new toys. A little later their uncle returns, to find that, having reinvented the municipal dustbin as a fort, John Stuart Mill as Marshal Saxe, Robert Raikes as Louis XIV, and Mrs Hemans as Madame de Maintenon, they are using the toys of peace to make war.

'Louis orders his troops to surround the Young Women's Christian Association and seize the lot of them. "Once back at the Louvre and the girls are mine," he exclaims. We must use Mrs. Hemans again for one of the girls; she says "Never," and stabs Marshal Saxe to the heart.'

'He bleeds dreadfully,' exclaimed Bertie, splashing red ink liberally over the façade of the Association building.

'The soldiers rush in and avenge his death with the utmost savagery. A hundred girls are killed.' (ibid. 11.)

In Saki's world, boys left to their own devices will want to fight, and boys in whom the desire to fight and a feeling for the 'Romance of war' are squashed will be anything but natural and normal.[2]

Hector's time at Bedford Grammar School was short because in 1887 Colonel Munro retired, returned to England, and carried him off, away from Bedford, Broadgate, schoolwork, restraint, and England. The liberation extended to Hector's sister, who was also rescued from the Aunts, but not to their elder brother. While Charlie was expected to begin the transition to adult life and responsibilities by completing his studies at Charterhouse and preparing to take the army exams, the 17-year-old Hector was allowed the irresponsibility of youth. The family's first destination was Etretat, in Normandy. A beach holiday spent bathing with congenial Russian and French visitors was followed by educational and recreational trips to Dresden, Berlin, Munich, Nuremburg, Pottsdam, and Prague, and a restorative stay at Davos, in Eastern Switzerland. Charlie joined them in Dresden during his school holiday, but left to enter an army crammer (Munro, p. 26).

Early repression and ill-health followed by sudden release appear to have delayed Hector's development. His sister remarks that although 'he was then eighteen, he was still a boy, with no intention of growing up' (ibid.). Newly untrammelled energies found an outlet in practical jokes of the most childish and sometimes crass kind. Ethel describes one of these with breathtaking smallness of mind. The girls are ugly, and so are fair game; the landlady is

German, and so has no sense of humour; a politely insincere note from the English party should more than satisfy the schoolmistress, and close the matter, in spite of their public demonstration of its insincerity.

On the flat beneath us was a girls' school, all of them ugly. One day, when my father was out, the boys made a weird figure of his bathing costume, stuffed out with paper and clothes, with a sponge for a face, and a rakish-looking hat. This they lowered into the balcony below. The school-mistress happened to be giving dinner to a pastor, and to them, instead of to the girls, was vouchsafed this appalling vision.

When the boys thought enough time had elapsed, they swiftly drew up the figure. Swiftly, also, a note of complaint arrived for our landlady, who, being German, saw no fun in the affair, not even with the figure sprawling at her feet. It was the convulsive laughter of a hitherto rather unbending American woman (in fact the only time we ever knew her to laugh) that thawed her, and a note of apology was sent—insincere, as the school ma'am must have guessed, from the shouts of laughter above. (ibid. 26–7)

Also in Germany, Hector wandered about in parks, accosting strangers to discover the location and German names of birds (according to Ethel) by drawing their outlines in the gravel of the paths (pp. 27–8). Then followed a lordly 'strenuous' progress through Europe, in which they refused to go over the Palace of Sans Souci at Potsdam until a keeper could show them where Frederick the Great's chargers and dogs were buried, they laid bets on the number of representations of St Sebastian they would find in the galleries and museums (Berlin won, with eighteen), vandalized a statue in Prague (Ethel distracted the guard while Hector cut a hair from the tail of Wallenstein's charger), and delighted in medieval towns and by their first sight of snow-capped mountains, on their way to Prague. In the castle of Wallenstein they were shown a window in a high chamber from which, they were told, obstreperous councillors were thrown. They leant out to see how far the victims had to fall, and Hector stored up the memory and later used it in his play *Karl-Ludwig's Window* (p. 28).

After an exhausting tour, they settled in Davos for several months, at the Belvedere (now the Steinberger Belvedere). This was on the main street, less than fifteen years old, and already the town's grandest hotel. Robert Louis Stevenson stayed there in 1881, though a verse letter to his friend Dew-Smith professes less satisfaction with his surroundings than Ethel's account.[3] The stay began with a week of lying low, drinking milk and recovering from the rigours of the tour: 'then we let ourselves go!' They encountered a number of what Ethel describes as 'middle-aged, self-sacrificing men' who 'tried to be extra fathers to us, but it was no use. Swiss air and freedom went to our heads—nothing but an avalanche would have stopped us' (ibid.). Ethel describes Davos (now a busy resort and conference venue) as 'a friendly, jolly place, not at all fashionable', but its high altitude, sunny climate, and clean dry air made it a popular resort for the convalescent, and for the location of sanatoria offering respite from tuberculosis. It had already had its share of famous visitors, including the poet and critic John Addington Symonds and his many distinguished visitors, and Arthur Conan Doyle was to ski there in 1899. Fashionable or not, there was plenty to do. Ethel lists the Munros' physical occupations as tennis, paper-chases, riding, dancing, climbing, and searching for marmots on the high reaches, and their mental occupations as lectures and painting lessons, but adds that Professor Meyer, a painter of birds of prey and a teacher after their own hearts, 'understood that we *had* to play some wild game before settling down to work' (p. 29). The wild games she describes have a Lawrentian feel. 'Usually we got to his flat before he was ready for us, and crept into his bedroom; presently a search began, and before he knew where he was he found himself in the midst of a pillow-fight—that or a wild scrimmage round the studio, and then we settled down' (ibid.).

Symonds gives a detailed contemporary description of the area in 'Our Life in the Swiss Highlands'.[4] Symonds took a house at Davos and was there during the Munros' stay, which was towards the end of his life (he died in 1893). Colonel Munro might be expected to have considered the author of *A Problem in Greek Ethics* (written in 1873 and published in 1883), a history of and apologia for homosexual love, an undesirable acquaintance for the 17-year-old Hector, and Hector himself, a snobbish Tory from infancy, might be expected to have little in common with the 'bourgeois radical', but the two did meet on several occasions. Ethel sums up the relationship in one line: 'he and Hector played chess together, and found they had a taste for heraldry in common' (ibid.), but it is possible that Symonds's work left a trace on Saki's, in particular in the portrayal of men. Many of Symonds's poems depict young men in languorous recumbent poses, often asleep.[5] The use of animal imagery makes the men's poses suggestive of latent strength in utter abandonment rather than weakness. This is perhaps echoed in Saki's descriptions of young men in garden chairs or by rock pools, reminiscent of Wilde's requirement of idleness for the condition of perfection, and his assertion that the aim of perfection is youth.

In his autobiographical writing, Symonds refers to his homosexual desire as a wolf within: 'Since the date of my marriage I had ceased to be assailed by what I called "the wolf" — that undefined craving coloured with a vague but poignant hankering after males'.[6] Symonds's memoirs remained unpublished until fifty years after his death, and then were published only in part, but one of his poems refers to a chimera, a hybrid lion-goat-serpent winged monster (Symonds's has bat's wings) which Rictor Norton has suggested is a further encoding of the wolf. Saki's wolves, werewolves, and other beasts within may originate from this source.

Childhood brings flowers to pluck, and butterflies;
Boyhood hath bat and ball, shy dubious dreams,

Foreshadowed love, friendship, prophetic gleams;
Youth takes free pastime under laughing skies;
Ripe manhood weds, made early strong and wise;
Clasping the real, scorning what only seems,
He tracks love's fountain to its furthest streams,
Kneels by the cradle where his firstborn lies.
Then for the soul athirst, life's circle run,
Yet nought accomplished and the world unknown,
Rises Chimaera. Far beyond the sun
Her bat's wings bear us. The empyreal zone
Shrinks into void. We pant. Thought, sense rebel,
And swoon desiring things impossible.

The Munros left Davos in April, after which they stayed at Schloss Salenstein, on the Swiss side of Lake Constance, in the home of 'some very charming people' they had met at Davos (Munro, 30). They then returned to England and took a large old house, Heanton Court, near the Taw estuary in North Devon, whose long history would have appealed to Hector. It was the seat of a branch of the Basset family from the fifteenth to early nineteenth century and features in R. D. Blackmore's novel *The Maid of Sker*, a name Hector was later to bestow on a pony when he was far away from the Court, Devon, England, and his family. (The house is now a pub.) By late 1891, they had moved a few miles away to Wrafton House, in Heanton Punchardon, in which they were looked after by servants at a ratio of 1 : 1. The 1891 census shows that the house was occupied by Charles A. Munro, then 57: 'Army Colonel—Indian Staff Corps'; Ethel M. Munro, 22: no employment listed; Hector H. Munro, 20: no employment listed; Ellen Petherick, 47: Cook—Domestic Servant; Gertrude M. Lawrence, 21: Housemaid—Domestic Servant (not the famous Gertrude Lawrence of stage and screen—she was born in 1898); and James Lethaby, 29: Private 1st class Army Reserve, Gardener—Domestic Servant. The servants do not much figure in correspondence between the Munros, but far away in Burma a few years later Munro perhaps had Ellen Petherick in mind when he sent his sister a sketch which featured a plump woman wearing an apron over a long dress. The sketch illustrates a report of the intrepidity of his current servant:

Fancy saying to an English cook 'Dinner at 7 sharp, and I've three guests coming; and by the way, just see if the buzzard's nest in the high elm has any eggs in it; and while you're about it find out if there is any gambling going on in the Red Lion, etc., etc.' Pedrica would have wept scalding tears at such requests.   (ibid. 52–3)

'Pedrica' is shown, hands on hips, confronting a woman with a dog at her heels who points behind her up to a nest in a high tree; she is saying: 'What! <u>ME</u> Mum?' (p. 52).

Hector explored the Devon countryside, learned the local folk-lore and superstitions, and heard of the incident which became 'The Blood-Feud of Toad-Water'; they got a dog and lost a cat and her kitten, probably to 'some beast of a keeper'. After the sublime landscape of the Alps, Devon perhaps seemed a little flat and parochial, even claustrophobic. Ethel reports: 'For two years we lived at Heanton, studying under my father's direction, then left it for a season in town. Then back to Davos for the winter' (p. 31). Heanton was four miles from Barnstaple and four miles from the Aunts, who were permitted to visit, singly, but not encouraged to stay for long.

On the whole we were far too kind to them—so much water had flowed under the bridge since Broadgate days, and we were now topdogs [sic] and they knew it. Moreover, they had mellowed a bit, and Aunt Tom especially was devoted to Hector. She was such an original character we had to forgive her much, simply because of her unusualness.   (ibid. 30–31)

Charlie, having been turned down by the army on the grounds of his poor eyesight, left to join the Burma (later Myanmar) Police, but though he was now out of his teens, Hector's extended youth continued. Ethel reports that, back in Davos for the winter, he was the leading spirit of a 'Push' and that on more than one occasion they literally painted the place red, and blue, with enamel. He also organized six people to keep guard while he painted devils 'in every state of intoxication' on the Hôtel des Îles. That hotel is censured by Ethel as 'very pious', but to her brother it had committed a less forgivable crime, it was mean (p. 32). They therefore plotted 'a gorgeous hoax' on its guests. The four English hotels of Davos habitually selected an 'amusement committee' at the beginning of each winter season to organize dances, concerts, and other entertainments. Each hotel would contribute to the costs, and each would invite the others' guests to the entertainments. The Hôtel des Îles invited no one, collected money, and spent it on a dinner for themselves. Ethel writes that 'naturally' this they could not stand, so they appointed themselves agents of Nemesis. Hector wrote invitations as from the Hôtel des Îles to the other English hotels and a selection of visitors, asking them to a performance of 'Box and Cox'.[7] Ethel blithely records that they had heard this was an improper play, so had chosen it to attract the foreigners. Self-righteously, she remarks that they left out the distant chalets so that no one would be put to the expense of hiring a sleigh (p. 33). Hector decreed that they did not have the nerve to look innocent, so they didn't stay to see the 'fun' but got it at second-hand from another member of the 'Push'. The English hotels got wind of what was going on, but not the Kurhaus, whose guests arrived expecting an entertainment. 'Then there was pandemonium, and a babel of imprecations assailed the chaste ears of the innocent inmates. "I know who did it," shouted an irascible man, and rushing home for a horsewhip he hurled himself into the room of a guiltless American. I mean he was not one of the "Push"' (p. 34). No more than he had grown out of practical jokes had Hector grown out of the conviction that he had the right to wield the flaming sword (or brush) of justice. Ethel's remark about the falsely accused American is interesting gloss on the siblings' view of people; the man is assumed not guiltless even if he is innocent of this particular prank.

After this last stay in Davos, the three returned to North Devon in the spring of 1893, and in June 1893, at the age of 22 and 6 months, Munro took up paid employment for the first time. Too prone to ill-health for a commission in the regular British army, he was nonetheless considered fit for duty in a colonial police force, and was sent out to follow his brother to Burma, and a new kind of hell. He might have reflected that since this was the Burmese mounted police, he would at least be able to ride.

3

Burma, Devon

To what extent Hector chose to join the Burma police is impossible to say. Perhaps he conformed to the family tradition to please his father, or because at the time he had no other way of earning a living. Though 'gentlemen', the male Munros had little beyond their salary to support them, and Colonel Munro had been keeping six dependants before the death of his mother, and five since, and his pension would have been linked to the value of the rupee, which had fallen considerably.[1] Ethel Munro's report of her brother's time in Burma, like his letters to her, make it sound all very cushioned and jolly, but Munro was later to say that the picture he drew in *The Unbearable Bassington* was closer to the truth, even though the exile in the novel is sent to West Africa rather than Burma. The story's anti-hero, the indelibly urban prodigal Comus Bassington, contemplating his forthcoming translation to the tropics on his last night in Town, reflects:

He would be in some unheard-of sun-blistered wilderness, where natives and pariah dogs and raucous-throated crows fringed round mockingly on one's loneliness, where one rode for sweltering miles for the chance of meeting a collector or police officer, with whom most likely on closer acquaintance one had hardly two ideas in common, where female society was represented at long intervals by some climate-withered woman missionary or official's wife, where food and sickness and veterinary lore became at last the three outstanding subjects on which the mind settled, or rather sank. That was the life he foresaw and dreaded, and that was the life he was going to. (*Bassington*, 239–40)

One sensible woman refrains from the usual blindly optimistic nothing-sayings.

'I'm not going to talk the usual rot to you about how much you will like it and so on. I sometimes think that one of the advantages of hell will be that no one will have the impertinence to point out to you that you're really better off than you would be anywhere else.'   (ibid. 241–2)

As far as the Munro brothers were concerned, Burma was British; a possession of the Empire controlled from India. Although the possibilities for commercial exploitation were strong (especially for the export of tea and rice), Burma's main importance was strategic; it was a buffer zone between India, Thailand, and China. Throughout the eighteenth century the British East India Company steadily acquired Burmese territories. More lands were taken in the First and Second Anglo-Burmese Wars of the 1820s and 1850s and in January 1886 the British formally annexed Burma. France had gained control of Indochina, consisting of Annam, Cambodia, Cochinchina, Laos, and Tonkin, by 1887. During the time that Hector and Charlie were in South East Asia, only Thailand remained independent of European rule. The Burmese monarchy was abolished and all political power was appropriated. The country was ruled from Calcutta, and the administrative mechanisms imposed were those of India. While the lower part of the country was ruled directly by the colonial powers, the upper, more ethnically diverse, part was ruled indirectly and allowed to retain its social and administrative structures. This led to ethnic and political division. The British encouraged migration from the dryer northern parts of Burma to the wetter Myanmar Delta, and organized the building of roads and bridges, docks, warehouses, and all the apparatus of modern international trade. Though the greater rainfall made the area fertile, it was covered with jungles and swamps infested by mosquitoes. Those who worked on it during the 1850s and after were vulnerable to various diseases, including malaria.

British administration and British rule were supported by the army and the police force. Though the rank-and-file were largely Indian or from the ethnic minorities of Burma, they were supervised by Anglo-Burmese bureaucrats and British officers. Hector joined his brother to be one of these.

Charlie met Hector on his arrival and they both stayed with the Deputy Inspector-General of Police in Rangoon before Hector left for his station. On arrival in the Singu province, Hector almost immediately fell ill. Comus Bassington's first experience of fever has an enervating and lowering effect and, in a landscape he detests, among people with whom he cannot communicate, in a climate he cannot tolerate, he rapidly sinks into apathy and depression.

The procession of water-fetchers had formed itself in a long chattering line that stretched riverwards. Comus wondered how many tens of thousands of times that procession had been formed since first the village came into existence. They had been doing it while he was playing in the cricket-fields at school, while he was spending Christmas holidays in Paris, while he was going his careless round of theatres, dances, suppers and card-parties, just as they were doing it now; they would be doing it when there was no one alive who remembered Comus Bassington. This thought recurred again and again with painful persistence, a morbid growth arising in part from his loneliness.

Staring dumbly out at the toiling, sweltering human ant-hill, Comus marvelled how missionary enthusiasts could labour hopefully at the work of transplanting their religion, with its home-grown accretions of fatherly parochial benevolence, in this heat-blistered, fever-scourged wilderness, where men lived like groundbait and died like flies. Demons one might believe in, if one did not hold one's imagination in healthy check, but a kindly all-managing God, never. Somewhere in the west country of England Comus has an uncle who lived in a rose-covered rectory and taught a wholesome gentle-hearted creed that expressed itself in the spirit of 'Little lamb, Who made thee?' and faithfully reflected the beautiful homely Christ-child sentiment of Saxon Europe. What a far-away, unreal fairy-story it all seemed here in this West African land, where the bodies of men were of as little account as the bubbles that floated on the oily froth of the great flowing river, and where it required a stretch of wild profitless imagination to credit them with undying souls! In the life he had come from Comus had been accustomed to think of individuals as definite masterful personalities, making their several marks on the circumstances that revolved around them; they did well or ill, or in most cases indifferently, and were criticized, praised, blamed, thwarted, or tolerated, or given way to. In any case, humdrum or outstanding, they had their spheres of importance, little or big. They dominated a breakfast table or harassed a Government, according to their capabilities or opportunities, or perhaps they merely had irritating mannerisms. At any rate it seemed highly probable that they had souls. Here a man simply made a unit in an unnumbered population, an inconsequent dot in a loosely-compiled death-roll. Even his own position as a white man exalted conspicuously above a horde of black natives did not save Comus from the depressing sense of nothingness which his first experience of fever had thrown over him. He was a lost, soulless body in this great uncaring land; if he died another would take his place, his few effects would be inventoried and sent down to the coast, some one else would finish off any tea or whisky that he left behind—that would be all.   (ibid. 294–5)

Like Hector in Pilton and perhaps in Burma, Comus is dying of the claustrophobia of monotony; of his sense of being unwanted, unremembered, and unloved. Like Hector in Burma, he is dying of homesickness for an England which has suddenly become unbearably beloved and necessary to him; dying simply of being in an alien world which cannot support his kind of life. It is hard to believe that the phrase 'the beautiful homely Christ-child sentiment of Saxon Europe' passes through the mind of a Saki character, even indirectly, yet it is used straight-facedly.

Comus carries with him a disintegrating novel whose plot is so bad that even in his almost bookless state he cannot plough through it. What he reads are the advertisements:

and these the exile scanned with a hungry intentness that the romance itself could never have commanded. The name of a shop, of a street, the address of a restaurant, came to him as a bitter reminder of the world he had lost, a world that debated and intrigued and wire-pulled, fought or compromised political battles—and recked nothing of its outcasts

wandering through forest paths and steamy swamps or lying in the grip
of fever. Comus read and re-read those few lines of advertisement, just as
he treasured a much-crumpled programme of a first-night performance at
the Straw Exchange Theatre; they seemed to make a little more real the
past that was already too shadowy and so utterly remote. For a moment
he could almost capture the sensation of being once again in those haunts
that he loved; then he looked round and pushed the book wearily from
him. The steaming heat, the forest, the rushing river hemmed him in on
all sides.   (ibid. 296–7).

For Comus, the wild forest is a claustrophobia-inducing cage,
while the city represents openness and freedom. The longed-for
land is not the west country with its green water meadows and
rose-covered rectories, but the West End of London, which is
Comus's native land, and for some years Hector Munro's; not an
idealized, pastoral England, but the material world of commerce
and commodity. Comus knows that he will never return; in striving
to recall it he is already 'haunting' it. In his bleakest moments,
Munro may have felt the same way. Once again he was both
locked in a place he did not understand and could not control and
locked out of a wider world he had just begun to visit. Where
the Devon countryside beyond the windows of Broadgates had
represented the as yet unexplored outdoors, now the entirety of
England, countryside and city, was a lost Eden.

He once told me of the feeling of loneliness he experienced when he first
arrived in Burmah, using almost the same words in which he described
Bassington's sense of isolation in the colony to which he was sent. That
account of the young Englishman looking enviously at a native boy and
girl racing wildly along in the joy of youth and companionship, is one of the
rare instances of autobiography in Munro's works.   (Reynolds, p. xiii)

Charles Gillen relates Munro's unhappiness less to isolation from
his family, friends, and country than to the place to which he was
exiled. Perhaps projecting onto Munro some imperialist sentiments
of his own, Gillen remarks that 'he may have felt a mixture of
fascination and repulsion for its vile greenness, its heat, its filth, its
stench, its noise of humanity'.[2]

Munro was not entirely cut off; he corresponded with his family and occasionally met other English-speaking people. Reading his letters we feel irritation at the blind adherence to divisions that made natives ineligible, unthinkable, as equal friends. On 26 July 1893 he writes to his sister: 'Mr Carey arrived by the boat and paid me a long visit—it was a relief to have someone human to talk to' (Munro, 37). Comus is a party to the same prejudices, more so, in fact, and we judge him accordingly. He is never a sympathetic character even before, entirely unqualified and unfit to run anything, he goes out to command an outpost of empire. Yet *Bassington* does generate sympathy for him and his story becomes a tragedy, as Hector Munro's very nearly was.

We can perhaps get a sense of Burma through Munro's eyes by reading his late story 'The Comments of Moung Ka', an elaborate platform for a trite remark about the government's failure to hold a referendum on partition, but set in a scene that must have been more than familiar to Munro.

Moung Ka, cultivator of rice and philosophic virtues, sat on the raised platform of his cane-built house by the banks of the swiftly flowing Irawaddy. On two sides of the house there was a bright green swamp, which stretched away to where the uncultivated jungle growth began. In the bright-green swamp, which was really a rice-field when you looked closely at it, bitterns and pond-herons and elegant cattle-egrets stalked and peered with the absorbed air of careful and conscientious reptile-hunters, who could never forget that, while they were undoubtedly useful, they were also distinctly decorative. In the tall reed growth by the riverside grazing buffaloes showed in patches of dark slatey blue, like plums fallen amid long grass, and in the tamarind trees that shaded Moung Ka's house the crows, restless, raucous-throated, and much-too-many, kept up their incessant afternoon din, saying over and over again all the things that crows have said since there were crows to say them.   ('The Comments of Moung Ka', *Square Egg*, 161)

Ethel Munro was perhaps not sensitive, and read her brother's letters at face value. She records that he 'got a lot of enjoyment from the animal life surrounding him—to be on a horse was one great delight, and to be at close quarters with wild animals was another' (Munro, 34). It is likely that by 1924, when her memoir was published, she was also already actively censoring the letters and shaping the image of her brother that she wished posterity to receive. She says that she has quoted 'almost exclusively the bits dealing with animals, because they are the most characteristic of him' (ibid.). The first letters, from Singu, are breezy, affectedly cynical, and humorous, even about Munro's illness. Rather than Comus Bassington, Munro seems to be writing in the persona of Bertie Steffink, a young scape-grace as welcome to his relations as Comus, and like him got rid of abroad by a substitute father, though, since he has survived and escaped from Ceylon, British Columbia, Australia, and Canada, presumably more robust. This later story is comic, of course, but its irony nonetheless indicates its narrator's opinion of the use of the colonies as a dumping-ground for unwanted youths.

At the age of eighteen Bertie had commenced that round of visits to our Colonial possessions, so seemly and desirable in the case of a Prince of the Blood, so suggestive of insincerity in a young man of the middle class. He had gone to grow tea in Ceylon and fruit in British Columbia, and to help sheep grow wool in Australia. At the age of twenty he had just returned from some similar errand in Canada, from which it might be gathered that the trial he gave to these various experiments was of the summary drum-head nature. ('Bertie's Christmas Eve', *Toys*, 97–8)

There is a nice contrast between a prince touring the margins of empire like a squire riding the boundaries of his estate, being fêted, lionized, and entertained, and inspecting 'our' (his) colonial possessions from within a cocoon of English comforts, and the middle-class boy whose 'round of visits' should not have been a round but a one-way trip, and which will not occasion cheering crowds at either end. Bertie regards with deep gloom the prospect of being sent off again (this time to 'a distant corner of Rhodesia, whence return would be a difficult matter'), but cheers himself up by wreaking havoc on a Christmas house-party. Though his journey to 'this uninviting destination' is imminent, we feel that he will survive, if just to return to plague his uncle.

In Munro's letters from Burma, people are on the whole dismissed as causes of one kind or another of social nuisance: babies cry, children scream, middle-aged ladies match-make and make personal comments (in a letter of 25 August 1893 he compares one to the Queen in *Alice in Wonderland*), men demonstrate either turpitude, cowardice, or cupidity; people en masse require him to be on parade in sweltering heat. He is 'agreeably surprised with' his servants, even though he never refers to them by name. They are 'quick, resourceful, seem honest, and are genuinely attached to my interests' (letter to Ethel Munro, 5 June 1893, Munro, p. 36). 'My boy continues to give satisfaction in regard to cooking, the way he serves up chicken as beefsteak borders on the supernatural' (letter to Ethel Munro, 17 June 1893, ibid. p. 37). Animals are sources of refreshment, apart from the local dogs, which 'go on at intervals during the twenty-four hours, like the Cherubin which rest not day or night. Have you ever seen a dog bark and yawn at the same time? I did the other day and nearly had a fit; it reminded me of a person saying the responses in church' (ibid. pp. 35–6). Munro himself may already have been censoring his records of his activities, and he selected his subjects to suit his recipient, which in Ethel's case meant pets.

I had quite a nursery establishment last week; I found a little house-squirrel which had just left its nest, on my verandah; it is like a large dormouse, silver grey with a mauve grey tail, and orange buff underneath; it lives upon milk and is very tame and snoomified . . . [EM's omission] Then there was a duckling; I thought of putting it with the squirrel, but the latter looks upon everything as meant to be eaten, and the duck had broad views on the same subject, so I thought they had better live in single blessedness. As the squirrel occupied the only empty biscuit tin the duck had to go into the waste-paper basket where it was quite happy.   (Letter to Ethel Munro, 5 June 1893, ibid. 36)

Later he adopted a tiger cub, a chicken dropped by a raven, and a darter (a large bird) (letter to Ethel Munro, 6 September 1893,

ibid. pp. 43–4). The next letter is in a similar vein; the interests
are those of the nineteenth-century Englishman abroad; local flora
and fauna, and the pursuit of gentlemanly studies not incompatible
with distance from the British Museum.

I am rather excité over a pony I have unearthed with zebra markings
on its legs; Darwin believed that the horse, ass, zebra, quagga and
hemonius were all evolved from an equine animal striped like the zebra
but differently constructed, and in his book on the descent of domestic
animals he attached great importance to some zebra-like markings which
he observed on an Exmoor pony; so my discovery may be of some
interest . . . [EM's omission] This is a disappointing place as far as the flora
is concerned; I have not seen any decent flowers or shrubs, except a kind
of magnolia which is common here [. . .]
    I amuse myself by painting, when the midges are not too troublesome.
I am doing a picture of the coronation of Albert II, Archduke of Austria,
in 1437; not a proper picture but a sort of heraldic procession like you
would see in old tapestries. The arch-bishop of Trèves looks very smart
on a fiery bay; I shall never forget the trouble I had to find his arms at the
Brit. Museum.   (letter to Ethel Munro, 17 June 1893, ibid. 36–7)

Surrounded by torrential rivers, swamps, forests, temples, and
other artefacts of ancient cultures, Munro chooses a subject from
medieval northern Europe. Aunt Tom, similarly blinkered, writes
to her nephew blithely disregarding any possible interest in his
discoveries in a wonderful unfamiliar country, still less his possible
discomforts, and entirely taken up with her own concerns. 'Aunt
Tom's first letter was full of her grievances—so interesting to read;
really if Providence persecuted me in the way it does her, I should
be too proud to go to Heaven. Her complaint of loneliness amused
me. If she is lonely in a place with 13,000 inhabitants, it's her own
fault' (ibid. p. 37). In July he writes from Mwéhintha Outpost that
he has taken up district visiting by boat, but reports that The Maid
of Sker[3] (his pony) 'is charmed with her new quarters, she sees
so much more life than formerly, and instead of having to thump
on the earth floor when she wants anything, she can now rap her
fore hoofs against the wooden partitions, which makes fifty times

as much noise and ensures a prompt attention' (p. 38). Though for a painter he seems blind to local culture, he is a keen observer of indigenous nature.

There are most charming birds here now the rains are on, egrets, bitterns, pelicans, storks, pond-herons, etc. Shwepyi (the 1ˢᵗ guard on my route) is a great stronghold of these birds, as in the dry weather there are 2 large lakes there and in the rains it is all one big swamp; so when I arrived there last night I determined to make a hurried excursion next morning before leaving for this place. Accordingly I went forth this morning in a small sort of canoe with my boy and two men in a row. We saw lots of pelicans and other birds but no nests, as most of them don't breed till August, As we were getting back, a Malay spotted dove flew up from a nest in a tree, which hung just over us. I sent one man up to get the eggs but he could not get at it, so I gave it a prod with an oar. There was a yell from the men and as I stood back I saw an enormous snake rise 'long and slowly' from the nest and glide into the branches. The man in the tree came down with the agility of three apes. It was a monster snake and looked very venomous.   (ibid. 38–9)

He continues with a mixture of unconscious imperialism and consciousness of its ridiculousness,

As we were coming here in the big boat we passed a tree on which were several nests with darters sitting on them (the darter is a sort of cross between a gannet and a cormorant) a frightful tree to climb, but one of the natives ran up it like a cat and brought me down a lot of eggs and some young birds for them (the natives) to eat; fancy eating unfledged cormorants—oo-ah! When I got here I found the stockade was ankle deep in water; I had to be dragged up to the guard house in a small boat, which had to be carefully led round various shallows; it was like the swan scene in Lohengrin.   (ibid. 39–40)

The only sign of his pining for London life is in the final two lines of the letter: 'Owl and oaf thou art, not to see "Woman of no importance" and "Second Mrs T." *The* plays of the season; what would I not give to be able to see them!' (p. 40). Munro very rarely mentions Wilde's (or Pinero's) work, though he does mention Mrs Erlynne in another letter to his sister (17 September 1893, ibid. p. 45). We don't know whether he went to see any of Wilde's plays on his return to London, but both the writing and the subsequent trial must have left their mark on him.

A month after writing the letter from Mwéhintha, Munro was in a place whose name he could not recollect, six miles from Mandalay, attending a religious festival which he describes, in *Alice in Wonderland* style, as being in honour of two local deities of great repute called the Nats.

Their history is briefly this: they were two brothers who were ordered by the king to build a temple here, which they did, but omitted two bricks, for which reason the king killed them, in the impulsive way these Eastern monarchs have. After they were dead they seemed to think they had gone rather cheap and they made themselves so unpleasant about it that the king gave them permission to become deities, and built them a temple, and here they are, don't you know. Just that. The original temple with the vacant places for the missing bricks is still here; this is not an orthodox Buddhist belief but the Nats are held in great esteem in Upper Burma and parts of China, and this show is held here every year in their honour. The whole thing is so new to me that I will describe it at some length.   (Letter to Ethel Munro, 25 August 1893, ibid. 41).[4]

Again, Munro veers between a sense of himself as an official and representative of the Empire and a sense of the ridiculousness of his position, and perhaps betrays greater respect for local culture than he would admit in letters to Ethel. He remarks that 'Of course' he had to come, 'as the presence of a European officer is necessary to keep order, and twenty-five police had to be drafted here', but later adds:

to my horror I found a solitary chair had been placed on an elevated platform for my especial use, to which I was conducted with great ceremony; I am not sure the orchestra did not try to strike up the National Anthem. I inquired wildly for Carey, but was told he was with his wife somewhere. I was in terror lest they might expect a speech, and how could I get up and tell this people, replete with the learning of centuries of Eastern civilization, 'this animal will eat rice'?   (letter to Ethel Munro, 25 August 1893, ibid. 41)

He watched bouts of wrestling, imagining himself as a presiding emperor like his own Placidus Superbus ('The Gala Programme'),

quite disappointed to see them stop as soon as one was scratched. I had hoped (such is our fallen nature) that they would fight to the death and was trying hurriedly to remember whether you turned your thumbs up or down for mercy. Some of the encounters were very exciting, but I had to preserve a calm dignity befitting the representative of Great Britain and Ireland, besides which my chair was in a rather risky position and required careful sitting. Noblesse oblige.   (letter to Ethel Munro, 25 August 1893, ibid. 41–2)

Though he points up the ludicrousness of his position and describes the festival as though it were a concert in the West End, like many of his duties, it was exhausting, particularly for a frail young man not inured to the humidity and heat.

Carey came and told me that he had got me a house adjoining the show place . . . [EM's omission] Not only does it adjoin the building, but it forms part of it and opens on to the arena! The hours of performance are from 10 am to 3 pm and from 8 pm to 6 am. There are two bands. During performances my dining room is a sort of dress-circle, so I have to get my meals when I can. As to sleep, it's not kept on the premises, while the heat is so great that you could boil an egg on an iceberg. There are also smells.   (letter to Ethel Munro, 25 August 1893, ibid. 42)

However dutiful Munro was and however conscious of his position as a representative of English governance, as Saki he had no reverence for the position. 'Cousin Teresa' concerns two half-brothers. Basset, the doggedly faithful servant of empire, returns to 'the home of his fathers' after four years of 'useful service in an out-of-the-way, though not unimportant, corner of the world' in which he has

quieted a province, kept open a trade route, enforced the tradition of respect which is worth the ransom of many kings in out-of-the-way regions, and done the whole business on rather less expenditure than would be requisite for organising a charity in the home country. In Whitehall and places where they think, they doubtless thought well of him. It was not inconceivable, his father allowed himself to imagine, that Basset's name might figure in the next list of Honours. ('Cousin Teresa', *Beasts*, 143)

Basset returns to find his half-brother, Lucas, 'feverishly engrossed in the same medley of elaborate futilities that had claimed his whole time and energies, such as they were, four years ago' (ibid. pp. 143–4). Lucas has an idea that, he claims, will be 'simply It'. It is a couplet that is to form the basis of a revue; a piece of nonsensical doggerel which Basset and their father receive with pitying contempt. But the idea catches on, the revue is a success, the couplet becomes the catch-phrase of the day, and the silly, lazy, plump sibling with the complexion of intensively cultured asparagus gains fame, fortune, and a knighthood.

Back in Singu, Munro found the 'tiger-kitten' had forgotten him. It was

quite wild; pretended it had never seen me before, so I had to go through the ceremony of introduction again. I soon made it tame again, and we have great games together. It has not learnt how to drink milk properly yet and immerses its nose in the milk, then it gets mad with the saucer and shakes it, which sends the milk all over its paws, upon which it swears horribly. I have another queer creature in the shape of a young darter (same species of bird as the self-hatching one) which I saw sitting on the river bank en route for here: the men rowed to shore and just picked it up and put it in the boat where it sat as if it didn't care a twopenny damn. What blasé birds these darters are. Then there is the crow-brought chicken which was carried here by a crow and rescued by the syce; crows often run off with one's chickens but it is not often they add to your poultry. I feel quite like the prophet Elijah (or was it Elisha?) who was boarded by ravens. Milk is scarce now, but the kitten has to have some of my scanty store, while the ponies feel very annoyed if they don't get a bit of bread now and then; I believe I am expected to share my sardines with the darter, but I draw the line there!   (letter to Ethel Munro, 6 September 1893, Munro, 43)

Ethel Munro had clearly passed on to her brother some impertinent speculation about his matrimonial prospects. He responds in a letter from the Hôtel de France in Mandalay with what sounds like asperity, and quickly displaces the question of his relations with women on to flippant and hyperbolic anecdotes which leap by association across a variety of subjects, ending far from the original point.

Tell Mrs Byrne there is no immediate danger of my marrying a Burmese wife; there was a woman at Singu—ugly as a fury—who, I think, had great hopes, but my boy, always ready to save me trouble, married her himself; he had one wife already, but that was a trifle. I impress upon him that he may have as many as he likes, within reasonable limits, but no babies. To this rule there is no exception. When I was out in the district if a child howled in any neighbouring hut men were sent at once to stop it; if it wouldn't stop it was conducted out of ear-shot; wouldn't you like to do that with English brats! How rabid the mothers would get!   (letter to Ethel Munro, 24 October 1893, ibid. 46)

The tiger cub accompanied Munro to the Hôtel de France in a specially made cage with an upper sleeping compartment, but 'every afternoon it comes out into my room for an hour or two and has fine romps' (letter to Ethel Munro, 24 October 1893, ibid. p. 46). The romps got Munro into some trouble later that week. He recounts the incident in a manner of superior indifference to the conventions or convenience of others, designed to amuse Ethel.

An old lady came to the hotel last week, one of those people with a tongue and a settled conviction that they can manage everybody's affairs. She had the room next to mine—connected by a door—and I was rather astonished when the proprietor came that evening, and with great nervousness, said that there was an old lady in the next room, and er—she was rather er—fidgety old lady and er—er—er—there was a door connecting our rooms. I was quite mystified as to what he was driving at but I answered languidly that the door was locked on my side and there was a box against it, so she could not possibly break in. The proprietor collapsed and retired in confusion; I afterwards remembered that the 'cub' had spent a large portion of the afternoon pretending that this door was a besieged city, and it was a battering ram. And it does throw such vigour into its play. I met the old lady at dinner and was greeted with an icy stare which was refreshing in such a climate. That night the kitten broke out in a new direction; as soon as I went up to bed it began to roar; 'and still the wonder grew, so small a throat could give so large a mew.' The more I tried to comfort it the more inconsolable it grew. The situation was awful—in my room a noise like the lion-house at 4 p.m., while on the other side of the door rose the beautiful Litany of the Church of England. Then I heard the rapid turning of leaves, she was evidently searching for Daniel to gain strength from the perusal of the lion's den story; only she couldn't find Daniel so she fell back upon the Psalms of David. As for me, I fled, and sent my boy to take the cage down to the stable When I came back I heard words in the next room that never came out of the Psalms; words such as no old lady ought to use; but then it is annoying to be woken out of your first sleep by a rendering of 'Jamrach's Evening Hymn.'[5] She left. The beast has behaved fairly well since, except that it ate up a handkerchief . . . [EM's omission] It also insisted on taking tea with me yesterday and sent my cup flying into my plate, trying meanwhile to hide itself in the milk jug to prove an alibi. I am getting as bad as Aunt Charlotte with her perpetual cats, but I have seen very few human beings as yet, everyone being away, as this is a sort of holiday time . . . [EM's omission].   (letter to Ethel Munro, 30 October 1893, ibid. 47–8)

The following February, Munro is smugly condescending to the possessor of a mere domestic pet. His 'tiger-kitten' is now half-grown and has become less manageable.

I hear you have a Persian kitten; of course I, who have the untameable carnivora of the jungle roaming in savage freedom through my rooms, cannot feel any interest in mere domestic cats, but I am not intolerant and I have no objection to your keeping one or two. My beast does not show any signs of getting morose; it sleeps on a shelf in its cage all day but comes out after dinner and plays the giddy goat all over the place. I should like to get another wild cat to chum with it, there are several species in Burma: the jungle-cat, the bay-cat, the lesser leopard-cat, the tiger cat, marbled cat, spotted wild-cat, and rusty-spotted cat; the latter, I have read, make delightful pets.   (letter to Ethel Munro, 1 February 1894, ibid. 49)

The expression 'to chum', meaning to live with, was later to be employed by Ethel of her brother's sharing rooms with other young men. The 'boy' who has featured in most of Munro's letters appears immediately after and about on a level with the tiger cub, as part of the domestic impedimenta.

I hope you have no more bother with servants; my boy gives me notice about once a month but I never think of accepting it; if he doesn't know a good master I know a good servant, to paraphrase an old remark. He has a great idea of my consequence and of his own reflected importance; I sent him to a village with a message, and Beale A.S.P., who was expecting some fowls from that place, asked if they had been sent by him; he told me he should never forget the tone in which he said 'I am Mr Munro's boy!' Civis Romanus sum.   (letter to Ethel Munro, 1 February 1894, ibid. 49–50)

This is the first in a succession of 'my boys' which included a 14-year-old who is said to have constituted himself Hector's valet in Warsaw, and who on hot days would turn a soda-siphon on his employer's back, and 'a very good little servant' in St Petersburg. A Registry Office in Paris offered a number of servants for Munro's inspection, but he rejected them all as perfectly correct and probably excellent, but not original, until he found Marcellin, 'an invaluable valet [...] with a taste for cooking and an imperturbable temper' (pp. 79–80). The only female servant hired to wait on Munro seems to have brought out the worst in him. Ethel reports that he and the friend with whom he was 'chumming' found that the servant took food, so opened a mince pie and inserted mustard under the filling (p. 79). Ethel's references to the men who shared her brother's lodgings are few and not elaborated. Only one is named, presumably to explain a reference to 'Tockling' in a letter to Ethel from London.[6]

Apart from a few references to the lack of conversation, Munro does not mention his loneliness, or the bouts of fever he suffered. The tone of the letters quoted continues flippant and the subjects remain animals, jokes, and Munro's alleged callous disregard of the world. He certainly showed a cavalier attitude to the interests of the birds whose eggs he collected, and their significance to the local people. In March, he writes that his boy has brought him some crows' eggs:

the Burmans don't quite approve of my taking them as they have an idea that the spirits of their grandmothers turn into crows, but I cannot be expected to respect the eggs of other people's grandmothers. Some absurd owls built themselves a nest inside my roof, which was a rash thing to do; of course I promptly took care of their eggs for them. Where would one find English servants who, besides cooking one's food and bottle-washing generally, hunted for birds' eggs and routed out police cases (my boy is of more use to me in that way than any of my police men, and is invaluable in the witness box, as he will swear not only to what he saw, but to what he thinks I should like him to have seen)? Fancy saying to an English cook 'Dinner at 7 sharp, and I've three guests coming; and by the way, just see if the buzzard's nest in the high elm has any eggs in it; and while you're about it find out if there is any gambling going on in the Red Lion, etc., etc.' (letter to Ethel Munro, 30 March 1894, ibid. 51–3)

The following month he was in Maymyo, and writes that he is delighted with this much more convivial and comfortable place:

it is delightfully cool and we have whist every night and dine and breakfast in each other's houses rather more frequently than in our own; not much work to do, and a fair amount of sport to be had . . . [EM's omission] [. . .] My goose has hatched out a brood of goslings in spite of 40 miles in a jolting bullock cart. (letter to Ethel Munro, 23 April 1894, ibid. 53)

A month later, he was regretting having counted his chickens, or goslings, after they had hatched, and enclosed a sketch, an 'allegorical picture representing my geese floating to Paradise on the tears of a weeping syce' (letter to Ethel Munro, 26 May 1894, ibid. pp. 54–5).

Munro always writes as though he were in Burma for the first time, and shows no attachment to or inclination to revisit his birthplace. Presumably, for the son of servants of empire, location of birth is irrelevant provided that his pedigree is impeccably British. Seven bouts of fever left him weakened, and a bad attack of malaria in August finally forced him to resign and to return home. Ethel Munro recounts an unpleasant incident during the long journey back to England that confirmed Hector's (and her own) anti-German prejudice.

He told me that while lying in bed, feeling wretchedly ill, in some hotel, he heard footsteps passing in the corridor and called out. A German, a visitor like himself, and a stranger to Hector, came in and asked what was the matter? Hector told him he wanted a servant to bring him something to drink; the German stood and argued that it was not his business and he could not attend to sick people, neither should he give a message to anyone, and then departed. Of course he may have been mad, or madder than usual. It was some time before Hector attracted the attention of a servant passing by and got what he wanted.   (ibid. 54–5)

There seems to be no record of the brothers having corresponded or met again during their time in Burma. It is of course possible that the exigencies of their respective duties precluded much travelling, and that such precious leave as they had would not be wasted on long cross-country treks, even for the prospect of fraternal meetings. It is difficult from this side of time to gain much sense of what Charlie Munro was like as a young man, but recollections of him from the 1920s challenge the more sympathetic portrait given by Langguth. Charlie left the Indian (Burma) Police to join the Irish Prison Service in 1902, becoming Governor of Derry Prison, and was made Governor of Mountjoy Prison (Dublin) in 1911. He was still in post at the time of the Troubles. Tim Carey finds that the Mountjoy staff at that time were 'at the uncomfortable coalface of the government's prison policy' and were 'very worn and harassed'.[7] He suggests that Governor Munro suffered more than most.

In his mid forties, Munro was described by Sean Milroy as 'a diminutive, shrivelled, ill-tempered shrew, trying to look severe and stern, but only succeeding in giving an impression of waspish insolence'[8] [. . .] Before the War of Independence Munro had dealt with many difficult prisoners in Mountjoy but the large-scale confinement of Republicans strained his abilities to near breaking point. Apparently incapable of delegating authority and intent on running the prison as if everything were normal, Munro was ill from nervous tension and exhaustion. Shortly before the Anglo-Irish Treaty was signed in London, Munro, in what was yet another plea to the GPB in Dublin Castle for assistance, expressed his worry that with the Sinn Féin prisoners, 'proper supervision is impossible without resorting to drastic measures'. On the verge of losing patience with Munro's neurotic concerns, Green writes that in the prevailing circumstances, 'we must use all our ingenuity to cope with dissatisfaction since we cannot transfer it elsewhere, or put an end to it'.[9]

Munro lost his first Republican prisoner in March 1919, when Robert Barton climbed over the back wall after cutting the bars of an infirmary window, leaving a note in his cell addressed to 'The Governor'. Later that month, Patrick Fleming, Piaras Beaslaí, and J. J. Walsh used a rope ladder to get over the prison wall, and in a break-out organized by Michael Collins, another twenty were lost.[10] The following May there was an unsuccessful escape bid by twenty-one prisoners in which Munro and his staff were confined in the Governor's office. A sentry arrived, fired a shot and was captured. A raiding party, hearing the shot, left. Munro, also hearing it, assumed that the shot was a general attack, and things seem to have degenerated into farce. Carey reports that the incident closed with 'something like internecine warfare at the Governor's door; the Governor holding it against what he thinks are rebels, and the party in the passage actually consisting of soldiers and wardens battering in the door under the impression that the Governor and staff are still at the point of a revolver inside.[11]

Having been invalided home, Hector was met by his father in London. They had planned to travel back to Devon together immediately, but Hector's condition must have been bad, because his father quickly realized that he would not last the journey. The Colonel engaged a nurse and stayed with Hector in town until he was strong enough to travel to Buckleigh, near Westward Ho!, where the family had taken another house, Hilcrest. An unnamed neighbour, quoted in *John Lane and the Nineties*, recollects Hector's second sentence of death: 'He was a wreck from fever and was supposed to have come home to die.'[12] He recovered, however, and entered his father and sister's social circle. The neighbour describes him as 'always interesting to meet, and a clever, witty talker in the quiet, condensed style of his literary work. He might be doing something as ordinary as handing the cake plates at an "At Home", but his originality flavoured most of his brief remarks and most people found it worthwhile to listen to him.' Interesting and original are not the same as amiable. The neighbour admits to having seen little of Saki, but is nonetheless willing to analyse his character.

He must often have mightily irritated the stodgy and slow-in-the-uptake; what he said was sometimes so keen and double-edged. The cynicism that came out in his stories always seemed to me a mask to hide another and a different man. He had many friends and one who was poor, ill or otherwise down on his luck might have surprised [*sic*] anyone who knew only 'Saki'. Small animals, kittens and birds would only have agreed with the friends.[13]

There seem to be words missing which we can only conjecture, but the suggestion is that Hector was a good friend, if a cynic who did not suffer fools gladly. After a summer of horse-riding and swimming, as well as handing cake plates and being moderately polite to neighbours, Hector was restored to health. Having discharged his duty in the family occupation, in 1896 he moved to London to become a writer.

4

London, the Balkans, Russia

THE first three years of Munro's London life were spent largely in the British Museum Reading Room, where he was researching his first book, *The Rise of the Russian Empire*, completed in 1899 and published by Grant Richards in 1900 as by Hector H. Munro. The style of the book is largely that of contemporary works of history, but there are touches of Saki. An epigraph from Le Père Pierling appears under the title on the frontispiece: 'On se flatterait en vain de connaître la Russie actuelle, si l'on ne remontait plus haut dans son histoire', and the bibliography of works consulted is idiosyncratic, as the books are arranged 'somewhat in the order in which they have been found useful, precedence being given to those which have been most largely drawn upon'.

A review by Edward Garnett in *The Bookman* of August 1900 finds that Munro had made 'a courageous and intelligent effort [. . .] to give the English people some notion of the tangled web of early Russian history',[1] and suggests that in making a survey of existing histories he had taken a sensible course, 'perhaps the best one available to the intelligent foreigner who, in dealing with a strange country, cannot claim either the learning or the range of outlook necessary for the survey of the specialists' vast domain.' Hector was prickly under criticism, and, in the persona of wide-travelled cosmopolitan polymath, likely to have been irked by being described as without first-hand experience of his subject, even though he had not been to Russia when the book was published. He made the mistake of responding to another review which, though far from hostile (it called the book 'learned and interesting'), had raised some minor quibbles about the spelling of Russian names, the relations of the early Great Russians to the early European Finns, and the extent of the Christianization of Russia.[2] His letter, which appeared in *The Athenaeum* a fortnight after the review, begins amiably enough, but descends into irony and even condescension. [3]

Not all of Munro's time was spent at the British Museum Reading Room. He returned to Devon to take over housekeeping from his sister when she went on visits (mostly, Ethel reports, to prevent Aunt Tom from taking over), and had his own town amusements (Munro, pp. 58–9). Ethel gives an extract from a letter 'written when he was chumming with a friend, one Tocke', a phrase perhaps borrowed from her brother's remark about the wild cat he had adopted (letter to Ethel Munro, 1 February 1894, ibid. pp. 49–50), but reveals that she destroyed some of her brother's correspondence because their father insisted on reading any letters from him 'and Hector and I sometimes had plans which we did not divulge to him at once' (p. 58). Munro writes inconsequentially in a train of thought that leads from duck to duckling to 'Tockling', and then is diverted to betting.

MY DEAR E.

The duck was a bird of great parts and as tender as a good man's conscience when confronted with the sins of others. Truly a comfortable bird. Tockling is looking well and is in better health and spirits generally, and everything in the garden's lovely. Except the 'Cambridgeshire' which we all came a cropper over. We put our underclothing on the wrong horse and are now praying for a mild Winter.   (ibid. 58)

Tockling was probably Albert Tocke, a barrister, 28 at the time of the 1901 census, who was sharing Munro's lodgings at 1a Middle Temple Lane. Like Munro a child of imperial service, he was born in Ceylon (Sri Lanka). Munro alludes to two other friends in the next letter Ethel Munro quotes, written from the house in Westward Ho! during one of her absences. One is 'Ker', who has left the day Aunt Tom arrived to visit, and one is 'Bertie', with whom Munro drove to 'Bucks' (presumably Buckinghamshire). (Bertie, in name at least, was later immortalized as Bertie Steffink as well as a number of other characters called by this popular Victorian diminutive.) They allowed a travelling menagerie to pass them on the road, and later tracked it down. 'Bertie and I went in on both nights to see the beasts, and made friends with the young trainer, who was quite charming, and had sweet little lion cubs (born in the first coronation week) taken out of their cage and put into our arms, also seductive little wolf-puppies which you would have loved' (p. 60). Throughout her memoir, Ethel Munro emphasizes her brother's love of animals domesticated and wild, and Munro was clearly attracted both to animals and those who lived with and trained animals, provided they maintained conditions he considered suitable. In a letter from Warsaw on 1 August 1904, he was jokingly to recommend that Ethel get a wolf instead of a hound, since 'there would be no licence to pay and at first it could feed on the smaller Inktons, with biscuits sometimes for a change [. . . .] you and Aunt Tom could do the marketing in comfort, as under' (p. 71). Below, a sketch shows one woman prodding trussed birds and another (presumably Ethel) sniffing flowers while other shoppers flee in terror from a large wolf with dangling tongue.

Through Devon connections Munro gained an introduction to the political cartoonist Francis Carruthers Gould (Sir F. C. Gould from 1906), who had been with the *Westminster Gazette*, having moved from the *Pall Mall Gazette*, from its earliest days. Gould took Munro to meet his editor, John Alfred Spender, and together they persuaded Spender to commission a series of pieces which would use Lewis Carroll's *Alice* stories as the basis for political lampoons. Spender recollected that Munro left most of the talking to Gould, 'and at the beginning one had to dig hard to get a word out of him. But the word when it came was pungent and original, and in a few minutes I came to the conclusion that Gould was justified in his "find".'[4] Spender had initially had misgivings, since most other parodies offered to him had proved 'dismal failures', since such things 'must either succeed perfectly or fail lamentably, and to succeed perfectly meant not merely copying the form but catching the spirit of the inimitable fantastic original'. Saki succeeded, however. As Spender remarks: 'Political parodies are generally dead within a few months of their first appearance, but *The Westminster Alice* is alive and sparkling after twenty-five years.'[5]

This was the beginning of a fruitful relationship with Gould and a long association between the arch-Tory Munro and the Liberal *Westminster Gazette*, though in mitigation of this seemingly odd coupling, it should be remembered that the *Westminster Gazette* published both articles that satirized the government and those that lampooned the Liberal opposition. Saki and Gould's satires, mostly concerned with the Boer War, appeared during 1900 under the name SAKI in uppercase letters. In 1902 they were collected as *The Westminster Alice*, initially as a pamphlet, then as a 'library edition', a very slim volume bound in blue leather and inscribed: 'With apologies to Sir John Tenniel and to everybody else concerned, including Messrs. Macmillan and Co., Limited, to whose courtesy we are indebted for permission to publish these political applications of the immortal adventures of Lewis Carroll's Alice.'[6]

The *Alice* stories were still familiar to Hector when he was in his twenties, and he assumed that his sister still remembered them as well. Hector's letter describing the festival of the Nats, reports that he was 'worried to death by princesses', including an old lady who took an annoying interest in him. 'She asked me, through Mrs. Carey, how old I was, and then told me I was too tall for my age, obligingly showing me the height I ought to be. It reminded me of another royal lady's dictum, "All persons above a mile high to leave the Court"' (Munro, p. 40). The stories provided a ready-made familiar register as the vehicle of satire. The collection opened with five quatrains parodying the author's dedication of the work to the dream-child, and making it clear that Alice is to be the *ingénue* whose straight-faced questions will provide the satire.

> "Alice", Child with dreaming eyes,
>   Noting things that come to pass
> Turvey-wise in Wonderland
>   Backwards though a Looking-Glass.
>
> Figures flit across thy dream,
>   Muddle through and flicker out
> Some in cocksure blessedness,
>   Some in Philosophic Doubt.
>
> Some in brackets, some in sulks,
>   Some with latchkeys on the ramp,
> Living (in a sort of peace)
>   In a Concentration Camp.[7]
>
> Party moves on either side,
>   Checks and feints that don't deceive,
> Knights and Bishops, Pawns and all,
>   In a game of Make-Believe.
>
> Things that fall contrariwise,
>   Difficult to understand
> Darkly through a Looking-Glass
>   Turvey-wise in Wonderland.   (*Alice*, 4)

The collection opens with 'Alice in Downing Street'. The Cheshire Cat asks Alice if she has ever seen an Ineptitude, and directs her to 'the most perfect specimen we have', who is A. J. Balfour, First Lord of the Treasury 1895–1900.

Alice followed the direction of its glance and noticed for the first time a figure sitting in a very uncomfortable attitude on nothing in particular. Alice had no time to wonder how it managed to do it, she was busy taking in the appearance of the creature, which was something like a badly-written note of interrogation and something like a guillemot, and seemed to have been trying to preen its rather untidy plumage with whitewash. 'What a dreadful mess it's in!' she remarked, after gazing at it for a few minutes in silence. 'What is it, and why is it here?'

'It hasn't any meaning,' said the Cat, 'it simply *is*.'
'Can it talk?' asked Alice eagerly.
'It has never done anything else,' chuckled the Cat.
'Can you tell me what you are doing here?' Alice inquired politely.
The Ineptitude shook its head with a deprecatory motion and commenced
to drawl, 'I haven't an idea.' (ibid. 4–5)

The imitation of Lewis Carroll's style is spot-on: the narration is
both innocent (the perspective and questions are Alice's) and knowing (the satirical descriptions by the narrative voice); the satirical
nonsensicality (sitting uncomfortably on nothing in particular) and
far-fetched comic similes (nothing could actually be something like
a badly-written note of interrogation and something like a guillemot, yet somehow this describes the untidy, vaguely apologetic
figure brilliantly).

Balfour is criticized as an inept and ineffectual party leader who
has failed to bring an end to the war in South Africa, but the
Secretary of State for War (1895–1900) and Foreign Secretary (from
November 1900), the Marquess of Lansdowne, is held up as the
chief cause of the long drawn-out campaigns. In 'Alice in Pall
Mall' he is represented as the White Knight, mounted on a horse
wrapped round with swathes of red tape and hung about with
numbers of obsolete appliances. The Knight tells Alice that he once
read a book written to prove the point 'that warfare under modern
conditions was impossible'. He remarks that she may imagine how
disturbing this was to a man of his profession, and invites her to
guess how he dealt with it. 'Alice pondered. "You went to war, of
course—" "Yes; *but not under modern conditions*" ' (ibid. pp. 10–11).[8]
He then invites Alice to examine a little short-range gun hanging on
his saddle. 'Why do you suppose I sent out guns of that particular
kind? Because if they happened to fall into the hands of the enemy
they'd be very little use to him. That was my own invention'
(ibid. p. 11). Representing characters as smugly self-congratulatory
for acts of great stupidity (as judged by the author) is a favourite
device of both Carroll's and Saki's work.

Joseph Chamberlain smashes through a wood crying out at the top of his voice. 'What a dreadful lot of unnecessary business we're talking!' said the White Queen fretfully. 'It makes me quite miserable—carries me back to the days when I was in Opposition' (ibid. p. 22). Required to sing something soothing, Alice offers the 'Intercessional', and produces a fragment of Kipling parody:

> 'Voice of the People, lately polled,
>   Awed by our broad-cast battle scheme,
> By virtue of whose vote we hold
>   Our licence still to doze and dream,
> Still, falt'ring Voice, complaisant shout,
>   Lest we go out, lest we go out.'

Alice looked anxiously at the Queens when she had finished, but they were both fast asleep. 'It will take a deal of shouting to rouse them,' she thought.[9]

If Munro's real name had ever been a secret when the pieces appeared in the *Westminster Gazette*, it ceased to be one now, since the title page has 'Hector H. Munro ("Saki")'.[10] In 1901 'SAKI' dedicated two parodies of the *Rubáiyát* of Omar Khayyam to an attack on prominent political figures of the time, and the following year another series illustrated by Carruthers Gould, initially under the title 'The Political Jungle Book', later as the 'Not-So-Stories', also in the *Westminster Gazette*, made ironic play with Kipling's *Just So Stories* (1902). These were ephemeral pieces whose humour, dependent on readers' recognition of characteristics or alleged characteristics of public figures, is now largely lost, since the necessity of constantly referring to a key makes the satire limp, but they were the *Spitting Images* of the time. Particularly effective is the representation of 'the big tiger, Sheer-Khan't, who had his den up in the Council Rock, and claimed the position of first Lord of the Jungle' (*Westminster Gazette*, 23 May 1902, p. 2).

The *Westminster Gazette* now also began to take Munro's fiction. 'The Blood-Feud of Toad-Water' (26 January 1901) appeared over his initials again, but the author of 'Reginald' (25 September 1901), was established as the same as the political satires, 'Saki'. There is some crossover between the political satires and the early stories, especially when Reginald breaks into verse in 'Reginald's Peace Poem'.

In writing about Peace the thing is to say what everybody is saying, only to say it better [. . . .]

> 'When the widgeon westward winging
> Heard the folk Vereeniginging,
> Heard the shouting and the singing—'
> [. . .]
> 'Mother may I go and maffick,
> Tear around and hinder traffic?'

> ('Reginald's Peace Poem', *Reginald*, 35–6)

Joseph Bristow provides a gloss on the verb 'to maffick', a Cockneyism which entered the language after the public celebrations of the relief of Mafeking in May 1900.

At this time, working- and lower-middle-class support for the empire was at its height. Members of the educated middle classes deplored the noisy masses taking to songs and chanting out of doors. Two years later, the liberal *Fortnightly Review* carried an article revealing the deep impression left by the ostentatious behaviour of the crowds on that day:

We have always known that the worst part of the London mob could be a disgrace and a danger if it got out of hand. 'Mafficking' has simply shown with formidable clearness the force of that suggestion. We may be absolutely certain that in times of public excitement, with peril nearer home, the brutal side of this huge rowdyism, if it should once break out, will be as menacing as its levity is uncouth, unwholesome and repellent.[11]

A cousin (son of Munro's mother's brother), C. W. Mercer, known as 'Willie' to the family but later better known as the author Dornford Yates, has left a description of Munro from around this time. The distance that had grown up between the two sides of the family during Charlie, Ethel, and Hector's childhoods seems to have persisted into adulthood, even without the Aunts' interference, because Mercer records that he didn't meet his cousin until he was 15 or 16 and Munro was 30 or 31.

My Mother and I were staying with an uncle and aunt of mine at their house in Phillimore Gardens, Kensington. I rather think he was asked to dinner for our sakes: that thereafter he was asked for theirs goes without saying, for Hector has beautiful manners, talked easily and well and possessed the precious gift of adaptability. He was then thirty or thirty-one—a spare man of average height, brown-eyed, clean-shaven, with a ready smile and a most intelligent face. His hands were sensitive, and he kept them very still. His complexion was sallow. He was well-groomed and neat in his attire. Always wore a bowler in London. Never careless or untidy in his dress. Brilliant satirist as he was, you would never have believed this to look at him. In repose, he looked his best. In conversation, he had a trick of using his mouth and lips too much, to emphasize some point.

I never heard him speak sharply to anyone; his conversation was always interesting and amusing, but seldom displayed the brilliance of his written words. He was much liked by Lady St Helier—a widow, old enough to have been his mother—and frequently visited her at her country house. A very fine Bridge player, he would play the game to all hours. From time to time I met some of his friends, either in his club, the Cocoa Tree, or at one of his parties at Soho; but none of them approached him in intellect or personality. The women between whom I sat were invariably precious and spoke much of 'values', and I sometimes think that Hector invited me out of mischief, to enjoy my reactions to such, to my mind, pinchbeck company. His personality stood right out always. But among those of his friends or acquaintances that I met, I cannot remember one man or woman who registered. Some may have been mentally attractive, though, if they were, they concealed their attraction from me; there was not one that was physically attractive among them.

That first evening in Phillimore Gardens, I remember that he said that the ballet 'Old China,' then running at The Empire, was exceptionally good, and that if my Mother and aunt did not mind visiting a music hall, they would be entranced. Such was his enthusiasm that my uncle declared that he would take seats the next morning. My aunt at once invited Hector to make one of the party, and an evening was fixed. So a few days later he dined with us again, and went with us to The Empire. The ballet was exquisite. Mme Adeline Genée was the *première danseuse*. To this day I remember how the curtain rose upon a vast marble mantelpiece upon which there stood three great pieces of Dresden china—a clock in the middle, with a shepherd (life-size) on one side and a shepherdess (life-size) on the other. The clock declared the time to be a few seconds to twelve. Then it struck the hour and, as its notes died, the figures on either side came to life and began to dance. Hector, who had already seen the ballet more than once, sat between my Mother and my aunt, continually indicating to them certain features which they might otherwise have missed [. . .] unhappily I seem to remember so little of him. I remember him as very gentle, gay, smiling, but never laughing outright. I never saw or heard him laugh, but a smile was nearly always on his face. I think his personality must have been elusive.[12]

Montague Summers also recorded memories and anecdotes of Munro from this time.

I took him to a dinner of honour with the promoters of the *Quad* [an undergraduate magazine]; for although he had not yet written of the famous Reginald or of Clovis, his political satires in *The Westminster Gazette*, illustrated by Caruthers Gould, were attracting a good deal of attention. The 'Quaddites', whom he voted delightful, hung on his words.[13]

The term 'anecdotes' might be more appropriate than memories in this case, because, for example, Summers writes that as well as dining with him in Soho restaurants, Saki also attended mass with him when he (Summers) was staying in London, which seems a little unlikely. Summers writes: 'often he would pleadingly say: "Shall we make it a pious intention?" But I was always adamant.'[14]

Munro could have remained in London as a whimsical satirist and that useful social functionary, a presentable bachelor. Instead, he chose to leave London, and England, again by becoming foreign correspondent of the *Morning Post*. Ethel Munro suggests that her brother had always envisaged himself going abroad again, and that it became feasible after he emerged from a severe attack of double pneumonia stronger than ever before and robust enough to face the hardships of travel (Munro, p. 64). Certainly, reporting on 'The Balkan Troubles' from Albania, Bulgaria, and Macedonia entailed visiting some dangerous places, and someone identified only as 'Wyntour' in a letter to Ethel sent Munro a tiny silver crucifix to ward off vampires, but he rarely had to rough it, and much of his time was initially spent playing Bridge with the English vice-consul (ibid.). His first piece as foreign correspondent was an interview sent from Belgrade dated 15 September 1902.

Munro's new employer, the *Morning Post*, established in 1772, has been described as 'possibly the best-written newspaper in England'.[15] Dr Johnson's *Journal of a Tour to the Hebrides* was first published there, Samuel Taylor Coleridge wrote a number of leading articles, Wordsworth published sonnets in it, Charles Lamb contributed jokes for sixpence each, George Meredith was a special correspondent during the Italian wars of liberation, and Thomas Hardy and Rudyard Kipling wrote verse for it.[16] Its fitness as a vehicle for Munro's writing was not its literary excellence, however. The *Morning Post* was High Tory, and the newspaper of the upper-middle classes. Its policies were monarchist, imperialist, and conservative, and it gained most of its revenue from the large number of advertisements for servants it carried. When Lady Bathurst, daughter of the editor-proprietor Algernon Borthwick, who became Lord Gleneck in 1908, sold the paper, she stipulated that its policy must be 'King and Conservative Party', and H. A. Gwynne, editor from 1911 to 1937, described the paper's tradition as 'King and Country'.[17] It was, above all, English. 'If the *Morning Post*'s unique reputation can be ascribed to any one cause, it must rather be to the peculiarly English savour of its independence; a "Be damned to you!" savour; the sort of savour that there was about Palmerston (with whom, incidentally, the *Morning Post* long maintained the closest connexions).'[18] As well as possibly the best-written paper in England, it was 'certainly the most English of English newspapers', even though 'Irishmen and Welshmen; Scotsmen and Jews, had done as much for the *Morning*

Post as Englishmen, and the Scotsmen had done most of all.'[19] The *Morning Post* and the patriotic, Tory Scottish-Englishman were a perfect match.

The patriotism of the *Morning Post* was not simply idealist and sentimental, but practical and militant. The success of Zeppelin I in 1909 fed British fears of a German threat. It was argued that Britain was no longer an island; it could no longer be defended by the navy alone. There were calls for an equivalent programme of dirigible-building. *Morning Post* leaders supported this, and on 21 June 1909 set up a National Airship Fund. The Fund's target of £20,000 to be raised by subscription (including generous donations from Lady Bathurst) was perhaps designed to shame the government, which had spent £1,980 on dirigibles and £5,270 on all forms of flight in the year before. It also emulated the *c*. £25,000 raised by public subscription in Germany for the construction of the Zeppelins.[20] The effort ended badly. A rival dirigible funded by the *Daily Mail* was delivered first, the *Morning Post*'s machine was damaged on arrival at its too-small hanger, and crashed on its first test flight. The affair led to accusations of financial mismanagement and neglect of editorial duties against the editor, Fabian Ware, who threatened libel charges, and was eventually given £3,000 and early retirement. Lady Bathurst returned the subscriptions, in spite of having lost a great deal of money herself. Keith M. Wilson gives an ironic epilogue to the story:

On the evening of 13 October 1915 a stick of bombs dropped by a Zeppelin straddled 346 Strand and caused the death of twelve people. The former premises of the *Morning Post*, on the junction of Houghton Street and Aldwych, were also partly demolished. The archives of the *Morning Post* contain a piece of shrapnel found imbedded in a bookcase.[21]

Like the *Morning Post*, Munro was to show that his love of England and England's possessions entailed being willing to demand favourable, if unfair, legislation (as when the *Morning Post* supported imperial preference), and to go to war for them.

Munro was in Belgrade in 1902, Uskub (later Skopje, Yugoslavia) in the spring of 1903, and Belgrade again in June of that year, in between visiting Sofia, Rustchuk, and Monastir.[22] Though past 30, he was still youthful in appearance. At the Turkish border he and Henry Brailsford, correspondent of the *Manchester Guardian*, were taken to be sons of the older Viennese journalist travelling with them. The Turkish border guards wrote in their passports that they were being taken to school in Salonica, and Brailsford was later arrested as a runaway.

Munro's letters to Ethel from Eastern Europe play down the tension and danger. His accounts of violent, nation-shaking events tend to be based on an observation of something ridiculous or entirely domestic in scale, and have the flavour of some-one likely to be seriously discomposed by clashing colours in the counterpane and rug but left unmoved by assassins in the wardrobe.

The only hotel in the place is full. I am in the other [...] I was walked upstairs and offered the alternative of sharing a bedroom with a Turk or a nicer bedroom with two Turks.
I pleaded a lonely and morose disposition and was at last given a room without carpet, stove, or wardrobe, but also without Turks [...] The country round is 'apart'; lovely rolling hills and huge snow-capped mountains, and storks nesting in large communities; everything wild and open and full of life. There are two magpies who seem to have some idea of living in this room with me. (letter to Ethel Munro, 20 April 1903, Munro, 65).

Munro was later to be remembered as both courageous and modest, but his modest reticence did not extend to occasions which afforded him the chance to prove his superiority to foreigners or kindness to animals, and especially occasions which afforded both. 'In the stampede here the other day when the attempt was made on the Telegraph Office I picked up a tiny kitten that was in danger of being trampled on and put it in a place of safety' (letter to Ethel Munro, dated 9 May 1903, ibid. p. 66).

His style of journalism was almost a parody of the stiff-upper-lipped understatement of British diplomacy. Though it was spiced with quirky observation and dialogue, sometimes flippant and occasionally satirical, it was neither vivid nor emotive. His most detached style was reserved for violent upheavals and atrocities, and he rarely reported the sufferings of civilian casualties.

In April 1903, word reached Uskub of the blowing up of the Ottoman Bank and of attempts to dynamite the railway line to Salonica. Munro and an American reporter went south by train to investigate, but on arrival were ordered by officials to remain at Salonica station, as the town was in a state of siege. They tried to slip away into some wasteland and move for the town. A letter to Ethel written from the station at midnight describes, humorously, the narrow escape that followed.

As a slight precaution against being taken for prowling Komitniki we turned down the collars of our overcoats so as to display the white collar, if not of a blameless life, at least of a business that did not call for concealment.

About four hundred yards of the distance had been covered when a frantic challenge in Turkish brought us to a standstill, and five armed and agitated figures sprang forward in the starlight and began to interrogate us at a distance, which they seemed disinclined to lessen. As five triggers had clicked and five rifles were covering us we dropped our valises and 'uphanded', but without reassuring our questioners, who seemed to be possessed of a panic which might more reasonably have been displayed on our part.

Neither of us knew a word of Turkish, and Bulgarian was obviously unsuited to the occasion. Never in my study of that tongue have its words come so readily to my lips, and every French sentence I began became entangled with the phraseology of the debarred language.

The men had reached a point whence they were unwilling to approach nearer, and for a minute or two they took deliberate aim from a ridiculously easy range in a state of excitement which was unpleasant to witness from our end of the barrels.

At last two lowered their rifles, and after stalking round us with elaborate caution managed to secure our hands with a rope or sash-cord, which was hurriedly produced from somewhere. The operation would have been shorter if they had not tried to hold their rifles at our heads at the same time. (letter to Ethel Munro, 30 April 1903, ibid. 66–8)

Munro's chief emotion appears to be his irritation at the inefficiency of his captors, and the pose of *sangfroid* is maintained at all times. He explains that having been accepted as 'Inglesi effendi' and released, he asked why he had not been shot, and was told that 'they had only hesitated on seeing our collars, which made them doubt if we were Bulgarian desperadoes' (letter to Ethel Munro, 30 April 1903, ibid. pp. 66–8). Once again, the Englishman is saved by his impeccable dress and phlegmatic poise. In Saki's work, the loss of either condemns him. In 'The Lost Sanjak' (*Reginald in Russia*, pp. 13–24), a man on trial for the murder of himself is given the opportunity to prove his identity, and therefore innocence, by answering some questions whose answers would allegedly be simple for any man with an English public school education. He fails, and is hanged.

During a break from his foreign correspondent days, in London, Munro continued to write for the *Morning Post*, which printed political satires 'Written by H. H. Munro'.[23] In 1904, he returned to Belgrade, then moved on to Warsaw, from where he was writing in March 1904. Ethel Munro remarks that his experiences of young men in Poland and Russia were always the same, 'he could not get them to be energetic' (Munro, p. 69). His sense of innate superiority persisted, as did his evident sense of being always on show and therefore always obliged to present a perfectly formed picture of English superiority to the world at large. Writing to tell his sister that he has bought some old coins from a man with an immense collection, he remarks that his superior knowledge of medieval history fairly had taken the man's breath away, since Englishmen are expected to be profoundly ignorant of such matters (letter to Ethel Munro dated 1 August 1904, ibid. pp. 70–1). He also seems unperturbed by what he refers to as the 'nice feudal ways' of some of the poorer people of Warsaw, who 'kiss your hand on the least provocation' (ibid. p. 71).

In the autumn of 1904, Munro moved to St Petersburg, where Ethel joined him for a holiday in January 1905.[24] On 22nd January (New Style), the Socialist priest Father Gapon led a march to the Winter Palace to take the demands of the labouring classes (a shorter working day, better pay, and better conditions) to Tsar Nicholas II. This was the beginning of 'Red Sunday'.

In expectation of dramatic events, Munro took his sister to the Hôtel de France to be sure of a good view, and after lunch left her in a smoking-room while he and a friend went out. The two men came running back across the snow, pursued by the cavalry, swords drawn. A woman in the crowd struck at an officer and the rest pulled him from his sleigh and beat him almost to death. The troops then sealed off the square and Cossacks whipped back rioters and passers-by alike. Munro and his friend used another exit from the hotel to get to the Moïke Embankment and sent for Ethel to join them. Ethel soon returned to the hotel, and immediately soldiers of the Ismailoffski Guards fired on the place where they had been standing. The two men took shelter in a doorway and a bullet whizzed past Munro's head and embedded itself in the wall. The soldiers were firing on the crowd and Cossacks were laying into them with sabres. More than a thousand were killed and many more wounded. Ethel found the whole thing 'exciting', and recalled it as 'with the exception of Davos [...] the most perfect time we had together' (p. 72). She found the next two days exciting, 'the Cossacks were doing some killing on their own account, and murdered some unfortunate students merely because they had called out insults to them' (p. 74). With a Victorian faith that physiognomy is a reliable guide to character type, she describes the Cossacks as 'an evil-looking lot, pronounced Mongolian type, with criminal faces'. There seems to have been an exchange of scowls between Hector and the Cossacks as they passed one another, the Munros in a sleigh, the Cossacks presumably mounted, but Ethel hurried to distract her brother's attention.

Ethel Munro's account is in its way even more detached than her brother's. She seems to have felt neither fear nor outrage, and to have regarded the riot as a good show, the high spot of the holiday entertainment. A curfew was imposed and since the electricians were on strike the streets were in darkness. Foraging for food, Munro heard an officer shout that anyone on the street after two minutes would be shot. He stayed long enough to buy eggs, tongue, sweet biscuits, and Bessarabian wine which Ethel declared made the best dinner she had ever had, 'with excitement as a sauce' (p. 75). The image of the celebratory feast spiced by the excitement of the carnage is singularly distasteful. Ethel seems to have been permanently entertained and amused by her encounters with hilarious and excitable foreigners. She describes local friends of her brother's dashing in to his rooms and pacing the floor whilst giving them news of the latest atrocities.

It was more exciting than any play. On the second evening, after telling us harrowing tales of searching hospitals for his friend, whom at last he found dead, one Russian calmly invited us to go to the opera with him that night! It was such a jump from horrors to frivolity that I could hardly keep grave, especially as Hector was making signs to me, behind the man's back, to refuse.

Hector's reports, sent to the *Morning Post* from the telegraph office in the evening, were as often made up of his impressions as they were of news, and like many foreign correspondents of the time, he rarely hesitated to generalize on the basis of brief impressions. On 29 August 1905, he sent a long-distance contribution to an exchange in recent editions of the paper about 'the existence and causes of physical deterioration', asserting that Russian men were inert, enervated, and torpid (quoted pp. 77–8). The ridiculousness and offensiveness of the passage is somewhat leavened by its deliberate absurdity. He describes the habits of young Russian officers as not widely different from that of an old lady at Bath with a taste for cards, and blames the national obsession with military-style dress for our misguided notion of the national character.

And in their peaked caps, gay shirts, and high Blücher boots, they convey the impression of a sort of Praetorian Guard in undress.

Probably the custom of dressing nearly every male civilian, from small errand boys to postmen and such minor officials, in high military boots is responsible for many of our earliest notions of the Russians as a stern truculent warrior breed. An army, it has been said, marches on its stomach; the Russians for several generations have lived on their boots.   (quoted pp. 78–9)

There follows an immediate comparison with British (rather than English this time) boys, who, it is imagined, would make proper use of such dashing and manly attire.

If an average British boy were put at an early age into such boots he would become a swashbuckling terror to his family and neighbourhood, and in due course would rove abroad and found an Empire, or at any rate die of a tropical disease. A Russian would not feel impelled by the same influence further than the nearest summer garden.

H. W. Nevinson, who was in St Petersburg in 1905, and staying in the same hotel as Munro,[25] includes Munro among 'the few English left in the city' in his memoir, *More Changes, More Chances*.[26] Munro is described as an adjunct of Rothay Reynolds, and said to be 'lately from Malay', which suggests that Nevinson was not well acquainted with him, and he is mentioned only briefly. The 'most notable' of the correspondents is said to be Dr Emile Dillon, of the *Daily Telegraph*. 'Rothay Reynolds was there, favoured in Russian society, though a Liberal and lately converted to Roman Catholicism. And hunting in couple with him was Hector Munro ('Saki'), lately from Malay, shrewd, cynical, abhorring all Liberalism and sceptical of all enthusiasm, a joy in conversation, and a master of the short story, whether charming or satiric'.[27] By 28 April 1905, as Thrane notes, Munro's byline in the *Morning Post* had become 'our own correspondent', and the *Morning Post* obituary of 25 November 1916 reports that 'he became our Special Correspondent in Russia in the troublous years of 1903–5'.[28] The Tory, establishment, journal was claiming him as one of its own.

There was an initial S at the end of the April 1905 piece, which may have been meant to advise *Post* readers of the author's identity, 'for "Saki" was well known in London for his *Westminster Alice* (1900–2) and *Reginald*' (September 1904). [29] If so, Munro's resistance to the anonymity of a staffer got past the copy-editor, and H. H. Munro and Saki were blended, as they were, curiously, by the subtitle of the *Morning Post* obituary: 'Lance-Sergeant "Saki" '.

Eight years after the revolution of 1905, Reynolds was to give a fictional portrait of Munro as 'our man in St Petersburg' in his novel *The Gondola*. Munro appears as Hugh Blair, whose physical appearance is not described at all, but who describes himself as 'a young man with an agreeably misspent past and a taste for absinthe' (p. 260). The hero of the novel, Venning, finds Blair as he expects, at five o'clock, sitting at a table in the window of a dining room in the Hôtel de France. ' "You remain a good Parisian," he said, sitting down. "Yes," said Blair; "the only thing I am really regular about is the sacred *heure de l'absinthe*" '. Blair (here referred to like Reginald's anonymous companion as 'the other') summons a waiter by shouting 'Human being', complains of the slowness and slackness of Russian people, and wonders why his paper keeps him on when there is so little to report. ' "Give me the good old days of bombs and assassinations. I haven't sent a wire for three days, and there's not a thing in the papers to-day" ' (pp. 260–1). This enables Venning to feed Blair a report which he wants to ensure will appear in the British press. The story is thin and the source uncertified, but Blair says that he can 'fake something' from it (p. 263). Venning, determined to run no risks, then 'deliberately [lays] himself out to be entertaining' in order to distract his friend long enough for Blair to have to leave for his evening engagement (the French theatre) in a hurry, and for himself to have an excuse to send off the wire (p. 226). Blair is shown as lazy and easily duped, but punctilious about money (he offers to pay for drinks, and counts up the cost of the telegram) and polite in his thanks.

Munro left Russia again in the summer of 1905, but was back at the end of August. The New Year of 1906 was almost as turbulent as 1905. Ethel must have regretted having left Russia for England. On New Year's Eve (13 January 1906 in the western calendar), Munro dined at the Medvyed, the largest restaurant in St Petersburg, where, at midnight, the Imperial Hymn was played as usual. One guest, a student, refused to stand, and another fired five bullets into his head. Hector's report takes a characteristic fastidious but unshocked tone:

Nearly every woman in the room had fainted . . . . Although the restaurant is in the centre of the city 70 minutes elapsed before the police appeared, during which time several parties resumed their supper within a few feet of the weltering corpse.

The melodramatic nature of the scene was heightened by the intermittent arrival of groups of the victim's friends, who exchanged furious denunciations across his body with equally vociferous partisans of the assassin who indecently gloated over the tragedy.

Naturally the superstitious Russians regard the episode as a terrible portent for the New Year and doubly deplorable from the fact of its being enacted before a large assembly of foreign witnesses.[30]

Later, however, he allowed some feeling to show in repeating the story about the well-connected Russians who, he said, had continued to eat and drink with the body practically at their feet. 'What particular stage of civilisation has Russian society reached?'[31] A few months later he reported that the killer received a sentence of only four years.[32]

There were clearly a number of English writers dining at the Medvyed that night. Munro's friend Rothay Reynolds, who was to write a memoir of Munro in September 1918, tells the same story in his *My Russian Year*, and remarks 'I once read a description of this scene in a book on Russia with a flaming title. The author made the band go on playing many a merry cake-walk and those Russian men and women sit down again to supper, while all the time lay—that, and he had the pronoun printed in capital letters' (p. 67). Reynolds records that the police took forty-five rather

than at least 70 minutes to arrive, and that the body was covered
with a tablecloth. Though people did not continue to eat supper,
a woman known in Bohemian circles as 'La Truite de Gatchina'
who vociferously defended the murdered student's actions in a
loud exchange over his body abruptly turned away and drank
champagne (pp. 67–8). Perhaps it is not surprising that she felt in
need of a drink. Reynolds describes a young actor 'whose face was
as pale as death' who, far from gloating over the corpse, confronted
the woman, 'confuting her statements in an oration delivered in a
tone of white-hot passion' (p. 67). He also records that the Russians
'did exactly what English men and women would do if a man was
murdered at supper in the Ritz. Some of the ladies fainted, people
took their wives and daughters home, without even waiting to
pay their bills, and the musicians fled and did not return' (ibid.).
Munro's account was published in a newspaper rather than a book,
but, if Reynolds's more temperate version is accurate, Munro's
account of the scene contains the same error or exaggeration as the
censured author's. Reynolds himself, however, adopts an almost
Saki-esque tone in describing one incident. 'One woman was so
frightened that she got under a table and besought the man she
found there to take her home if he loved her as a husband should.
She probably recovered her nerve when they crawled out together
and she discovered her companion to be a Tatar [sic] waiter' (ibid.).
It is tempting to imagine Munro to be the 'young Englishman
of my thoughts' who told Reynolds that 'he could not determine
which is the greater bar to human happiness, religion or the family'
(p. 160) and whom Reynolds believes would have been encouraged
by some of the opinions of contemporary Russian youth. He
'would certainly have been encouraged at finding Russian boys
and girls who accept as axiomatic the principles that sound so
startling when enunciated at an English dinner-table. His cup
would overflow when he discovered that *Mrs Warren's Profession*
was being played night after night at one of the state theatres
in St Petersburg' (pp. 160–1). The ironic mention of admiration

for Shaw strengthens the possibility that Reynolds was thinking of Munro, but Munro, of course, had already discovered Russian youth and Russian theatres for himself. Reynolds's comments follow a description of the strong-mindedness of young Russian girls who take themselves and their studies very seriously, and some anecdotes about a precocious Russian boy, Shura, who might be a character from a Saki story.

Shura took the opportunity to give a full account of a play he was about to write. The action took place in the Paris of Louis XIV, and all the characters were excessively immoral. The three of us supped together in a restaurant, and Shura laid down the law on politics, religion, and the problems of life with amazing assurance. He was not called upon to take any active part in politics, he told us, but when obliged to do so, he should certainly give his support to the Socialists. He further stated that he was a Lutheran, but had long since lost his faith.

'You see,' he explained, ''it is obviously absurd to believe in the existence of God.' [...]

'When I am twenty-five I shall shoot myself,' he remarked [...]

'Why?' I asked.

'Well,' he answered, 'what would life be after twenty-five?'

Then he went away, for, as he mentioned, his father was annoyed if he stayed out later than two in the morning.   (ibid. 158–9)

Similarly, a 17-year-old gives Reynolds 'a picture of the progressive boys and girls of the little town in which he lived' which represents the Saki youths' hedonist pleasures and casual misogyny. 'They went out to parties in the woods at night and stayed there until dawn, playing cards, eating and drinking, and making love. He thought that love-making was bad for the health, and blamed the girls for his downfall' (p. 159). It was to be some time before Saki's women ceased to be despoilers of men.

The portraits of Munro at this time left by Reynolds seem slightly odd for a close friend, and at odds with the portrait left by his employer. 'In all these adventures Mr. Munro displayed an undaunted courage and an enterprise that no discouragement of circumstance could quench. Again and again he took with a frolic welcome the gravest risks in order to serve the newspaper to which he was accredited.'[33] An obituary is no place to stint on praise, but the references to Munro's energy and courage seem to be in too great contrast to the studied laziness of Blair.

In 1907, Munro left Russia for Paris, where his duties were more those of theatre critic and occasional columnist than political commentator, though he did report on rioting which threatened the government of Premier Clemenceau. He was called home in March by the illness of his father, who died two days after his arrival. Later that summer, he and Ethel took a holiday in Pourville, in Normandy. Munro often recycled places and experiences, if not too personal, in his stories, and Pourville later became 'a little watering-place' whose small casino proves irresistible to a newly rich old lady, and devastating to the hopes of her nieces in 'The Way to the Dairy' (Clovis, pp. 176–87). Here Hector demonstrated that his love of practical jokes was still intact. Ethel reports:

Next door to our caravanserai was a post-office which sold odds and ends as well as stamps. Choosing some picture post-cards one day I asked how much they were and was answered from behind the counter by Hector, who sold them to me, and some stamps to another customer, suggesting further outlay on his part on various goods, the owner looking on and beaming. (Munro, 81).

It is not clear why Munro found this amusing or what the point was. Probably it was along the lines of 'funny foreigners'. The Munros still saw 'types' everywhere and Hector at least still took upon himself the role of judge and executioner of the kinds he found less acceptable. Ethel describes Pourville as 'thick with types', one of whom provided the original of 'The Soul of Laploshka', in Reginald in Russia. He had a reputation for meanness, so 'in the fullness of time Hector played a hoax on him; if there were a crime on which he had no pity it was meanness, and this man had apparently plenty of money, so there was no shadow of excuse for him' (ibid. pp. 81–2).

How elaborate the hoax was, or how painful or embarrassing to the hoaxed, Ethel does not say. Implicit, as in her description of any of her brother's enterprises, is that it was a success, of course. Perhaps it is the way Ethel tells it, but somehow Munro's solemnly planning, patiently awaiting the opportunity for, and finally carrying out a hoax on a stranger, on the basis of a reputation for meanness and a rumour of wealth, is just not funny, as the elaborate hoaxes in the stories are.

As 'our own correspondent' in Paris, Munro reviewed some plays and exhibitions, recorded mounting concern about the increasing incidences of violent attacks by 'Apaches', described an attempt to launch a flying machine, and reported on a Parisian waiters' strike, an 'exceedingly Parisian decision' in a court case. He also wrote about Franco-German relations, in a piece headed 'Is an agreement possible?', and ending: 'And the question comes back again and again with disagreeable persistence, in certain phases of our recent statecraft and foreign policy: have we been complacently building a hedge around a cuckoo?' (*Morning Post*, 8 April 1907, 7).

From Pourville, Munro returned to Paris in September, presumably to settle his affairs there, and Ethel presumably settled family affairs in Devon. Though he continued to publish fiction in newspapers and magazines, and wrote a 'Potted Parliament' column for *The Outlook* from 2 February to 8 August 1914, Munro was never again 'our special correspondent' or 'foreign correspondent'. Perhaps a small inheritance from his father enabled him to give up the life of a foreign correspondent, or perhaps, as Ethel Munro says, journalism had lost its appeal for Munro now that he had lost his most appreciative reader (Munro, p. 81). Perhaps with the death of his father he no longer felt the need to repay the Colonel's years of support with visible diligence and fiscal responsibility, by holding down a regular job, and could at last become a fiction writer, the fluctuations of whose fortunes were his own concern.

5

London Again

SAKI'S first full-length collection, *Reginald*, had been published by Methuen while Munro was in Russia, and he stayed with Methuen for his second collection, *Reginald in Russia*, which was published six years later. *Reginald* had received some fair notices, which Munro's devoted sister had forwarded to him, and a characteristically crushing reception from Aunt Tom, as Munro reported:

Thanks for your letter and the cuttings. The Athenaeum consoled me for Aunt Tom's remark that it was a pity the book had been published as, after the 'Alice', people would expect it to be clever and of course be disappointed. The 'of course' was terribly crushing but I am able to sit up now and take a little light nourishment.   (letter to Ethel Munro, no date given, Munro, 72).

Neither collection made much money, and Methuen were slow in sending the small royalties that were due. Langguth quotes from correspondence between the author and publisher. A letter from Methuen refers to a cheque for £4. 1s. 1d. which has been lost in the post, and promises a new one. A few days later, Munro wrote: 'The fresh cheque for £4. 1. 1. of which you speak in your letter of the 4th instant appears to have had no better luck than its predecessor" (letter to Methuen & Co., no addressee or date given, Langguth, 166).

In 1908, Munro settled in London, in the rooms at 97 Mortimer Street where he was to write most of his best-known stories, and bought a cottage in the Surrey hills, twenty-three miles away, where he installed his sister and various pets (Munro, 82). Hugh

Walpole describes him at this stage in his life as: 'to be met with at country houses and London parties apparently rather cynical, rather idle and taking life so gently that he might hardly be said to take it at all. Certain intimate friends of his knew that that was not the truth but they supported the disguise and encouraged it; it saved him, we cannot doubt, a number of tiresome obligations.'[1]

A similar account of Saki about Town a little later is given by Thomas Anstey Guthrie (writing as F. Anstey) in a memoir published twenty years after Munro's death. Anstey describes Munro as giving 'an extremely funny imitation of Sarah Bernhardt reciting a French version of "The Walrus and the Carpenter" at an evening party in December 1912, and refers to him as one of the country's most brilliant humorists',[2] but also recalls an anecdote told by Munro at their first meeting that gives a hint of the *schadenfreude* attributed by a number of people to both the characters and their creator.

One day that March [1912] I met Hector Munro (Saki) at the Ladies Park Club; he was rather short, dark-haired, and clean-shaven, with one side of his face very slightly out of drawing and he had a soft and remarkably pleasant voice. Find a note of an anecdote he told that afternoon of a man who when seized by a sudden and violent hunger found that he had nothing but a penny in his pocket. Fortunately, however, he came upon an automatic chocolate machine outside a shop, eagerly put in his penny and got a box of matches.[3]

Rothay Reynolds tells a similar story, citing it as an instance of the way in which the wealth of others did not excite Munro's envy. 'I remember his coming home from a ball and relating that he had sat at supper next a millionairess, whose doctor had prescribed a diet of milk-puddings. "I had a hearty supper," he said gleefully, "and for all her millions she was unable to eat anything." '[4]

Munro's London life was organized around a series of routines: lunch at his club or a Lyons corner café, evenings playing whist or bridge at the club, or at the theatre, or dining with a small circle of friends, or at home working on a 'tapestry painting'. Having ceased to be a foreign correspondent, he seems to have given up foreign travel. From the outside, his London life seems narrow, comprised of the predictable round made so horrific in 'The Mappined Life', in which a young girl draws a parallel between the life of the average middle-class family and that of captive animals on the new concrete 'Mappin terraces' at the zoo. Perhaps, though, there were excitements, high-spots, and unrest-cures. Perhaps to relieve the tedium and to convince himself that he was not becoming middle-aged, in his early forties, Munro was still given to pranks, jokes, caricature sketches, and apparently spontaneous bursts of elaborate make-believe. When Ethel deplored the effect of a sunless summer on the Surrey garden, her brother insisted that they would invoke the aid of Apollo, round a bonfire. 'So, with a guest who was with us, we draped sheets round to make us look more Grecian and therefore more pleasing to Apollo, while we craved the boon of sunshine. The next day there was a brilliant sun and every day after for three weeks' (Munro, p. 83). There is an invisible, 'of course' before the full stop. Ethel had complete faith in Hector. Perhaps at 40 Munro was still desperately trying to be a spontaneous, authority-challenging, irresponsible youth, which would have been a hideously embarrassing spectacle, but one wonders how fully he entered into the spirit of the ritual, and how much of him was watching his sister and his guest, and wondering how far he could make them go.

Sending some stories to John Lane, Munro explained that Methuen 'have published two previous books [storie] of mine, but they are dreadfully unenterprising in the way of advertising'.[5] Methuen also appears to have been ignorant of the publication that year of *The Chronicles of Clovis* (1911). More than a year after they had brought out *Reginald in Russia*, and when Clovis had been in bookshops for some time, they wrote to solicit a new collection, in lukewarm and, as Langguth points out, condescending terms. 'We write to ask if you are likely to have another volume of stories ready before long. We like your stories very

much, and we should be glad to make them better known' (letter
to H. H. Munro, no date given, Langguth, p. 166). Munro's reply
is superficially polite but dripping with irony. He sends thanks for
the offer but informs Methuen that sales of *Reginald in Russia* were
so limited that he assumed they could not be interested in his
next two, which are bespoken (letter to Methuen & Co., quoted
ibid.). Another letter, telling John Lane that he would be amused
to hear of Munro's first ever, if belated, complimentary letter from
Methuen, suggests his real response, and provides an opportunity
to hint to his new publisher that he is a sought-after commodity.[6]
Methuen may have tried to fill Saki's place in their list with P. G.
Wodehouse, whose novel, *The Little Nugget*, about attempts to
kidnap a spoiled and loathsome child of wealthy parents, they
published in 1913.

Once established with The Bodley Head, Munro did not give
up his journalism, but continued to review books for the *Morning
Post* and, Thrane persuasively argues, to write unsigned occasional
pieces under the heading 'At the Zoo' (one of which, 'The Mappin
Terraces' (*Morning Post*, 21 January 1913), seems very likely to have
been by Saki),[7] and he continued to publish stories in the *Bystander*
and elsewhere. In spite of the time and income these cost him,
however, he did continue to collect the short stories into volumes,
for which he wrote additional stories, and to produce a second
novel after *Bassington*.

The pseudonym under which Munro published his stories might
come from the last stanzas of *The Rubáiyát of Omar Khayyám*, in
which 'Sáki' is a cup-bearer.

> Yon rising moon that looks for us again—
> How oft hereafter will she wax and wane;
>   How oft hereafter rising look for us
> Through this same Garden—and for one in vain!
>
> And when like her, oh Sáki, you shall pass
> Among the guests Star-scattered on the Grass
>   And in your joyous errand reach the spot

Where I made One—turn down an empty Glass!

(trans. Edward Fitzgerald, 1859)

Saki's obituary in the *Westminster Gazette* stated off-handedly that it was 'a pen name adopted, by the way, from Nagasaki'.[8] Whatever its source, the pseudonym could not have been intended to conceal Hector Hugh Munro's identity as the author of the stories, since 'H. H. Munro' is credited on the title pages. Saki did not treat the probable source very reverently. Evidently, the *Rubáiyát* had become the obvious gift for a modern young male relative. For an older generation it still had enough of a whiff of perfumed orientalism about it to feel faintly daring and advertise avant-garde taste, but the book was quite respectable and even scholarly, so for the younger generation, of course, it was a damp squib. In 'Reginald on Christmas Presents', Reginald remarks: 'I am *not* collecting copies of the cheaper editions of Omar Khayyam. I gave the last four that I received to the lift-boy, and I like to think of him reading them, with FitzGerald's notes, to his aged mother. Lift-boys always have aged mothers; shows such nice feeling on their part, I think' (*Reginald*, p. 15). In 'Reginald's Rubaiyat', the Duchess has asked Reginald to write something in her album: ' "something Persian, you know, and just a little bit decadent" ', and Reginald obliges with verses about rotten eggs (p. 106). Quatrains rhyming *aaba* pop up all over the collections after that. The avant-garde aesthetic had become blunted and ubiquitous.

The choice of John Lane as publisher was in a way predictable and in a way daring, as was Lane's choice of Saki as an author. Lane had been Wilde's publisher and had suffered from Wilde's fall. Though Wilde had died ten years before, repercussions of his trial were still felt. Christopher Lane reminds us of the 'bizarre libel case' that followed the first performance in England of Wilde's *Salomé* eighteen years after its author's death, and that in 1918, the trauma Wilde had allegedly caused England was scandalously invoked as a reason for the country's not (at the time) winning the war.[9]

As a satirist, playwright, and epigrammatist, Saki would have had some affinity with Wilde. Munro was an admirer of Wilde's plays,[10] and comes close to quoting him, as when one character remarks to another: ' "To lose an hotel and a cake of soap in one afternoon suggests wilful carelessness" ' ('Dusk', *Beasts*, p. 130).

Wilde's trial would have had a tremendous impact on him whether he was a practising homosexual or not. After Wilde's imprisonment, there could have been a powerful temptation to follow 'St Oscar' in openly declaring one's sexuality and proclaiming it no crime, and an equally powerful imperative to conceal any sexual 'deviance', adopt protective colouring, and keep a low profile.

According to the playwright Ben Travers, who worked for Lane from 1911 to 1914, Lane was a 'bigoted Liberal' who poured scorn on Travers's inherited Conservatism, but was 'not the man to let political bias interfere with a good bargain'.[11] Saki was evidently a good bargain.

No Conservative writer of the day was a better marksman than H.H. Munro. Without ever going out of his way to lug a political allusion into his beautifully polished *Morning Post* stories he could release an occasional arrow of satire at the Asquith government and its ministers which would wring a yelp of indignant pain from such Liberals as Mr. Crockett, the town traveller. But Lane, puckering his beard in forbearance, appreciated 'Saki's' wit and encouraged and exploited him for all he was worth.[12]

Travers remarks that having consulted the *Oxford English Dictionary* for the definition of a wit, and been told that it is 'a person with the capacity for making brilliant observations in an amusing way', he finds it a fair description of Munro 'at a time when, it is interesting to note, Noël Coward, as a late-teenager, was one of his most fervent admirers'.[13] Tantalizingly, Travers recalls Coward as 'an occasional visitor to the Bodley Head in his Saki researches' but says no more of them.[14]

In an interview with Langguth, Travers recalled that Lane had allowed him to choose his favourite Saki story to appear in full in the Bodley Head monthly promotional circular, the *Bodleian*, as a promotion for *Beasts*. Lane disapproved of Travers's choice, 'Dusk', on the grounds that it was unrepresentative of Saki's characteristic style. 'Dusk' is a twist-in-the-tale story, dependent on the structural irony of the final paragraph for its effect rather than for the epigrammatic and ironic style of the narrator and characters, and is not among Saki's best works, but Travers presumably chose it for what he felt was its characteristic portrait of a disenchanted, cynical, ex-romantic. (See *Beasts*, pp. 125–32.)

Lane's exploitation of authors probably consisted in paying very low royalties, very slowly. Most of Munro's extant letters to him and other members of the firm are requests, demands, and pleas for payment, which continued through his publication of *Bassington* and *William* and into his enlistment. Late payer or not, Lane made a handsome job of *Clovis*. No attempt was made to maintain the pseudonym, and every attempt was made to appropriate any success of the *Reginald* books. The author's name was given as 'Saki' on the cover and 'Saki/H. H. Munro' on the spine. The dust jacket cover was grey/green printed in black and it featured the same illustration as the hard cover, a young man reclining in a hammock, his socks and cuffs picked out in bright blue, with a book raised in one hand and a cigarette between the fingers of the other. His likeness to Clovis and co. is proclaimed by his centrally parted wet-look shiny black hair and the large, floppy, checked bows on his shoes, but even so he looks slightly more tweedy than dandy, particularly as he is slightly plump and appears to have no neck. The collection is dedicated:

TO THE LYNX KITTEN,
WITH HIS RELUCTANTLY GIVEN CONSENT,
THIS BOOK IS AFFECTIONATELY
DEDICATED.

H.H.M.
August, 1911

Whether the Lynx Kitten is child, adult, relative, friend, lover, or even anthropomorphized animal, is unknown.

The Chronicles of Clovis was not Munro's first choice of title, and was presumably chosen to match the alliteration and style of *Reginald in Russia*. In February 1911 Munro had submitted some stories, addressing the editor as 'Dear Mr Lane', and signing himself 'Very sincerely yours'.[15] A sheet headed 'Sketches to form volume with suggested title "Tobermory and other Sketches"', written in Munro's hand, may have accompanied this letter. It lists the stories as 'Tobermory, Wratislav, The Matchmaker, Hermann the Irascible, The Unrest-Cure, Adrian, Sredni Vashtar, The Quest, The Jesting of Arlington Stringham, The Background, The Stampeding of Lady Bastable, Filboid Studge, Esmé'.

On 26 April of that year, Munro wrote in cooler, more formal terms ('Dear Sir' and 'Sincerely Yours') to note that he had not yet received an opinion of the stories he had sent, which he describes as '"Tobermory and other Sketches"', and to send four more, which he lists as 'The Easter Egg', 'The Chaplet', 'The Peace of Mowsle Barton', and 'Mrs Packletide's Tiger'. He adds that four or five of the stories deal prominently with animals, and suggests 'Beasts and Super Beasts' as a better title than 'Tobermory'.[16] These stories were published with others as *The Chronicles of Clovis*, and Munro had to wait for his next collection to use *Beasts and Super-Beasts*, which seems strange, as many of the stories concerned with beasts natural and supernatural appear in the former volume. *The Chronicles of Clovis* was evidently foisted on to him, and he prophesied that it would damn the collection. A letter of October 1911 quotes a, possibly apocryphal, elderly gentleman who had announced that he could not read such remote French history.[17] Munro, a student of medieval European genealogy, would have known the legends and history of the Frankish king Clovis, whose predilection for swift and nasty vengeance and what he considered poetic justice (he split the skull of a soldier who had split a looted vase with an axe) would have appealed to him. The addition of

Sangrail is also allusively medieval, suggesting perhaps one without a quest, or ideal, or indeed any elusive, unattainable goal; someone more concerned with the material things of life, as well as someone with royal blood.[18]

He had been working fast. A letter of 9 June 1911 records the delivery of 'A Clovis story' and promises a 'longish' story in a day or two. Ten days later, he wrote again, enclosing 'a long Clovis story, 'the Story of St Vespaluus' [sic].[19] He continued to add to the collection until close to the end of August, but the same letter turns down a request for a story on a topical theme, such as the Coronation, on the grounds that such a story would give the collection an out-of-date feel almost as soon as it was published. It was one thing to publish political satire in a daily or even weekly newspaper, and even to allow publication in book form of the *Alice* articles, but Munro clearly expected his short stories and novels to have a longer shelf-life. The idea of bringing out collections of themed stories seems to have appealed to him, but he decided against it. In July 1911, sending 'The Way to the Dairy', he announces that he has decided against bringing out a separate volume of saint stories, so his 'St Vespaluus' is to be included in *Clovis*.[20] This seems a pity; an anthology of anti-hagiography by Saki would have been worth reading.

Though his publishers may not have allowed Munro to veto the title of the collection, they clearly did ask for his opinion about the cover. A letter dated 13 Aug. 1911 shows that he scrutinized the versions offered with minute attention. He notes that he found the version with a red background and white lettering the most desirable in all particulars apart from the amended drawing of a leg which appeared on a version with a green background, except that he perceived some additional shading in that cover as detracting from the simplicity and spoiling what he called the white flannel effect. To be absolutely sure, he listed his requirements: the cover he had marked 'I' with the amended leg but without the additional shading of the cover that he had marked no. II.[21] He also paid attention to the order of the stories within his collections. When he sent a new story on 24 August 1911, he stipulated that it should be inserted before 'Ministers of Grace' because the latter made a more effective wind-up to the volume.[22]

A description of Munro at this time appeared in an interview in *The Bodleian*.

To look at, Mr Munro is what nice old ladies would call 'interesting'. He is very slim and straight, and well-groomed; his eyes are shadowed and mysterious; his mouth has ironic curves, and there is a delicate lack of energy about his movements that is rather charming. He does not upset chairs, talk in a loud voice, drink excessively, or get on one's nerves. So he is an excellently worthy companion; withal, studiously and unobtrusively observant. But the personality of the man is frankly baffling, and he declines to talk about himself.[23]

The pose is affected, slightly languid, and distancing, and the interviewer is obviously in on the joke.

We began.
'Do you know anything about interviewing?'
'No,' I replied with brutal frankness.
'Well, I don't either.'
There was a silence of about an hour and a half.
Then Mr Munro went on:
'My favourite flower is the periwinkle; my favourite animal is the kingfisher, my favourite bird is the hedge-sparrow, and I like oysters, asparagus and politics. Also the theatre.' [24]

He was pleased with the reception of *Clovis*: critics had been kind; booksellers had done well; friends had promised to read it if he would send them copies. The interviewer remarked that he liked the way Saki mixed the 'weird with the winsome'. Munro seemed surprised. ' "Do you? I was a little surprised to see how well it has come off. Many of my critics want me to devote a whole book to tragic stuff." The interviewer suggested that it was a compliment for a man whose wit is admired to be asked to do purely serious work. "Yes," replied Munro, "a humorist is almost invariably expected to be funny for life." '[25]

A photographic portrait of Munro from a year or so later is also in existence. E. O. Hoppé represents him looking into the far distance, his lips just parted, one eyelid slightly drooping and one eye slightly lower than the other.[26] His hair is thinning and his brow faintly creased, but the overall impression is of a well-groomed and immaculately shaved, relatively young-looking man. He is dressed conservatively, in a dark coat, waistcoat and stiff collar, and seems to be in a black tie.

J. W. Lambert sees Munro as rather a misanthrope, perhaps similar to Norman Gortsby in 'Dusk', disillusioned by the pettiness and lack of nobility in society, which for him, was 'a breeding-ground of inanity' (Lambert, p. 59). He suggests that when Saki 'turns from the attack' he turns into 'a celebrant of loneliness', and points out the lack of close human relationships in the work. For Lambert, Saki's writing points 'with hypnotic glee, towards the fragmentation of established, steady, solid society, the confusion of the bourgeoisie' (p. 60). The glee was as horrified as it was hypnotic. A true conservative, Munro valued an imaginary, unchanging England imbued with noble ideals and organized in a rigid hierarchy.

By 1912, Saki was writing for the *Outlook, Morning Post, Daily Express,* and *Bystander. The Bystander,* then edited by Vivian Carter, would have been particularly congenial. Deciding to extend the magazine's coverage and give it a more cosmopolitan flavour, Carter set up successive temporary offices in several European cities so that his staff could produce the respective special issues within authentic local colour. As a freelance, Munro did not go with them, but he did mark the occasion in a story.[27] When Sir Lulworth Quayne's nephew expounds on the animal instinct to migrate, Quayne retorts that the phenomenon is also observable in human affairs, and that an instance has occurred recently in this country.

I mean the wander fever which suddenly displayed itself in the managing and editorial staffs of certain London newspapers. It began with the stampede of the entire staff of one of our most brilliant and enterprising weeklies to the banks of the Seine and the heights of Montmartre. The migration was a brief one, but it heralded an era of restlessness in the Press world which lent quite a new meaning to the phrase 'newspaper circulation'.   ('The Yarkand Manner', *Beasts*, p. 152)

Though the publications from this period (1910–14) made his pen-name famous, and are littered with Duchesses, Baronesses, Arch-Dukes, and Gräfins, Munro was living a fairly modest and private rather than public life, and did not move in exalted social circles. His milieu was the West End and Bloomsbury; Gentlemen's Clubs and Bond Street shops, which Ben Travers describes as quite exalted in themselves.

I can still feel the exhilaration with which I would step out of the office into Burlington Gardens and walk across Bond Street into Albemarle Street to spend my luncheon hour at the Public Schools Club, of which I was an original member. It always delighted me to realise that it was all part and parcel of my job to be situated here, in the heart of the West End, with all the delectable air of expansive Edwardian luxury which still clung to it; to know that I belonged to it and that it belonged to me.
    [...] The Albany itself and Burlington House are over forty years older but still present much of their sedate tranquillity to the pandemonium of a modernized Piccadilly, like two very old members blinking in stolid abstraction through their club windows at the extraordinary procedures of a changed world. Burlington Arcade, too, with its gay little shops tinkling with allurement as of old, still fills my nostrils with the nostalgic redolence of patchouli [...] Bond Street suggests to my mind a pre-eminently aristocratic dowager (opposite number to the two old club members) preserving her spirit of dignity and nursing her poor worn-out old complexion in a charabanc-load of trippers. Its wares—pictures, jewellery, hats, scent—are now, as then, among the most exquisite and exorbitant that London has to offer. But the pavements which today are pervaded by a fleeting succession of noses, being poked into shop windows and whipped away again ('Hurry up, Jennifer, or we'll miss the bus') were then a privileged parade-ground, where the hobble-skirted

ladies of fashion, escorted by bespatted and buckskin-gloved attendant nuts, lingered in appreciative bemusement.[28]

This was the London Munro knew.

Munro was not in London or Caterham all the time. Charlie had left the Burmese Police and become a prison governor in Ireland, and his wife's family had a house, Carrig Cnoc, on the shore across the bay from Portstewart in the north of the country. From 1908, Munro and his sister would holiday there during August, walking, swimming, and playing with Charlie's first daughter, Felicia. Later, Munro was to write to Felicia from the front, telling her that he had been crawling between the British trenches and no-man's-land very much as they had when they played at being wolves on the hunt for farmers' wives.[29]

Events in Britain before, during, and after Munro's time abroad help to contextualize, though not of course excuse, the anti-Semitism represented in a number of his stories. By the time Munro was born, the Emancipation Act had enfranchised Jewish male householders, and by the time he returned to England, as Alderman says, the Jewish vote had come of age. 'The generation of the emancipation was giving way to its successor, the emancipated generation, the members of which exercised their rights without any special regard for the feelings of the Gentile majority.'[30] Fear about the political power of 'the Jewish vote' interacted with fear that the Jewish community was growing. Approximately 150,000 Jewish Russians came to Britain between 1871 and 1914, many fleeing the pogroms, and, Antony Taylor argues, were often associated in the public mind with anarchism, since in the Tsarist Empire, anarchism had become the means of revenge against the state which had encouraged anti-Semitic purges in the 1880s and 1900s. This association led to what Taylor calls scapegoating of the Jewish community following anarchist atrocities. It was argued that legislation should be put in place to prevent Britain from becoming a haven for fleeing anarchists and revolutionaries.

In 1905 the Anti-aliens Act provided one such response to rising concerns about anarchists in Britain. Overturning centuries of tolerance the Act introduced limitations on incomers. Outraging much liberal opinion at the time, and offending some European neighbours, after the Siege of Sidney Street in 1911 there were further debates about beefing up the Act and controlling the circulation of firearms which continued until the eve of the Great War.[31]

Anti-Semitism was further stoked by suggestions that the immigrants were stealing British workers' jobs, and undercutting prices through the sweat-shop system. In 1888, a Select Committee on Alien Immigration was appointed from the House of Commons, and another on the Sweating System from the House of the Lords. Alderman reports that the Lords 'gave the immigrants a reasonably clean bill of health', concluding that ' "undue stress has been laid on the injurious effect on wages caused by foreign immigration, inasmuch as we find that the evils complained of obtain in trades which do not appear to be affected by foreign immigration" ', while the Commons found that 'the immigrants were "generally very dirty and uncleanly in their habits" but none the less showed themselves to be "quick at learning, moral, frugal and thrifty and inoffensive as citizens" '.[32] In spite of this, opposition to Jewish immigration persisted, and in 1892 Salisbury's government announced that an Aliens Act was in preparation. Salisbury lost the general election which followed soon after, and the Liberal government which followed him did not pursue the issue, but he reintroduced it as a private member's bill that passed all the required stages in the House of Lords before it was dropped, only to be revived again at the next General election, in 1900. In 1901, the British Brothers League, a group with links to the TUC and other labour organizations, and the ancestor of the British Union of Fascists, was established; in 1902, an Alien Immigration Committee of fifty-two MPs was set up, and an abortive attempt was made to pass another bill in 1904.[33] 'All this agitation was taking place against a background of mounting, country-wide anti-Semitism, fostered by the right-wing jingoism and left-wing anti-capitalism which accompanied the Boer War.'[34]

The Aliens Act was finally passed in 1905. It established a new system of immigration control and registration, and gave the Home Secretary responsibility for all matters relating to immigration and nationality in Great Britain. It did not preclude the possibility of asylum in Britain for émigrés escaping persecution, but it did make asylum a matter of discretion.

The opposition to unrestricted immigration by Jewish refugees came largely from the Conservative party and in particular from a group of MPs with constituencies in the East End of London. Major Williams Evans-Gordon, MP for Stepney, united some of these as leaders of the British Brothers League. Evans-Gordon supported denial of entry to Britain and relocation in British colonies for Jewish migrants. The existing Anglo-Jewish community was not necessarily opposed to the Act or to the BBL's position. It was supported by the Jewish Conservative MP for Limehouse, Harry Samuel, and the Liberal Jewish MP for Wolverhampton South, Henry Norman. There were twelve Jewish MPs in the House of Commons when the vote was taken. Four voted for the bill, four against, and there were four abstentions.

The attitude of the existing Anglo-Jewish community of some 60,000, newly emancipated by the Whigs, was to fear that the backlash against the refugees—who unlike themselves were not anglicized, dressed differently, spoke Yiddish, etc.—would spill over into hostility towards themselves. They were for the most part prosperous and newly accepted within the innermost circles of the British bourgeoisie. Why jeopardize their class position for the sake of religious brethren with whom they had so little in common? Their attitude was best summed up by the Conservative Chief Rabbi of the time (some things never change) Hermann Adler: 'We [Anglo-Jewry] must frankly agree, that we do not desire to admit criminals, and that there is force in the argument against the admission of those [Jews] mentally or physically afflicted.'[35]

As Home Secretary, it was Balfour who gained the power of veto over Jewish and other immigration into Britain. Later, as Foreign

Secretary, he was to issue the Balfour Declaration in support of the Zionist movement, implicitly arguing that Jewish immigration into Britain should be discouraged in favour of immigration to Palestine. Balfour's extreme xenophobia was exhibited in his *Decadence*.[36]

In Saki's 'The Unrest-Cure', Clovis uses a pretended massacre of Jews as a comic device by which a staid middle-aged man, J. P. Huddle, and his sister are shaken out of a rut. Clovis masquerades as a private secretary arranging a secret meeting at an out-of-the-way country house. Amid a flurry of telegrams and elliptical messages, the unwilling and unwitting hosts are told that 'the Bishop' and 'Colonel Alberti' are in conference in the study and must not be disturbed. They then learn that their house is to be the headquarters of a massacre; a massacre of Jews, and that it is surrounded by armed men who will shoot on sight anyone attempting to leave. Through the afternoon, Jewish people from the neighbourhood arrive, called by urgent telegrams ostensibly sent by Huddle. Clovis departs, leaving the Huddles and their guests to a night of conjecture and terror, in which 'every creak of the stairway, every rustle of wind through the shrubbery was fraught with horrible meaning'. On his way back to town, Clovis reflects that he doesn't suppose they will be grateful for his Unrest-cure (*Clovis*, p. 84–5). There is of course never any intention to kill anyone, and in a less prejudiced writer the comedy would come from the victims of the hoax being prejudiced enough to believe that such a massacre might be planned, but in Saki's story the Huddles are not anti-Semitic, or not actively against the continued existence of the respected Sir Leon Birberry, the alleged first victim. Though Huddle expostulates when he hears that the leader of the plan is the Bishop: 'But—the Bishop is such a tolerant, humane man', and insists 'He will be hanged', the plot is clearly not so outrageously ridiculous as to be entirely implausible. That Saki employs his usual kind of humour—the juxtaposition of urbane language and manners and outrageous circumstances—for such a distasteful subject could make the story even more offensive.

In a penetrating and illuminating account of the story as part of his exploration of 'The Unrest-Cure According to Lawrence, Saki, and Lewis', Christopher Lane identifies the problem that readers encounter with this story: 'the effects of under- and over-reading'. He continues: 'Downplay its subject and one risks trivializing the prejudice it exploits; focus only on its anti-Semitism, by contrast, and one misses its comic pretensions.'[37] Lane's inclusion of the story, with D. H. Lawrence's *Women in Love* and Percy Wyndham Lewis's *Apes of God*, in the category of 'anti-identitarian fiction' draws out the possibility of a less damning reading.

[W]e could read the story counterintuitively, in ways similar to Lawrence's postwar narrative, as alerting us to the catastrophe it seems to present. Like *Women in Love*, and *The Apes of God*, 'The Unrest-Cure' draws on eschatology without countenancing extinction; it does so by nudging Huddle and his sister towards 'self-abolition' while ultimately protecting them from that catastrophe. The postman's arrival the next day 'finally convince[s] the watchers that the Twentieth century was still unblotted', but of course we can't read this line (or the story overall) and share the characters' relief [...] Perhaps only in hindsight, Saki's short story resembles a 'hygienic practice of nonviolence', a phrase that Leo Bersani uses when arguing that the ego represents difference as a menacing threat to its specious coherence. 'As soon as persons are posited,' he declares, 'the war begins'.[38] The point for Bersani is that anti-identitarian fiction [...] does more than betray the ego's violent appropriation of reality; it also compels the subject to establish a new relation to the world.[39]

The denouement of 'A Touch of Realism' depends upon a practical joke at once childish and horrible played on a Jewish couple, the Klammersteins (*Beasts*, pp. 133–42). Earlier, in 'Reginald at the Theatre', Reginald shocks the Duchess by insisting that what she calls 'the great Anglo-Saxon Empire' 'is rapidly becoming a suburb of Jerusalem' (*Reginald*, p. 29). In *Bassington*, the MP Courtenay Youghal alludes to the support by some Jewish groups for the Aliens Act and in a particularly nasty form of anti-Semitism, deplores Jewish culture as aesthetically objectionable, in deploring the Jewish as opposed to classical basis of Christian myth.

'Whatever else you take in hand', said Youghal, 'you must never improve this garden. It's what our idea of heaven might be like if the Jews hadn't invented one for us on totally different lines. It's dreadful that we should accept them as the impresarios of our religious dreamland instead of the Greeks.'

'You're not very fond of the Jews,' said Elaine.

'I've travelled and lived a good deal in Eastern Europe,' said Youghal.

'It seems largely a question of geography,' said Elaine; 'in England no one is really anti-Semitic.'

Youghal shook his head. 'I know a great many Jews who are.' (*Bassington*, pp. 101–2)

Later, Saki was to depict the occupation of Britain by German forces as bringing an influx of European Jews. A doctor, Holham, attending the central character of *William*, Yeoville, remarks that ' "There are more of them now than there used to be." ' He confesses that he dislikes Jews but concedes: 'I will be fair to them, and admit that those of them who were in any genuine sense British have remained British and have stuck by us loyally in our misfortune; all honour to them' (*William*, p. 57). The concession is not a great one, since it is clear that Holham's category of 'genuine Britishness' would exclude most of those he is thinking about, and Jews remain 'they' while the British are 'we' and 'us'. Holham continues:

'But of the others, the men who by temperament and everything else were far more Teuton or Polish or Latin than they were British, it was not to be expected that they would be heartbroken because London had suddenly lost its place among the political capitals of the world, and become a cosmopolitan city. They had appreciated the free and easy liberty of the old days, under British rule, but there was a stiff insularity in the ruling race that they chafed against. Now, putting aside some petty Government restrictions that Teutonic bureaucracy has brought in, there is really, in their eyes, more licence and social adaptability in London than before. It has taken on some of the aspects of a No-Man's-Land, and the Jew, if he likes, may almost consider himself as of the dominant race; at any rate he is ubiquitous.' (ibid. 57–8)

Jews are accused of being without the firm anchor of nationality, British nationality, which would give them moral purpose and rectitude. They are represented as what we might now call Euro-trash; rootless seekers of pleasure; the 'insidious leaven that will help to denationalize London' and degrade it from 'a world-ruling city with a great sense of its position and its responsibilities' to 'the centre of what these people understand by life' (pp. 58–9). As proof of this degeneracy, the narrative voice, describing the audience at a theatrical performance in honour of the new regime that sickens the patriotic Yeovil notes that it contains people from 'Paris, Munich, Rome, Moscow and Vienna, from Sweden and Holland and divers other cities and countries, but in the majority of cases the Jordan Valley had supplied their forefather with a common cradle-ground' (pp. 124–5).

The Jews are presumably represented as content to live under the Kaiser in spite of the anti-Semitic discourses he disseminated because, recognizing their economic importance, he allowed them to enter and to hold positions in the Second Reich. By the time this novel was published, there had been anti-Semitic riots in Great Britain. In 1903, fighting broke out between different immigrant groups in Merthyr Tydfil, and during the Tredegar 'Jewish Riots' of 1911, Jewish-owned businesses in the Welsh town of Tredegar were looted and burned.

When Saki's stories are familiar these days, it is mostly from the Methuen and Bodley Head collections, or from later anthologies, but those are not the forms for which they were initially designed and from which Munro's income initially derived. Most were written for publication in a newspaper, and the earliest (such as 'Reginald', 'Reginald at the Theatre', and 'Reginald on Christmas Presents') covered only a column or two. Even when Munro was writing to a book publisher, he tended to think in column lengths rather than in pages. Sending a further story to join some others delivered earlier, he writes that most of them represent about a column and quarter of the *Morning Post*.[40] In a way, publishing books was a distraction from his real job, or at least his main source of income. Part of the problem was the amount he could earn from writing fiction, and part how quickly he would be paid. Asking for an advance, he reminds his publisher that the payment is for work he had completed more than eighteen months ago, and that writing a novel takes him away from journalism which is paid both better and more quickly. He adds that there is little temptation for him to write books while it proves so difficult to get any money out of the work.[41] Four months later, he writes again, asking again for the £25 he has been 'clamouring' for, and reminding Lane again that working on a novel severely diminishes his income, so that he views with disfavour even successful novel-writing.[42] That Munro placed both his novels with The Bodley Head suggests that he was reasonably happy with John Lane as an associate. He nonetheless warned his young relative Willie Mercer against publishing with Lane. Though a keen seeker-out and promoter of new talent, Lane was notoriously bad at paying the talent once he had secured his or her publication. Munro had continually to plead for advances and royalties owed to him. A letter to one of Lane's employees calculates that Munro is fifty guineas out of pocket from having concentrated on *Bassington* to the exclusion of his journalism, and remarks that the clause in his contract stating that he will receive payment within three months from 30 June seems to mean 'any damned time'. The letter is justifiably waspish, but it is signed 'Very sincerely Yours' and includes a friendly postscript under Munro's signature, hoping that Willett had enjoyed a recent holiday novel.[43]

There had also been friction between publisher and author over the title, the publication date, and the cover of *Bassington*. It is mentioned as early as May 1911, in a letter in which Munro says that he has been busy both with 'the novel' and the sketches.[44] An undated letter enclosing 'the only copy in existence' gives 'Comus Bassington' as the best provisional title Munro can come up with at the time.[45] By January of 1912, when Munro sends an additional chapter (including Comus's visit to the gallery) and advises Bodley Head that he has some additional matter to work into the first chapter, it has become 'The Van Der Meulen'.[46] In August, a short note substitutes 'Blue Street, W.' as the best title Munro can think of, though under his signature are two further suggestions: 'The Bassington Boy' and 'The Passing of Comus'.[47] On 14 August, in an unaddressed note, he elaborates on his suggestions concerning the title of 'the ci-devant "Van der Meulen"'. He insists that everyone to whom he has offered 'The Bassington Boy' or 'Blue Street, W.' as alternative titles has unequivocally preferred 'Blue Street, W.', and adds that with Reginald and Clovis 'to misguide them', readers would assume that 'The Bassington Boy' was an extension of the short stories.[48] He was evidently determined that the novel should clearly be marked as something other.

The novel remains 'Blue Street, W.' on 26 August, though prefaced by a question mark, when Munro sends a sketch for the wrapper.[49] Willett seems to have replied to this with a suggestion of his own which found no favour with Munro. To his mind, he writes, 'Comus holds the Stage' is utterly meaningless and irrelevant to the novel. He sees no point in tacking a 'Charles Garvice sort of title' on to a book of a completely different kind written for a completely different public.[50] Publisher and author seem to be unable to agree on the kind of book they are publishing, or rather, Willett appears to think that he is publishing a novel about a light-hearted, amiable fop. A design for a dust jacket evidently seems to Munro so far from suggesting the kind of book he has actually written that he is prepared to sever his relationship with The Bodley Head if it is used. It seems to him monstrous, he writes, that an author should have to beg that his work not be disfigured by a grotesquely inappropriate dust jacket, and he gives Bodley Head an ultimatum: if they use the wrapper, he will refuse to do anything to help sales, and he will not submit any other of his work to the company.[51] Since The Bodley Head did publish other of Saki's books, presumably the wrapper design was changed, and the disagreement, as Lambert and Ratcliffe say, blew over.[52]

Bassington was originally to be published in the spring, but in February Munro was informed that publication would be deferred for some months. He wrote to Lane to say that since their conversation he had consulted several literary friends (who included Wilde's friend Robert Ross), all of whom had advised that the book be published as soon as possible, i.e. in March. His reasoning is that apart from the political content, the milieu of the novel means that it would benefit from the kind of word-of-mouth publicity it would receive during the London Season.[53] Although he was reserved to the point of self-effacement, Munro was not above hinting that as one who moved in both literary and society circles he knew better than most when a book should appear. Social status, however, had to come second to financial considerations. An undated letter to Lane, evidently written just before the one quoted above, shows that Munro would have been willing to overlook late publication in return for early payment. Though unconvinced of the wisdom of deferring the English publication of *Bassington*, he writes that he is not too bigoted to be bribed, and that it would be a real boon to him if he could be paid twenty-five pounds immediately.[54]

He was still asking for money owed to him a year later, and was evidently in need of it, since he took time from a visit to Barnstaple to write first to Lane,[55] and two days later to Willett, asking for fifteen pounds of the year's royalties, and to be advised when the sum had been paid, since, he says, his bankers, King and Co., are sometimes slow.[56]

Dispirited though this letter sounds, Munro had not ceased to write books. Eleven days earlier, he had written to John Lane (now 'Lane' rather than 'Mr Lane') to say that he was taking the manuscript of his next book, *William*, with him on visits in Staffordshire and Devonshire, and that he hoped to have it completed on his return to London two weeks later.[57] He evidently kept that promise, or came close to keeping it, since in September he was writing to Willett to urge an early publication date, on the grounds of the mortality of emperors. The death or critical illness of the Kaiser would, he suggests, spoil the book's chances, and while 'When William Went' would be a charmingly alliterative title, he would have to write an entirely new novel to fit it.[58] The Kaiser, of course, survived for more than long enough.

6

The Stories: The Young Men

BEFORE the publication of his first book, Munro had produced a slighter but more momentous piece, his first published story. 'Dogged' appeared in the *St Paul's* magazine of 18 February 1899. At a church bazaar, Artemus Gibbon is bullied by a species of Aunt—a 'severe-looking dame with an air of one being in authority',[1] but he is more Claude than Conradin:[2] 'Artemus Gibbon was, by nature and inclination, blameless and respectable, and under happier circumstances the record of his life might have preserved the albino tint of its early promise; but he was of timid and yielding disposition and had been carefully brought up, so that his case was clearly hopeless from the first.'[3] The 'albino tint of its early promise' is characteristic of the ironically portentous tone of the narrative voice, and the assertion that anyone 'carefully brought up' is a hopeless case one way or another was to echo through Saki's stories. A little later, however, in the phrase 'tray-bearing handmaiden', the comically portentous slips into the arch without being placed in a way that suggests it is a piece of free indirect style. The characteristic Saki voice was nascent but not yet fully developed.[4]

The dog forced on Gibbon is a 'rakish-looking fox terrier, stamped with the hall-mark of naked and unashamed depravity and wearing the yawningly alert air of one who has found the world is vain and likes it all the better for it'.[5] It is called Beelzebub, though Mephistopheles might have been more appropriate, since it leads Gibbon through a Faustian diary of dissipation without providing any real gratification. Gibbon's rake's progress is not extensive, and compares unfavourably with that of the old lady who takes to gambling in 'The Way to the Dairy'. It takes in being forced to move to more expensive rooms, frequenting restaurants, making some mildly disreputable acquaintances, graduating from beer to whisky, and receiving one kiss. At the end, even if the presiding demon has led Gibbon into bad habits, Gibbon has not colluded in them nor enjoyed them. He remains fundamentally good, and the conclusion is unsatisfactory. The story was signed H.H.M. 'Saki' did not yet exist.

Following the success of the 'Alice in Westminster' satires, the *Westminster Gazette* took Saki's next published short story, 'The Blood-Feud of Toad-Water', subtitled 'A West-Country Epic', in the spring of the following year. The story is slight, so the piece depends almost entirely on its style. When a neighbour's hen scratches up some seeding onions, mock-epic, biblical, and high-flown phrases are used to describe trivial events and petty responses.

Mrs Saunders sauntering at this luckless moment down the garden path, in order to fill her soul with reproaches at the iniquity of the weeds, which grew faster than she or her good man cared to remove them, stopped in mute discomfiture before the presence of a more magnificent grievance. And then, in the hour of her calamity, she turned instinctively to the Great Mother, and gathered in her capacious hands large clods of the hard brown soil that lay at her feet. With a terrible sincerity of purpose, though with a contemptible inadequacy of aim, she rained her earth bolts at the marauder.   ('The Blood-Feud of Toad Water', *Reginald in Russia*, 33)

If the mock-epic style comes from Pope or Rochester, the symmetrical syntax ('terrible sincerity of purpose' though 'contemptible inadequacy of aim') could be from Dr Johnson, perhaps by way of Austen or, more likely, Wilde. The narration is in the third person, and the lack of dialogue perhaps adds to the mock-epic and to the sense of the slow march of time during which the feud persists, but it does not add any liveliness to the piece, which ends without the anticipated climax.

The next ingredient in the polishing of the stories was the fully-formed Sakian youth. Ethel Munro declared that the eponymous protagonist of *Reginald* was 'composed of several young men, studied during his [Munro's] years of town life' (Munro, 72), but adds that her brother told her that more than one of his acquaintances considered himself to be the original, and various friends wrote to say that they had established the identity of the duchess who appears in several of the stories.

Though Walter Allen declares that '[i]t is scarcely possible to speak of development in Saki's art',[6] it is possible to see development and refinement between the first and subsequent *Reginald* stories. The first, 'Reginald', dilutes the hero's voice by giving it in reported dialogue. The first-person narrator, a typical Saki interlocutor who is a mere functionary, having taken Reginald to a tea-party, hardly dares let him out of his sight, steering him past potential wreckage and constantly monitoring him like an anxious pilot. Reginald is set up as a ticking social bomb, but he doesn't explode; he does nothing more outrageous than telling a Colonel not to admit to his age, talking about alcohol to the son of someone prominent in the Temperance movement, and discussing a risqué play. When he produces the opening to what sounds like a nursery joke: 'What did the Caspian Sea?', there are 'symptoms of a stampede' ('Reginald', *Reginald*, 8). In Reginald's second appearance, in 'Reginald on Christmas Presents', there is no interlocutor; no setting, and no story; it is a monologue represented in the third person by the interjection of three tags in parentheses: '(said Reginald)', '(he continued)', and '(concluded Reginald)' (pp. 3–9). The third story, 'Reginald on the Academy', is a dialogue in which the interlocutor reappears, not as 'I' but as 'the Other' and with some scene-setting (the two are dining together, at the expense of the Other). At this stage, Reginald has hit form and is producing memorable ripostes, epigrams, and aphorisms. 'To have reached thirty', said Reginald, 'is to have failed in life' (p. 23).

The early Reginald stories which are not simply first-person anecdotes open with a very lightly contextualized conversation which is a framing device to introduce Reginald's narration of a story, but 'Reginald's Drama' is closer to the embedded or second story type described by Armine Kotin Mortimer.[7] The opening conversation has substance. The subject of Reginald's imagined play could have carried a whole story, but it leads only to the narration of another story. This describes the parading at an at-home of a nearly reformed washerwoman, 'You can rescue charwomen by the fifties with a little tea and personal magnetism, but with washerwomen it's different; wages are too high' (p. 83).

Airy hyperbole ('charwomen by the fifties') is followed by litotes ('a little tea and personal magnetism'), and the reader expects more hyperbole to follow, but the opposing phrase simply states the obvious (because washerwomen have more money than charwomen they are less grateful for whatever they receive in exchange for being patronized). The humour comes from Reginald's stating of obvious facts about which the subjects of his anecdote were oblivious, and from the word 'rescue'. The ladies of the League of the Poor Dear Souls behave as though they were missionaries or surgeons rescuing the objects of their charity (there may be an echo in the 'personal magnetism' of the magnetism therapies of the nineteenth century. Mrs Mudge-Jervis, of the beautifully named League of Poor Dear Souls, has great hopes of the laundress, and

they thought at last that she might be safely put in the window as a specimen of successful work [...] it's sheer bad luck that some liqueur chocolates had been turned loose by mistake among the refreshments—really liqueur chocolates with very little chocolate. And of course the old soul found them out, and cornered the entire stock. It was like finding a whelk-stall in the desert, as she afterwards partially expressed herself. When the liqueurs began to take effect, she started to give them intimations of farmyard animals as they know them in Bermondsey. She began with a dancing bear, and you know Agatha doesn't approve of dancing, except at Buckingham Palace under proper supervision. And then she got up on the piano and gave them an organ monkey; I gather she went in for realism rather than a Maeterlinckian treatment of the subject. Finally, she fell into the piano and said she was a parrot in a cage, and for an impromptu performance I believe she was very word-perfect; no one had heard anything like it, except Baroness Boobelstein who has attended sittings of the Austrian Reichstath. ('Reginald's Drama', ibid. 84–5)

The substitution of 'whelk stall' for 'oasis' may denote a class stereotype, but it is funny. Reginald brings in a series of oppositions which denote the charwoman's low and his own high register and experience (since Agatha's and Baroness Boobelstein's reactions are clearly his own projections), and they are beautifully, ludicrously paired: dancing bear versus dancing at Buckingham Palace; a realistic organ monkey versus a Maeterlinckian staged version; a drunken laundress in a piano and the Austrian parliament.

In their account of Saki's publications with The Bodley Head, J. W. Lambert and Michael Ratcliffe take as given that Munro was parodying and pillorying the upper classes and the dandy-set. They suggest that G. S. Street's *The Autobiography of a Boy*, a 'sheaf of mockery' of Wilde and the decadents, was a precursor of *Bassington*, bracket *Reginald* (published by Methuen) with the slight, generic 'epigrammatic worldy-witty' stories of The Bodley Head's Mayfair Library series, and find Saki 'the most durable of the worldings'.[8] Munro is described as joining The Bodley Head 'with a series of books making mock of the upper bourgeoisie, involving them with the supernatural, and, in *When William Came* [...] pointing a sharp finger at those likely to be collaborators in the event of a German invasion'.[9] Munro's attitude to the upper bourgeoisie and aristocracy is more complex than straightforward mockery. The stories may scourge the Duchesses,

Aunts, tea-presiding women, tight-fisted millionaires, and other assorted hypocrites, but the tones in which Reginald and Clovis are described are those of their own self-admiration. It is hard not to imagine the author envisioning himself at a dull gathering in Reginald's description of himself (when being ragged by lesser mortals) as like a gad-fly surrounded by buzzing cows under the impression that they are teasing him ('Reginald on House Parties', ibid. p. 56).

Saki's critique was from within; the establishment satirizing the establishment (though never seeking to bring it down), or perhaps more accurately, the lower (active, intelligent, sharp, clear-sighted) rung of the upper rungs satirizing the failings (stupidity, philistinism, insularity) of the upper. There are exceptions, one of whom is Lady Carlotta in 'The Schwartz-Metterklume Method' (*Beasts*, pp. 97–105). She is one of Saki's agents of Nemesis, descending on the pretentious and pompous Quabarl family like a Goddess of Battles with the total confidence and rhino-hide of the born-in-the-purple.[10]

While Gillen's study of Saki's work places it in the tradition of Classical comedy, and Drake's article on Saki's irony regards it as an instrument of chastisement and normalization, Miriam Quen Cheikin argues that the stories should not be classified as satire but as comedy. She suggests that though the stories criticize British high society, and have a satiric tone, they are not satires because 'his interest centers on the people, not the exposure of follies'.[11] She draws attention to 'the awareness of the vast separation between what is and what should be' in satire, 'which evokes feelings of anger or bitterness', and asserts:

the satirist displays his wares to arouse us to the need for reform rather than acceptance, contempt rather than pleasure. In contrast, comedy, although it rouses our intellectual awareness that human life often falls short of expectation, tends to surround man with an aura of acceptance. Comedy balances itself between humor's loving embrace of mankind and satire's bitter and hostile thrust, and it is the realm of comedy that is Saki's domain.

Cheikin offers a *Reginald* story, the inverted parable 'Reginald on Besetting Sins' (pp. 71–7), as an example, arguing that the behaviour of the unnamed woman who tries to tell the truth all the time, rather than the idea of lying or truth-telling, is the focus of the story. Certainly, neither Reginald nor Clovis as narrator could get away with taking a moral stance on telling lies, since neither would think of sacrificing the effectiveness of an epigraph or anecdote in the cause of accuracy or veracity. The whole story functions in the same way as Wilde's inversion of the conventional attitude to work in *The Importance of Being Earnest*, but as Fogle points out, its defining quality is in the way in which elegantly and economically constructed line follows elegantly and economically constructed line, each of which could have served as a final flourish: 'The revenge of an elder sister may be a long time in coming, but, like a South-Eastern express, it arrives in its own good time'; 'Madame was not best pleased at being contradicted on a professional matter, and when Madame lost her temper you usually found it afterwards on the bill'; 'The cook was a good cook, as cooks go; and as cooks go she went'; 'Miriam Klopstock came to lunch next day. Women and elephants never forget an injury' (*Reginald*, pp. 74, 76–7, 77).

Cheikin identifies the characteristic features which define Saki's writing as comedic rather than simply humorous: 'the unexpected, the incongruous, and the action that breaks the rules of decorum. The characters are entertaining, but rarely sympathetic enough to engage our 'gut' feelings; the reader mimics Munro's detached manner, a manner that reflects his lack of emotional involvement.'[12] All these features and qualities are present in the first collection and are developed throughout *Clovis* and *Beasts*.

At this stage, the Saki youths are cynically detached from the interest of Empire and of people who overenthusiastically support those interests. Though not actively against either, they adopt an aloof pose. Rather than the Edwardian slang word 'nut' used by Travers, the epithet for the youths more likely to come to mind is 'dandy', and one obvious point of comparison is Wilde's *Dorian Gray*. Saki's youths are not artists, however; theirs is neither Wilde's aesthetic nor Baudelaire's intellectual dandyism; it is the dandyism of hedonistic narcissism. While Saki's young men may hint of experiences that go beyond the mere naughtiness they employ in the stories, readers are not, as in Wilde's novel, invited to indulge in lascivious imaginings of their nameless crimes. 'Innocent' in the stories seems simply to mean 'not yet experienced or knowing'. 'Youth,' said the Other, 'should suggest innocence.' 'But never act on the suggestion' ('The Innocence of Reginald', (ibid. p. 8). This is echoed in one of Reginald's effortless come-backs: 'When I was younger, boys of your age used to be nice and innocent.' 'Now we are only nice. One must specialize in these days' ('Reginald at the Theatre', ibid. p. 31). Even Bertie, who is 'so depraved at seventeen that he had long ago given up trying to be any worse' ('Tobermory', *Clovis*, p. 37), does not do anything so very terrible in the stories. Reginald advocates the imitation of the lilies of the field:

'[. . .]which simply sat and looked beautiful, and defied competition.'
'But that is not an example for us to follow,' gasped Amabel.
'Unfortunately, we can't afford to. You don't know what a world of trouble I take in trying to rival the lilies in their artistic simplicity.'
'You really are indecently vain of your appearance. A good life is infinitely preferable to good looks.'
'You agree with me that the two are incompatible. I always say beauty is only sin deep.' (*Reginald*, 42–3)

Perhaps Reginald is thinking of Wilde as well as the Bible when he mentions lilies, as his aphorism is so very Wildean, though to 'defy' competition suggests a latent energy, and 'competition' suggests that the beauty was directed at a specific audience or market. The beauty of Reginald's language should not blind us to the careful choices in Amabel's dialogue. She applies to 'vain' an adjective which in slang would be empty of its usual meaning and would function like 'very', but which Freud might have said reveals her unconscious knowledge and disapproval of the target of Reginald's carefully managed appearance. At this stage, Reginald is not unlike a Wilde dandy. As Fogle says, he believes in the unimportance of being earnest.[13] Later, when England was threatened, he was to become very much in earnest.

Reginald and the other Saki protagonists belong by birth to a privileged and wealthy class, but consider themselves not quite privileged or wealthy enough. Saki did create an ungilded youth, the son of a charwoman from Bethnal Green, but most of his exploits happen off-stage ('Adrian', *Clovis*, pp. 103–10). The earlier characters do not narrate their own tales except indirectly. They require an audience, preferably gasping in admiration or shock. An anonymous narrative 'I' expresses tolerant exasperation at the exigencies of Reginald, Clovis, or Comus, and when the story is told principally in dialogue there is 'the Other' to act as prompt and foil.

Though not necessarily or overtly homosexual, the heroes appear to have little interest in women for romantic or sexual purposes: ' "I know, you want one of her smoke Persian kittens as a prospective wife for Wumples—or a husband, is it?" (Reginald has a magnificent scorn for details, other than sartorial)' ('Reginald', *Reginald*, p. 3). Their main love-object is exclusively themselves. The effortless superiority and self-sufficiency of the dandy is for Simon Stern, 'homosexual' in the sense that he is literally the same as his sexual complement. Camille Paglia finds his paradigm in Dorian Gray, 'the oblivious beautiful boy [who] can fall in love with no one—except himself'.[14] This piece of perfection, it is argued, can be an object of desire but will neither require nor desire a sexual other. The more polished dandy-youths may be complete Narcissists, but it is not true of Bertie Steffink, the most bouncing and least aloof of them. Saki gives him one of his few overt, uncoded references to a same-sex desire (for a, presumably beautiful, young boy), and he makes it intelligible to the usual cast of dull relations.

'Come, Teddie, it's time you were in your little bed, you know,' said Luke Steffink to his thirteen-year-old son.

'That's where we all ought to be,' said Mrs Steffink.

'There wouldn't be room,' said Bertie.

The remark was considered to border on the scandalous; everybody ate raisins and almonds with the nervous industry of sheep feeding during threatening weather. ('Bertie's Christmas Eve', *Toys*, 99)

When Bertie switches the meaning of 'we should all be in our respective beds [asleep]' to 'we should be in Teddie's bed', and brings sex into the room, the group (or flock) turns away to food, just as Reginald and Clovis do in the earlier stories. Bertie is not a fully fledged Sakian dandy, therefore, in Simon Stern's terms, because he has desires beyond himself.

Obviously these beautiful young men greatly admire their own looks, which almost invariably comprise an athletic body and dark or Titian hair. Saki had a predilection for describing the kind of carefully brushed and parted, smooth, dark hair which appears on the heads of many male characters major and minor (as well as that of the character on the cover of *Clovis*), often evoking sleek fur. A page boy in 'The Jesting of Arlington Stringham' has 'sleekly brushed and parted hair' (*Clovis*, p. 89). The attractions of 'Adrian' for a silly woman are that he has 'delightful hair and a weak mouth' ('Adrian', ibid. p. 105). Clovis creates Vespaluus with 'an elegant, well-knit figure, a healthy complexion, eyes the colour of very ripe mulberries, and dark hair, smooth and well cared-for' ('The Story of St Vespaluus', ibid. p. 164). The Baroness says that this sounds like a description of what Clovis imagined himself to be at 16, to which Clovis replies: 'My mother has probably been showing you some of my early photographs.' Another nephew,

Cyprian, commandeered by an Aunt to carry parcels, may be two-dimensional, with few characterizing features other than a dreamy expression (and, as it turns out, a willingness to become an extra and unofficial middle-man in the commercial transactions of Walpurgis and Nettlepink), but his not wearing a hat in order to preserve his hair-style is enough to prompt his aunt to enquire anxiously whether he is going to be a 'Nut' ('The Dreamer', *Beasts*, p. 177). The hair is 'brushed back in a smoothness as of ribbon seaweed and seamed with a narrow furrow that scarcely aimed at being a parting'. Jocelyn in 'The Philanthropist and the Happy Cat' is attracted to a young man who evidently 'knew how to brush his hair' and is later described as 'the boy with the beautifully-brushed hair' (ibid. pp. 300, 301). The hair does not have to be natural. A Russian boy cited as an example of family affection for declaring only black suits in bridge for three months after his grandmother dies has 'hair that curls naturally, especially on Sundays' ('Reginald in Russia', *Reginald in Russia*, p. 5). Even a doom-laden story more concerned with atmosphere than character contains 'a rather good-looking youth of eighteen with very smooth, evenly parted hair' ('The Hounds of Fate', *Clovis*, pp. 228–9). 'Gabriel-Ernest' does not brush his hair, but accomplishes the same effect. 'His wet hair, parted by a recent dive, lay close to his head' ('Gabriel-Ernest', *Reginald in Russia*, p. 48). In contrast to all the attractive young men with dark locks, a repellent infant has a 'mop of tow-coloured hair' ('The Quest', *Beasts*, p. 124), and characters less than confident that their hair is unimprovable are inevitably despised. In 'Reginald's Christmas Revel', a young man 'whom one knew instinctively had a good mother and a bad tailor', as Reginald says, 'smooths his hair dubiously as though it might hit back' (*Reginald*, p. 101).

While spending a great deal of their time in other people's houses, at other people's social functions, and dining at other people's expense, the young men do not consider themselves freeloaders, but ornaments and social assets whose presence conveys prestige (at best) or entertainment (at worst). They have an unshakeable belief in the perfection of their taste in dress, wine, art, and design, and show a great deal of interest in food. In 'The Match-Maker', Clovis compares people who eat a healthy diet to the flagellants of the Middle Ages, except that:

'They did it to save their immortal souls, didn't they? You needn't tell me that a man who doesn't love oysters and asparagus and good wines has got a soul, or a stomach, either. He's simply got the instinct for being unhappy highly developed.'

Clovis relapsed for a few golden moments into tender intimacies with a succession of rapidly disappearing oysters.

'I think oysters are more beautiful than any religion,' he resumed presently. 'They not only forgive our unkindness to them; they justify it, they incite us to go on being perfectly horrid to them. Once they arrive at the supper-table they seem to enter thoroughly into the spirit of the thing. There's nothing in Christianity or Buddhism that quite matches the sympathetic unselfishness of an oyster.' (*Clovis*, 24–5)

Clovis is being facetious, of course, but rather than sympathetic unselfishness, what he describes is either masochism or a kind of solipsism. Disregarding the desire of the object (not to be eaten) and replacing that with a projection of his own desire (to enjoy eating) suggests a lack of empathic understanding (even if with animal life) that borders on autism and perhaps explains the youths' lack of pity. In *The Importance of Being Earnest*, the sensuality or sexuality of Wilde's characters Jack and Algy is displaced onto food. Whenever they are threatened with the perilous necessity of being required to act like suitors, or be intimate with Gwendolyn and Cecily, they stuff their mouths with cucumber sandwiches or muffins. Saki's restaurant scene goes further than Wilde in the use of food as both hedonistic indulgence and displacement, and he dispenses with the female juvenile leads. Clovis's tender intimacies are with the means of his gratification, and thus himself.

John Kaplan and Sheila Stowell point out that the denouement of *The Watched Pot* finds the characters celebrating the overthrow of an abstemious chatelaine and her replacement by a more generous hostess, with champagne for the house-guests and Moselle for the servants.[15] The play also depicts a kind of ordeal by food, in which Trevor, under siege by women who want to marry his fortune, makes eating rice pudding (which he detests) and hanging back from the pickled walnuts (which he likes) an acid test for a would-be wife (*The Watched Pot*, *Square Egg*, 258–61).

Saki's other young men share Clovis and Reginald's sense of proportion (as well as Reginald's sublime disregard of the gender of babies). Food of the right kind takes precedence over things they consider trivial.

> 'We've lost Baby,' she screamed.
> 'Do you mean that it's dead, or stampeded, or that you staked it at cards and lost it that way?' asked Clovis lazily.
> 'He was toddling about quite happily on the lawn,' said Mrs Momeby tearfully, 'And Arnold had just come in, and I was asking him what sort of sauce he would like with the asparagus—'
> 'I hope he said hollandaise,' interrupted Clovis, with a show of quick interest, "because if there's anything I hate—' ('The Quest', *Clovis*, 119–20)

(Another reference to the sauce for asparagus in Saki's writing is in the form of a fantasy about hanging a cook for sending up the wrong kind. (See 'The Mappined Life', *Toys*, p. 189.) Clovis would, of course, perfectly well have grasped the obvious interpretation of 'lost'. His lazy request for disambiguation and improbable illustrations of other possible meanings are affectations which relegate the absence of Baby, or indeed Baby's presence, to its proper place of unimportance. The possible absence of the correct sauce on the asparagus, however, is another matter, which elicits an (again possibly affected) energetic response, as Robert Drake points out in his article, 'The Sauce for the Asparagus'.[16]

Similarly, when Eleanor Stringham (who once served an indifferent curry to Clovis and Bertie van Tahn), believing that her husband is having an affair, commits suicide, Clovis, 'who perhaps exaggerated the importance of curry in the home, hinted at domestic sorrow' ('The Jesting of Arlington Stringham', *Clovis*, 92). The narrator allows that Clovis 'perhaps exaggerated'; Clovis would have stated as a fact that the food was enough to drive anyone to suicide.

Ellen Moers's definition of the dandy could usefully be applied to a number of Saki characters. She finds that the dandy is a man (though women could also be dandy-esque) 'dedicated solely to his own perfection through a ritual of taste'. He is 'free of all human commitments that conflict with taste: passions, moralities, ambitions, politics, or occupations'. This suggests someone entirely given over to surface and form; someone all style and no substance, as well as someone inhumanly detached from human ties. Reginald recommends that for a lesson in elaborate artificiality, Lady Beauwhistle should watch the studied unconcern of a Persian cat entering a drawing-room ('Reginald on Worries', *Reginald*, p. 52). Neither he nor Clovis would have needed such a lesson, and would have spent much energy in perfecting an elaborately artificial grace which they would perform whilst watching themselves being watched.

Taking part in outdoor amateur dramatics, Clovis ensures that the flamboyant young charioteer is the most prominent character in the story of Agamemnon's return, and 'his panther-skin tunic caused almost as much trouble and discussion as Clytemnestra's spasmodic succession of lovers' ('The Peace-Offering', *Beasts*, p. 193). A panther skin turned into a tunic, a tailored garment, rather than slung about the shoulders of the person who had killed and skinned, or at least was capable of having killed and skinned the creature, is a sign of the wild tailored to the decadent; the Dionysian dramatized. Similarly, in *The Watched Pot*, a party of house-guests make merry while their repressive hostess Hortensia is away, in a manner which she considers the last word in debauchery and describes as a Saturnalia and an 'abominable and indecent orgy' (p. 268), a costume party in which the costumes are sheets and pillowcases. Though the guests, whirling about in billows of white linen, several of them masked and one of them in a phantom hound mask, might look like participants in a Dionysian rite, their behaviour is no more unleashed than that of schoolboys raiding the biscuit-barrel. The party is 'flat', a 'frightful frizzle' (p. 239), and rather than frenzied, their movements are circumscribed by the steps of waltzes and lancers—Dionysus choreographed—apart from René St Gall, a Reginald, Bertie, and Clovis conglomerate, who, having refused to wear a pillowcase hood on the grounds that it would ruffle his hair, does a 'nautch girl' dance to the tom-toms (p. 261),[17] and describes to the outraged Hortensia the farce-like ingress and egress of characters through doors stage centre and left as 'Only were-wolves chasing goblins to the sound of unearthly music' (p. 267). As ever, the character whose milieu seems to be the antithesis of the wild has the Pan or Dionysian streak.

Neither Clovis nor Reginald, nor even Comus, is entirely concerned with dress and surfaces, however. In spite of the consumption of live oysters, and the suggestion that the oysters encourage it, the heroes are neither amoral nor testing diversion to destruction like Dorian Gray. They have been known to help a friend in need, and once or twice to do so without requiring dinner, a tie-pin, or a trip abroad in exchange. They also reveal the shallowness of the allegedly Christian virtues, in particular charity, of the characters who advertise strict moral principles.

The Duchess thought that Reginald did not exceed the ethical standard which circumstances demanded.

'Of course,' she resumed combatively, 'it's the prevailing fashion to believe in perpetual change and mutability, and all that sort of thing, and to say we are all merely an improved form of primeval ape—of course you subscribe to that doctrine?'

'I think it decidedly premature; in most people I know the process is far from complete.' [. . .]

'[O]ne is conscious of spreading the benefits of civilization all over the world! Philanthropy—I suppose you will say *that* is a comfortable delusion; and yet even you must admit that whenever want or misery or starvation is known to exist, however distant or difficult of access, we instantly organize relief on the most generous scale, and distribute it, if need be, to the uttermost ends of the earth.'

The Duchess paused, with a sense of ultimate triumph. She had made the same observation at a drawing-room meeting, and it had been extremely well received.

'I wonder,' said Reginald, 'if you have ever walked down the Embankment on a winter night?'

'Gracious, no, child! Why do you ask?'

'I didn't; I only wondered [. . .]' ('Reginald at the Theatre', *Reginald*, 27–30)

'Of course' is a red rag to Reginald's bull. He cannot but puncture the comfortable assumption of an older person that he will be a follower of any fashionable doctrine (fashionable, that is, in the older person's terms; we suspect that Reginald's fashion-sense will have a different time-scale). He seems to do this, by giving a negative, but in fact shows that he does subscribe to a theory of evolution, only holds certain people exempt from it.

The Duchess then makes a significant association of the Saki youth with Nietzsche. ' "Oh, you're simply exasperating. You've been reading Nietzsche till you haven't got any sense of moral proportion left. May I ask if you are governed by *any* laws of conduct whatever?" ' (ibid. p. 30). Reginald responds with studied flippancy.

The Duchess is not the only target for Reginald's social criticism. A number of characters who are less than generous to the poor are ridiculed or punished, by providence, the hero, or the deadly irony of the narrative voice, as in 'Mrs Packletide's Tiger'. 'Louisa Mebbin adopted a protective elder-sister attitude towards money in general, irrespective of nationality or denomination. Her energetic intervention had saved many a rouble from dissipating itself in tips in some Moscow hotel, and francs and centimes clung to her instinctively under circumstances which would have driven them headlong from less sympathetic hands' (*Clovis*, p. 48). Any sentimentality in this attitude is undercut, however, by the heroes' equally deploring any lack of generosity to themselves. As Clovis remarks in 'The Match-Maker': ' "All decent people live beyond their incomes nowadays, and those who aren't respectable live beyond other people's. A few gifted individuals do both" ' (ibid. p. 25).

A. A. Milne, a near-contemporary of Munro, compares his own and other Edwardian comic writers' techniques to those of Saki, and finds everyone else wanting. They, he writes, 'were so domestic, he so terrifyingly cosmopolitan. While we were being funny, as planned, with collar studs and hot water bottles, he was being much funnier with werewolves and tigers.'[18] He continues, however, on a note of disquiet, suggesting that he and his fellow writers may have wondered 'if Saki's careless cruelty, that strange boyish insensitiveness of his, did not give him an unfair start in the pursuit of laughter. It may have been so; but, fortunately, our efforts to be funny in the Saki manner have not survived to prove it.'[19]

It is clear that Munro was sensitive, but perhaps mostly about himself and the damage done to him. Saki's sensitivity is highly selective, and when his characters or his narrative voice are insensitive or callous, it is with the self-centredness of a very young child or animal, or the detachment of a surgeon wielding a scalpel. S. B. Mais, attributed by Ethel Munro with 'an uncanny insight into his [her brother's] character' (Munro, p. 91), suggests that Saki's humour 'connotes cruelty, and "Saki" seems to me to be, on occasion, one of the "hardest" writers I know [. . .] he is a sort of prose Pope'.[20] He envisages Munro as very like Reginald in his youth: 'sardonic and rude at garden parties, never losing an opportunity of revenge against his enemies, conversationally brilliant in a way that unfortunately reminds one of Wilde at very rare intervals'.[21] Mais declares *Clovis* to be Saki's best and most characteristic book, exhibiting not only his understanding of animals, his first-hand knowledge of house-parties and hunting, his astounding success in choice of names for his characters, his gift for epigram, his love of practical jokes, his power of creating an atmosphere of pure horror, his Dickensian appreciation of food and the importance of its place in life, his eerie belief in the supernatural, and his never-failing supply of bizarre and startling plots, but also 'his almost inhuman aloofness from suffering'.[22] Mais concurs with the view that Saki was cruel in a childlike way.

Saki was not only a child-lover, he was a child himself, with all the imagination, the irresponsibility and the harsh cruelty of children fully developed in him: there is nothing sweet or mellow or restful in his genius: he surprises us just as 'O. Henry' surprises us by turning a complete somersault in his last sentence after astonishing us with all manner of gymnastic capers in each paragraph before.[23]

William York Tindall also refers to this alleged childlike indifference to, or even enjoyment of, others' suffering, finding the 'callousness' of Saki's short stories

that of a sadistic child. His effect depends in part upon regarding the affairs of the adult world with the cold-blooded eyes of such a child and in part upon brevity and casual speed. Appalling practical jokes, infantile revenge, and meaningless horrors compose a world (not unlike that of Kipling) peopled by children, carnivorous animals, and the ruling caste.[24]

Gillen suggests that Munro's time in the Balkans, Poland, and Russia completed his disillusionment with human nature and fostered his cruel streak.[25] It would not be hard to imagine the things he saw during the Balkan disturbances or at the Winter Palace engendering disgust at humankind's inhumanity, and his later experiences in the trenches would have reinforced his sense of the superiority of animals to humans, but even if we accept the vengefulness and *schadenfreude* as aspects of Munro's own personality, that would not necessarily make him a sadist as Gillen asserts.

Other than Comus Bassington, the Saki youths show pleasure in their victims' discomfiture, but no evidence of the sensuous taking of pleasure in others' pain. Often, rather than seeming sadistic, or capriciously cruel in an unaltruistic, egotistical, childlike way, Saki's narrative voices and characters seem simply mildly amused and mildly satisfied at the outcome of their plans. 'Saki was a good "hater", and his "cruelty" is always directed toward the inflicters of cruelty. It is thus not really a morbid delight in the cruel act for its own sake, but, rather, a meting out of cold justice.'[26]

The callousness of characters such as Reginald and Clovis, or their refusal to enact the social hypocrisy of demonstrating sympathy for the travails of those with whom they have no connection, is quite different from the sanctimoniousness and hypocrisy of the assorted Duchesses, Baronesses, and family members of the short stories, and the audaciousness of it provides much of the humour. In 'Esmé', a hyena devours a gypsy child. 'Constance shuddered. "Do you think the poor little thing suffered much?" came another of her futile questions. "The indications were all that way," I said; "on the other hand, of course, it may have been crying from sheer temper. Children sometimes do." ' (Clovis, p. 19). Here, a woman's callousness to a child is not the culpable cruelty of an Aunt or guardian, but as with the unlamented fate of the Toop child, allowable. The Baroness demands no recompense for the parents of the lost child, but expects and receives a compensation for the hyena (which, with the Saki character's gift for on-the-spot improvisation, she passes off as a pet dog, Esmé) from the young man who runs over it with his car.

Jewels such as the diamond brooch accepted as a kind of heriot or blood-price for Esmé are a species of currency in Saki's stories, and his characters can evaluate their worth instantly. In 'The Secret Sin of Septimus Brope', Clovis's price for having helped his aunt and her friend is a 'really nice scarf-pin' (Clovis, p. 265). In The Watched Pot, Ludovic tells Mrs Vulpy that if she can help him to marry off Trevor, and thus depose the dreadful Hortensia Bavvel, his gratitude will take concrete shape, such as a commemorative bracelet. A nice exchange follows:

LUD. [. . .] have you any particular favourite stones?
MRS. V. I love all stones—except garnets or moonstones.
LUD. You think it unlucky to have moonstones?
MRS. V. Oh, distinctly, if you've the chance of getting something more
valuable. I adore rubies; they're so sympathetic. (*The Watched Pot*,
Square Egg, 202–3)

Ludovic refuses to lend René a 'thirty-guinea scarf-pin' and René immediately lowers his expectations to 'your pearl and turquoise one; the pearl is a very poor one, and it can't be worth anything like thirty guineas' (p. 220). René is adamant that he should be given something (which he is unlikely to return) because: 'I've lost a mother. I make less fuss about that than you do at the prospect of separation from a five-guinea scarf-pin. You might show a little kindness to a poor grass orphan' (pp. 220–1).

As well as the worth of characters' afflictions and the price of their actions (or silence), jewels also function as pricing characters' worth in themselves. Later in the same play, two young women are discussing Mrs Vulpy. Sybil describes her as a rough diamond, and Clare retorts: 'So many people who are described as rough diamonds turn out to be merely rough paste' (p. 210).

Gillen finds Reginald to be of the same 'idling nit-witted . . . type' as P. G. Wodehouse's young men.[27] This is surely mistaken. Saki's youths may have been the models for Wodehouse's young men of independent means and dandyish habits (his *Toys* story 'The Seven Cream Jugs' might be the origin of one of the trials with which Bertie Wooster is beset, and 'The Elk' and *The Watched Pot* might be the origin of the ordeals thrust upon him by matchmaking Aunts), but well-intentioned upper-class twits such as Bertie[28] are entirely without the Saki youths' feral quality and vengefulness (except through rather more harmless pranks involving, for instance, hot-water bottles), and Saki's youths are entirely without the Wodehouse heroes' ingenuousness. Clovis, Reginald, Comus, and the several Berties also lack an essential attribute of Wodehouse's Bertie, the servant as Superman. Bertie Wooster is one half of a duo; without Jeeves he would lose most of his comic effect. The aesthetes of Ronald Firbank's novels *Vainglory* (1915), *Inclinations* (1916), and *Valmouth: A Romantic Novel* (1919),[29] similarly lack the feral quality, as do the socialites of Evelyn Waugh's satires *A Handful of Dust* (1934) and *Scoop* (1938). Sir Percy Blakeney, Baroness Orczy's Regency dandy and Scarlet Pimpernel, who first appeared in 1905, could be a common ancestor, but while Sir Percy throws off his airs and graces to save aristocrats from the Guillotine, any Saki protagonist not on his way to it, deep in composition of a suitable last epigram, would be more likely to be offering a guided tour of the device to a repellent tow-haired child.

In his study of Edwardian novels, John Batchelor names the hero of E. F. Benson's *The Babe, BA* as the ancestor of Saki's youths.[30] The Babe (a 'cynical old gentleman of twenty years of age')[31] is an eccentric whose party-piece is cross-dressing and who enjoys food as much as Reginald or Clovis,[32] but described in the third person, he lacks Saki's youths' bite and his eccentricities seem contrived. 'In his less genial moments he spoke querulously of the monotony of the Church of England, and of the hopeless respectability of Mr Zola. His particular forte was dinner parties for six, skirt-dancing and acting, and the performance of the duties of half-back at Rugby football.'[33] As someone who plays Rugby-football without being forced to, Babe seems unlikely to have been part of the social circle of Reginald, Clovis, or Comus.

As mentioned above, in 'The Feast of Nemesis', Clovis fondly pursues a fantasy of poetic justice, elaborating a system that makes little distinction between the infliction of minor inconvenience and the infliction of painful death in tones both practical and urbane. He proposes a feast day which would work in the same way as Christmas, but instead of having to worry about choosing appropriate presents, one would have to

'transplant that idea to the other and more human side of your nature, and say to yourself: "Next Thursday is Nemesis Day; what on earth can I do to those odious people next door who made such an absurd fuss when Ping Yang bit their youngest child?" Then you'd get up awfully early on the allotted day and climb over into their garden and dig for truffles on their tennis court with a good gardening fork [. . .] You wouldn't find any truffles but you would find a great peace, such as no amount of present-giving could ever bestow.'

'I shouldn't,' said Mrs Thackenbury, though her air of protest sounded a bit forced, 'I should feel rather a worm for doing such a thing.'

'You exaggerate the power of upheaval which a worm would be able to bring into play in the limited time available,' said Clovis; 'if you put in a strenuous ten minutes with a really useful fork, the result ought to suggest the operations of an unusually masterful mole or a badger in a hurry.' (*Beasts*, 171)

The justification for inflicting the acts of Nemesis shifts from the requiting of earlier insults and injuries to being irritated by someone's behaviour, demeanour, or appearance, and the punishments range from inviting a greedy woman to a picnic and losing her before lunch to inveigling a lazy young man into a garden hammock and throwing a lighted fusee[34] into a nearby wasps' nest.

'They might sting him to death,' protested Mrs Thackenbury.

'Waldo is one of those people who would be enormously improved by death,' said Clovis; 'but if you didn't want to go as far as that, you could have some wet straw ready to hand, and set it alight under the hammock at the same time that the fusee was thrown into the nest; the smoke would keep all but the most militant of the wasps just outside the stinging line, and as long as Waldo remained within its protection he could escape serious damage. And could be eventually restored to his mother, kippered all over and swollen in places, but still perfectly recognizable.'

'His mother would be my enemy for life,' said Mrs Thackenbury.

'That would be one greeting less to exchange at Christmas,' said Clovis. (ibid. 174)

That off-handedly judicious line: 'Waldo is one of those people who would be enormously improved by death' is of course immortal.

The title *Beasts and Super-Beasts* is more than a parody of Bernard Shaw's *Man and Superman*. The collection has its own Nietzschean pecking order. Clovis is superior to Waldo and his ilk because he is wittier, better groomed, more sophisticated, and better-looking than Waldo. Above all, he is superior because he denotes his own superiority; his super-strong ego is capable of determining, observing, and insisting on that superiority. It is worth remembering that Darwin's *On the Origin of Species by Means of Natural Selection* was published only eleven years before Munro's birth. The Sakian youth could easily be persuaded that he was the product of natural selection, and the next stage in evolution.

Only the less than beautiful people in Saki's writing offend against the credo of Nietzsche's superman and the unsentimental youths by showing compassion or remorse. In the case of Octavian Ruttle, for removing something weaker than himself that was causing him some annoyance. The penance Ruttle undertakes is a rare occasion in Saki's stories of an adult gaining the full approval of the children he has hurt, because it is a rare occasion in Saki's stories of an adult admitting to a child that he or she was wrong, and apologizing for it. Significantly, Ruttle is 'one of those lively cheerful individuals on whom amiability had set its unmistakable stamp, and like most of his kind, his soul's peace depended in large measure on the unstinted approval of his fellows' ('The Penance', *Toys*, p. 67). He could hardly be more different from Reginald, Clovis, or Comus.

In exchanging a festival of revenge on those who have committed minor offences for one of love and friendship, Clovis draws attention to the solipsism of the Saki youths. In a period when it was permissible for literature to represent sentimental close male friendships it is notable that readers are not introduced to close friends of Reginald and Clovis, but only to their social circles, made up of acquaintances, fellow guests, rivals, and sparring partners. Reginald writes to 'his most darling friend' at the beginning of 'Reginald's Choir Treat', but only, it seems, in order to get in the aphorism: 'It's the Early Christian that gets the fattest lion' (which should surely be hungriest lion, unless it is that the Early Christian makes the lion fat?) (*Reginald*, p. 41).

When Clovis does help out an acquaintance, it is usually, though not inevitably, for a tangible reward or as part of a larger plot. As mentioned above, in 'The Secret Sin of Septimus Brope', Clovis gets himself one reward for putting an end to a love affair that never existed, and also gets himself another for transposing the name of the real woman involved in the imagined affair to a fictional character in lyrics which invert her position in the usual love song.

Brope, a staid and respectable editor of the *Cathedral Monthly*, and expert on Byzantine ritual and memorial brasses, is a Bunburyist. When he is overheard repeating 'I love you, Florrie', and he drops a piece of paper containing the same words and the message 'meet me in the garden by the yew', his fellow guest at a house-party, the aunt of Clovis, suspects him of having an improper liaison with her housemaid, Florinda. The supposed love-object never appears in the story and is not consulted. Clovis's aunt refuses to countenance the match; she won't let Florinda go; the maid understands her hair too well, so the hostess must put a stop to the liaison.

Clovis takes matters into his hands, and discovers that in fact the secret sin is the composition of popular nonsensical songs. Brope has made quite a good living from producing 'sentimental, sugary compliment with a catchy rhyme' which go to 'sickening namby-pamby waltz tune[s]'. He tells Clovis, 'Of course I loathe the whole lot of them; in fact I'm rapidly becoming something of a woman-hater under their influence' and adds: 'Can you wonder that I positively hate Florrie all the time that I'm trying to grind out sugar-coated rhapsodies about her?' (*Clovis*, p. 262). Clovis does nothing to discourage this misogyny, but turns it to good account, producing a refrain which

in Blackpool and places where they sing [it . . .] held undisputed sway:

> 'How you bore me, Florrie,
> With those eyes of vacant blue;
> You'll be very sorry, Florrie,
> If I marry you.
> Though I'm easy-goin', Florrie,
> This I swear is true,
> I'll throw you down a quarry, Florrie,
> If I marry you.'   (ibid. 265)

Wilde's *Earnest* and *An Ideal Husband* depict men becoming engaged to women whilst having closer (mock-antagonist) relationships with other male characters. Clovis's lyric anticipates a horrible (if comic) end to a loveless marriage, and then he and Septimus Brope go away together, as far as Ragusa. (See ibid. p. 264.)

On the other hand, in 'Shock Tactics' Clovis helps Bertie Heasant, asking for no other reward than the pleasure of it, and indeed not letting his friend know that he was going to help. The last line of the story, however, suggests that in this case he did not need to ask: 'And Clovis has no more devoted slave than Bertie Heasant' ('Shock Tactics', *Toys*, p. 226).

These heartless young men of Saki's writing are to be both pitied and feared. That their greed will only be amusing and their capriciousness indulged as long as they are young and beautiful is not made explicit, but is implicit. Munro said that what he cared for above all was youth, perhaps consciously aligning himself with Wilde's Lord Henry Wooton, who exclaims: 'Youth! Youth! There is absolutely nothing in the world but youth!'[35] or with Lord Illingworth, who remarks that youth is 'the most wonderful thing in the world, "the lord of life"'.[36] Reginald, 'in his wildest lapses into veracity never admits to being more than twenty-two' ('Reginald', *Reginald*, p. 6). The knowledge that their value is skin-deep and has a strictly limited shelf-life makes them both more inclined to exercise their temporary power to the hilt and pre-emptively vindictive both to those who will lose interest in and those who will supplant them. If the Saki youth is cast as an *eromenos*, there is no obvious older and/or more powerful *erastes* counterpart in the short stories, unless it is the (older) reader. The youths themselves could be seen as enacting that relationship with even younger boys, in terms of physical, if not sexual power, as with Reginald and the choirboys ('Reginald's Choir Treat', *Reginald*), Adrian and the Grobmayer child ('Adrian', *Clovis*, pp. 103–10), and Comus and Lancelot Chetrof (*Bassington*), but these relationships, unlike those of the *eromenos* and *erastes*, cannot be said to be mutually enriching; they are more like that of predator and prey, and a clear distinction is made between the practical joke and posturing of the archetypal Saki youth, Reginald, and the behaviour of the lower-class hooligan Adrian and the damaged and unpleasant Comus. In *Bassington* and *William*, the youth is shown in his grown-up amphibian mould of a man whom wolves have sniffed at, represented by Tom Keriway and Murrey Yeovil, but Keriway never encounters Comus either as his *erastes* or his competitor, while Yeovil, as a metonym of England, is too battered and humiliated by defeat to have the energy for physical desire.

Though the Saki youths are urbane, there is a whiff of the feral about them. They go for the throat of their prey (if only the bridge opponent) and for the essentials of survival (good clothes, fine wine, baubles) with all the single-mindedness of a ferret in a rat-hole. They leave Town only to rusticate, joining country-house parties given by reliable hostesses for the sake of the food and the cards or the chance to live cheaply and catch up on sleep. They abhor the usual country pursuits of the gentry and upper middle-class such as estate management, shooting, and fishing, and are soon bored by long damp walks, village philanthropy, and parlour-games. Characters in 'Reginald on House Parties'

(*Reginald*, p. 53–60) learn of the folly of ragging Reginald about his inability to hit anything. If they dislike and are out of place in the tamed, estate-managed, pastoral kind of landscape, however, they are attracted to the real, untamed wilderness. Their usual habitat may be the West End (of London) rather than the West Country, but they are associated with predators, danger, and the wild, which Saki's women characters almost invariably detest and fear, and which is discussed in more detail in the next chapter.

7

The Stories: The Men that
Wolves Have Sniffed at, the
Wild, and the Boys

THE feral aspect of the Saki ephebe has an affinity with the sublime
wild. The author of the letter describing the death of young
Lieutenant Munro in 1793 employed the contemporary register of
sensibility and sublimity: unutterable horror; overpowered senses;
an unimaginably terrifying adversary.[1] The animal he describes
is an Ur-tiger, a magnificent, supernatural entity like William
Blake's Tyger. The spelling of 'aweful' is telling; an encounter with
such an animal is overwhelming, in its presence human intellect
freezes; it is an aspect of the sublime. In contrast to the gently
rolling fertile landscape of the pastoral, or the sinuous curves and
artful naturalness of the picturesque, sublime nature is huge and
awe-inspiring; alpine passes, storms, cataracts, mighty waterfalls,
jungle; the untamed, dangerous, and unknowable. A picturesque
landscape was considered aesthetically pleasing, promoted mental
and physical well-being, and represented harmony, tranquillity, and
God's moral primer. To contemplate it was to experience beauty,
as Wordsworth did. A sublime landscape highlights the smallness
and fragility of humanity; to contemplate it is to experience a
feeling akin to terror. Pastoral Arcadias where sheep safely graze
are the traditional setting for comedy, sublime landscapes were

the traditional setting for the Gothic novel, and in the twentieth century deep countryside and wild animals became the settings and agencies for horror (as in Hitchcock's *The Birds* and many Hammer horror films). Critics have suggested that the tiger which killed Lieutenant Munro inspired 'Mrs Packletide's Tiger', but the jungle setting of that story is incidental; the tiger is old and enfeebled, and could equally have been another beast whose slaughter provided the de rigueur holiday souvenir of the time. It is a story about meanness, upmanship, and blackmail, not a tiger.

Other of Saki's stories, however, draw on the same tradition as *The Gentleman's Magazine*'s report of the death of Lieutenant Munro (see introduction, above). A great god, a quintessence of the animal spirit, is called into being out of a pet in a hutch to be the Nemesis of unkind urban grown-ups; a reminder that not even Aunts, guardian-cousins, and managing women are all-powerful.[2] That the boy who calls this spirit into being feels both adoration and fear of the animal indicates he is in the presence of the sublime.

Saki retains the sense of the sublime in landscape at a time when the ideal of England was represented as picturesque pastoral. The English countryside and English village life were being reinvented and idealized before and during Munro's lifetime by William Morris, Cecil Sharp, and the Folk Revival. Middle England was represented as composed of organic communities of unalienated workers and men of the soil, and invested with symbolic importance by writers such as Kenneth Grahame and Rudyard Kipling. In wartime, it became metonymic of England, the Empire, the English people, and the English way of life in a way explored by D. H. Lawrence in 'England, My England' (1915). Saki's writing ignores villages and depicts villagers only as crudely stereotyped peasants; his country-house characters explore and appropriate the countryside for their leisure pursuits and profit, and ignore or employ the inhabitants, who do not own it.

Landscape comes in three forms in Saki's writing, brutally tamed, natural, and a hybrid. The former is represented by over-composed and cultivated middle-class, Home Counties gardens with clashing plantations and manicured lawns, and the latter by the wilderness.[3] The former is the province of the female and the emasculated male, and the latter of the man.

These two worlds collide in a *Morning Post* story, 'The Holy War'.[4] Bevil Yealmton is returning from Russia to an old house he has known and loved since boyhood and inherited from an uncle before he left England, but which he has never inhabited. He spends the long journey visualizing every detail of the house and its farmyard, pond, woods, and orchard, lovingly dwelling on the memory of farm animals such as waterfowl, gamecocks, and pigs, and the surrounding wildlife, especially the goldfinches in the orchard. 'There were a hundred other heart-enslaving things that he remembered from his boyhood's days, and the wonder was that the glamour of them had stood the critical test of maturing years' (p. 145). The estate is a hybrid, partly trained and nurtured in order to be productive, but not entirely tamed, and it is set in and connected to the wild.

Yealmton reflects that he is 'impatiently counting the slow hours that separated him from the old homestead at the foot of the hill, but he could not assure himself that any of his impatience was honestly due to a desire to be once more in his wife's company and within the sphere of her organising genius' (p. 145). Thirza is a managing woman, a bully and busybody 'of the regrettable kind that can never realise that nature, and particularly human nature, is sometimes devised and constructed to be unmanageable, for its own happiness and its own good' (p. 145). She greets Bevis with the announcement that he will find a lot of 'improvements'. She has filled in the old pond, replaced the 'old stock' of game fowl with efficiently productive white leghorns, cut down the old trees and replaced them with neat young fruit trees in rows, banished Peterkin, the yellow cat of the house (a character's relationship with cats is always telling in Saki's work), and told the keeper to shoot the owls in the wood because she found their calls 'dismal' (p. 147). Everything denoted 'old' (including Peterkin, since Bevis has known him since his uncle's time) has been destroyed; everything mellowed by time and organic in form has been replaced by something neat, trim, utilitarian, profitable, and, to Bevis, horrible.

Bevis immediately initiates a campaign to eradicate all traces of modernity, and restore the house and land to its unmanaged state; unmanaged, that is, in the sense of not under the control of Thirza, and in the sense of left in a beautiful semi-natural state which gives bounty, rather than organized and exploited as a commercial concern. In his holy war, Bevis digs out the pond, reimports gamecocks, which kill the 'alien' white cockerels, forbids the gamekeeper to shoot any more owls, and reinstates Peterkin. 'Even the fruit paddock was induced to lose some of its nursery-garden air and to stray back toward the glory of a West Country orchard' (ibid.). He regards his wife's 'management' as a kind of defilement of a sacred old place. Among her most offensive suggestions, a sop to her husband's supposed sentimental nostalgia, is that the goldfinches she has driven out of the orchard could be kept in an aviary.

'Is there any other vile thing that you have done in this dear old place?' asked Yealmton. Then he added: 'Something dreadful must surely happen to you!'

Both 'vile' and 'dreadful' are well-chosen; 'dreadful' because of its association with holy dread, another version of the awe induced by the presence of the sublime. Thirza is of course insensitive to the wild that ought to induce feelings of worship, awe, and dread, but something dreadful does happen. Determined to make sure that the local children are not enjoying themselves on the ice forming at the shallow end of a mill-pond, Thirza is patrolling the water meadows, watched from the orchard gate by Bevis. He sees 'something white rush out of the bushes and come flapping towards her,' and 'Thirza start back, and fall on the slippery edge of the pond' (p. 148). She is found 'lying half under the scum of churned-up ice and slush at the pond's edge' (ibid.). Thirza has been killed by a wounded wild swan. The white rush might be reminiscent of Yeats's (later) 'Leda and the Swan', but the swan is not a god in disguise, it is a white spirit, a manifestation of the wild that Thirza has been trying to tame. Swans, associated with peaceful meandering Home Counties rivers, serenely graceful, protected possessions of the Crown, might seem an incongruous choice, especially as in *Bassington* we see Comus feeding swans the remains of a picnic tea from a silver basket, and in 'The Mappined Life' framed photographs of young women feeding swans stand for conventional, unimaginative wedding gifts heralding a conventional, unexciting life (*Bassington*, pp. 102–5; 'The Mappined Life', *Toys*, p. 191). Swans can be both powerful and dangerous, of course, and the killer of Thirza is specifically a wild swan. Their connotations in Saki's writing are clear from their coupling with a wolf to signify the association of Yeovil with the wild in *William*. ' "I know, I know," said the doctor, sympathetically; "life and enjoyment mean to you the howl of a wolf in a forest, the call of a wild swan on the frozen tundras" ' (p. 59).

The sublime, then, is evoked more through fauna than flora in Saki's writing. Animals or half-animals are the distilled essence of the wild and its guardians, and wild animals such as wolves evoke a thrilling sensation. In 'The Music on the Hill', the beloved country dwelling is a little larger and a little more wild than the unnamed place in 'The Holy War'. The female protagonist of the story, and the enemy of the wild, Sylvia Seltoun, is the archetypal middle-class Englishwoman who professes a love of the countryside but is 'accustomed to nothing much more sylvan than "leafy Kensington" ' (*Clovis*, p. 150). She congratulates herself on achieving a loveless marriage with a cold and indifferent man, and on then persuading her husband to go down to his ancestral home, Yessney, but the country manor is not what she expects.

In its wild open savagery there seemed a stealthy linking of the joy of life with the terror of unseen things. Sylvia smiled complacently as she gazed with a School-of-Art appreciation at the landscape, and then of a sudden she almost shuddered.

'It is very wild,' she said to Mortimer, who had joined her; 'one could almost think that in such a place the worship of Pan had never quite died out.'

'The worship of Pan never has died out,' said Mortimer. (ibid. 151)

Sylvia is perfectly placed both by her 'School-of-Art' casting about for the picturesque, and by the inappropriate use of 'sylvan' to apply to a London suburb whose usual clichéd epithet is put in inverted commas to indicate the ridiculousness of bracketing the place with a real wood. Exploring, Sylvia has a sense of an indefinable 'something'; a sinister presence at Yessney. Even the estate is not the picture-postcard farm with tidy, hen-pecked yard, picturesque duck pond, and sanitary Jersey cow that she expects, but a hostile, claustrophobic, brooding place. Animals slink away from her, and she is frightened by a large sow. Then: 'As she threaded her way past rickyards and cowsheds and long blank walls, she started suddenly at a strange sound—the echo of a boy's laughter, golden and equivocal' (p. 153). One day, following her husband, she comes across a clearing in which stands a small bronze figure of a young Pan at whose feet, as if in offering, have been placed a bunch of grapes. Since grapes are none too plentiful at Yessney, she snatches them angrily and returns homeward. As she turns, she sees a boy's face scowling at her from a tangle of undergrowth. He is brown and beautiful, but his eyes are 'unutterably evil' (p. 154). She finds that her husband, who wears 'a Jermyn Street' urbanity in the town, has another aspect in the country. He remarks dispassionately on the consequences of meddling with offerings to the Wood Gods, and suggests that she should avoid the woods and orchards, and give a wide berth to the horned animals on the farm. Nervous of the cattle and the ram, Sylvia skirts the farm meadows and the woods, and climbs the hill above Yessney, but is drawn onward by a stag apparently driven in her direction by a hunt, and by a low, fitful, reedy piping coming from a nearby copse.

The pipe music shrilled suddenly around her, seeming to come from the bushes at her very feet, and at the same moment the great beast slewed round and bore directly down upon her. In an instant her pity for the hunted animal was changed to wild terror at her own danger; the thick heather roots mocked her scrambling efforts at flight, and she looked frantically downward for a glimpse of oncoming hounds [. . .] in a flash of numbing fear she remembered Mortimer's warning [. . .] And then with a quick throb of joy she saw that she was not alone; a human figure stood a few paces aside, knee-deep in whortle bushes.

'Drive it off!' she shrieked. But the figure made no answering movement. The antlers drove straight at her breast, the acrid smell of the hunted animal was in her nostrils, but her eyes were filled with the horror of something other than her oncoming death. And in her ears rang the echo of a boy's laughter, golden and equivocal.   (p. 158)

The horned, goat-legged Pan was the deity of Arcadia, a peaceful pastoral land, but he has come to stand for the spirit of the wild. In his presence both animals and people were overwhelmed by a sense of awe close to terror which would immobilize them, cause them to tremble violently, and lose all sentient thought. The wild in Saki's stories is beautiful but violent and dangerous. It contains no trace of the myths of Nature as nurturing Mother. The supernatural force of the wilderness is associated with the beauty of an animal or a lovely, wild boy. The object of desire in Saki's stories is often adolescent and inhuman, or at least outside human society, and therefore constraints of class, manners, and mores. In 'Gabriel-Ernest', the beauty of the youth is described in terms suggesting both the feral and the urbane.

On a shelf of smooth stone overhanging a deep pool in the hollow of an oak coppice a boy of about sixteen lay asprawl, drying his wet brown limbs luxuriously in the sun. His wet hair, parted by a recent dive, lay close to his head, and his light-brown eyes, so light that there was an almost tigerish gleam in them, were turned towards Van Cheele with a certain lazy watchfulness.   (*Reginald in Russia*, 48)

Later, Van Cheele finds the boy 'Gracefully asprawl on the ottoman, in an attitude of almost exaggerated repose' (ibid. p. 54).

Assuming the boy is a poacher, Van Cheele tells him that he can't stay in the woods. ' "I fancy you'd rather have me here than in your house," said the boy.

The prospect of this wild, nude animal in Van Cheele's primly ordered house was certainly an alarming one.' Alarming, but also exciting.

The boy turned like a flash, plunged into the pool, and in a moment had flung his wet and glistening body half-way up the bank where Van Cheele was standing. In an otter the movement would not have been remarkable; in a boy Van Cheele found it sufficiently startling [. . .]

Almost instinctively he half raised his hand to his throat. The boy laughed again, a laugh in which the snarl had nearly driven out the chuckle, and then, with another of his astonishing lightning movements, plunged out of view into a yielding tangle of weeds and fern.

'What an extraordinary wild animal!' said Van Cheele.   (ibid. 48–51)

Van Cheele is correct; Gabriel-Ernest is a werewolf. Or so 'the artist Cunningham' says, after having seen boy transform into wolf as the sun set. Wolves don't swim like otters, nor sprawl languidly in the sun, lazily watchful, like cats, but Gabriel-Ernest is as much a creature of water as of the woods. Perhaps his metamorphosis is not solely a wolf-to-human, so that his boy manifestation has attributes of other animals, or perhaps the passage is more concerned with describing his physical beauty and grace than with accuracy (if werewolves can be described accurately). His nakedness is alluded to several times, sometimes archly, sometimes as through Van Cheele's prudish vocabulary: 'considering the nature of his toilet' (p. 50); 'this wild, nude animal' (p. 51); 'He was drier than when Van Cheele had last seen him, but no other alteration was noticeable in his toilet' (p. 48); 'Van Cheele hastily obscured as much of his unwelcome guest as possible under the folds of the *Morning Post*' (p. 48). The dive into the pool allows descriptions of his wet, glistening body and lithe movements. The eroticism is powerful, and part of it is the threat. Though it is not made explicit, the reader knows that Van Chele's instinctive feeling that this creature will go for the throat provides an erotic *frisson*.

The woman in the story, Van Cheele's aunt, is insensible of the erotic appeal or the threat, sees only an object on which to exercise her charity (always a crime in Saki's work), and infantilizes the 16-year-old youth by thinking of him as a child. 'A naked homeless child appealed to Miss Van Cheele as warmly as a stray kitten or derelict puppy would have done' (p. 49), whereas he both appeals to and terrifies Van Cheele in quite other ways. Miss Van Cheele covers the beautiful body in an inappropriate suit of clothing and the animal in an inappropriate name.

The comedic element of 'Gabriel-Ernest' is in Van Cheele's social discomfort when he finds an incongruously naked boy in his morning-room, 'in an attitude of almost exaggerated repose', and his stereotypically British embarrassment at the thought of dictating a telegram saying 'Gabriel-Ernest is a werewolf'. The comic and erotic elements are kept separate. In the denouement, Gabriel-Ernest is absent and the violence off-stage, marked only by 'a shrill wail of fear' (p. 59). Without either the disturbing bodily presence of Gabriel-Ernest or the disturbing things he says, for atmosphere and suspense the last part of the story relies on descriptions of Van Cheele's dash from London and through the woods, and of the sun racing him as it sets, rather like Van Helsing and his companions' race to reach the Count before sunset in *Dracula*.

On one side ran the swift current of the mill-stream, on the other rose the stretch of bare hillside. A dwindling rim of red sun showed still on the skyline, and the next turning must bring him in view of the ill-assorted couple he was pursuing. Then the colour went suddenly out of things, and a grey light settled itself with a quick shiver over the landscape. (ibid. 58–9)

Gabriel-Ernest's victim is described as 'the little Toop child' and in a couple of sentences whose confused pronouns are perhaps designed to indicate her general failure of perception and discrimination,

Miss Van Cheele says, 'It was getting so late, I thought it wasn't safe to let it go back alone. What a lovely sunset, isn't it?' (p. 58). One of twelve, a member of Miss Van Cheele's Sunday School infants' class, and subject to her patronage at a tea-party, the child is presumably a working-class villager. It is not worthy of a first name, or even a gendered pronoun, unlike the werewolf, and not of sufficient individuality or importance to be mourned or given a memorial, also unlike the werewolf: 'Mrs Toop, who had eleven other children, was decently resigned to her bereavement, but Miss Van Cheele sincerely mourned her lost foundling. It was on her initiative that a memorial brass was put up in the parish church' (p. 59). 'Lost foundling' is a very nice oxymoron, and, thanks to Saki's brisk thumb-sketch characterization, clearly typical of Miss Van Cheele's sentimental inaccuracies.

Gabriel-Ernest is attractive because of his beauty but also because of his class. He may be a werewolf, but he is an upper-class werewolf whose speech is impeccable Edwardian Standard English. 'It's quite two months since I tasted child-flesh' (p. 50); 'I fancy you'd rather have me here than in your house' (p. 51). As with Dracula, part of the appeal of this killer is clearly meant to be his exoticism, and part his casual and entirely justified arrogance. Like Dracula also, he is a lethal animal who looks good sheathed in tailored evening clothes. Gabriel-Ernest's werewolf side could be read as Darwinian (the trace of the ancestral beast), Freudian (the beast within the subconscious), or Nietzschean (the natural man untrammelled by convention and morality). That he is urbane in the drawing room yet undergoes a transformation at sunset would seem to link him to the Victorian, Darwinian dualism of Dr Jekyll and Mr Hyde. But is his nature divided? He is also urbane in his natural setting; he is a wild creature of the woods even when not in werewolf form. He is a fantasy of an amphibian youth; effortlessly superior in either drawing room or forest. Perhaps even his name, with its juxtaposition of archangel and the Bunburyists (as well as the foundling) of *The Importance of Being Earnest* indicates his duality.

Any reading of 'Gabriel-Ernest' makes puzzling Gillen's reference to the lack of sexuality in Saki's work, as well as Ethel Munro's
assertion that one subject her brother never wrote about was sex.[5]
There is no intercourse in Saki's writing, and little interest displayed
by the central characters in women, but there certainly is sexuality.

Even those boys who do not metamorphose sometimes show
a flash of the beast beneath the skin. Rollo, in 'The Strategist',
though fully human, has a flicker of Gabriel-Ernest. 'Rollo sank
into a chair and smiled ever so faintly at the Wrotsleys, just a
momentary baring of the teeth; an otter, escaping from the fangs
of the hounds into the safety of a deep pool, might have given a
similar demonstration of its feelings' ('The Strategist', *Reginald in
Russia*, 93).

When Cunningham sees Gabriel-Ernest on the hillside at sunset, he describes the boy's pose as 'suggestive of some wild faun
of Pagan myth' (p. 57). Fauns were half-goat, half-man spirits of
ancient woodland in classical myth, which, for many Victorian and
Edwardian authors, provided a rich vocabulary for evoking the
potent desirability of an adolescent male. Saki occasionally uses
the shorthand of a 'young boy-emperor', but elsewhere restricts
his use of such references and comparisons to fauns and Pan; the
presiding spirits of Roman *pagus,* or countryside beyond civilized
urban life. 'The Music on the Hill' has something in common
with E. M. Forster's 'The Story of a Panic' (1904), in which the
presence of Pan creates misrule and tumult. Unlike other late-
Victorian and Edwardian writers, however, Saki does not use
classical paganism for a whimsical effect. Kenneth Grahame, with
whose work Saki's has sometimes been bracketed, softens and
dilutes his pagan elements until they are acceptable for childhood reading, but Saki keeps his red in tooth and claw.[6] Jefferson
Hunter dismisses Saki's work as part of the coterie fiction which
extended and exploited audiences created by successful nineteenth-
century authors. He groups Saki's stories with 'Edwardian fiction
of fantasy of whimsy' such as Kenneth Grahame's writing,

E. Nesbit's works for children, Ronald Firbank's *Odette: A Fairy Tale for Weary People* (1905), Max Beerbohm's *Zuleika Dobson* (1911), and James Stephens's *The Crock of Gold* (1912). While some of the slighter stories could be seen as belonging in this category, others more properly belong with another touched on by Hunter, the ghost story (which includes manifestations of the supernatural other than human revenants). Again, Gillen's unequivocal statement that Munro 'was the only writer of his day who consistently used the unhackneyed subject of the uncanny and supernatural' is puzzling. He asserts that other writers 'were indifferent to this subject perhaps because they could not fit it into their work' and continues, 'by its nature the subject disqualified itself from use by the realists and social reformers, and probably could only be appreciated by a restricted and selective readership like Munro's'.[7] Many Edwardian writers used the uncanny and supernatural, and ghost stories were extremely popular, but perhaps the key word here is 'unhackneyed'. Gillen may be suggesting that for most of Saki's contemporaries, the supernatural was a trope, whereas for him it was an event of the plot. The 'whimsical' Edwardian authors' use of the supernatural could be considered hackneyed in the sense of utilizing stock or archetypal figures and forces. Grahame's Pan is a wild but benign animal-god. In *The Wind in the Willows* (1908), his piping is beautiful and enrapturing, and brings the hearer a new consciousness of the divinity of things.[8] His presence does engender an awestruck suspension of faculties; the rat and the mole have an overwhelming sense of godhood; but the 'panic' and 'terror' are explicitly refuted. This Pan is a strong, wise, and kindly protector, at least of animals. The animals have been in the presence of the sublime, and their mortal minds would not bear its loss, so Pan sends them forgetfulness.

The faun (Puck) in Kipling's *Puck of Pook's Hill* is similarly benign and de-sexed. Mildly mischievous but kindly, he functions as an 'Old Thing' who has lived through, and can guide the children of the story through, English history; and, with a panoply of fairies, goblins, wizards, gods, demi-gods, giants, and heroes, he represents a magical, symbolic Old England; a countryside both populated by and animated in these creatures, and that sends the children off singing

> Land of our Birth, our faith, our pride,
> For whose dear sake our fathers died;
> O Motherland, we pledge to thee
> Head, heart and hand through the years to be![9]

Kenneth Grahame's *Pagan Papers* (1893), published, like Saki's later work, by John Lane, similarly evokes an English countryside in which history is always on the threshold of the present, and significant history is made up of people, events, and places linked to the establishment and maintenance of English identity. Saki was to evoke the English countryside as a rallying-point in *William*, but as yet his copses, bracken, and hills were undifferentiated from any other landscape, and, though sometimes sinister, not invested with earth-magic.

Batchelor finds that Edwardian fantasy contains '[s]ome of the most vivid expressions' of nostalgia for a landscape threatened by modernity and war.[10] Citing E. M. Forster's comments on '[f]auns and dryads and slips of memory . . . Pans and puns, all that is medieval this side of the grave', he finds this 'an irresponsible form, retrogressive, infantile, seeking appropriate arenas in which to escape from the pressures of the day, but he also acknowledges that Pan can be an image of sexual freedom, as in Forster's 'The Story of a Panic' and Stephens's *The Crock of Gold*. He makes a distinction between Pan's 'more decorous literary role as great custodian of the natural world' and 'his phallic character', but in Saki's stories the two may be combined.[11] Perhaps Pan's horns and hairy legs, his unprettiness, vigour, and half-animal aspect distinguish him from the drooping, enervated, and sometimes androgynous qualities of classical archetypes employed by other writers. Though he is half-goat, he could almost be half-wolf.

Classical mythology provided a convenient register or code for Victorian and Edwardian literary homoeroticism. While Saki uses the code, he also laughs at it (in 'Reginald's Choir Treat') and adapts it. A young Pan might well have been an object of worship for the Saki heroes, with their cult of youth and beauty, their indifference to the fate of mere mortals, and their capricious hedonism, but the reference behind many of the objects of desire is not classical. Reginald, Clovis, and other Saki youths may look like and pose themselves like Ganymede, Hylas, or Hyacinthus, they may make us think of the Greek cult of the *kouros*, and they are certainly Narcissists, but Gabriel-Ernest is something else. Werewolves do not belong to classical myth, so Cunningham's shock is more complete as the boy who evokes an image of beauty from a familiar mindset transforms into something quite other. The wolf and werewolf seem to belong to a colder location and another civilization's myth-kitty. While Saki's writing often dwells on the beauty of the ephebe, the excitement he creates comes from the whiff of the feral, and the imagery calls on an eastern European register of wolves and steppes and icy spaces, particularly in *William* (discussed in Ch. 8 below). It is significant that when Van Cheele's pallid silence suggests a mind-paralysing encounter with the awe-inspiring sublime, his sister says that he looks as though he has seen a wolf, not a ghost ('Gabriel-Ernest', *Reginald in Russia*, 53).

Spears derides S. P. B. Mais's suggestion that the pagan elements in Saki's work indicate a form of nature-worship, conflating author, characters, and narrators to argue that Munro was no Pan-worshipper and used such elements only for comic exaggeration.

Frankly, we are inclined to be skeptical. We do not deny Munro's predilection for the ghoulish and sadistic. But when we are asked to swallow Munro's awe for Pan, we must beg to demur. We suspect that in this isolated instance even the keen-sighted Mr Mais has allowed himself to be hoodwinked by our master ironist, unless, of course, the critic himself is being ironical. At any rate, we must urge the caution that although Pan is indispensable to the understanding of D. H. Lawrence and Wallace Stevens, he is not at all germane to the comprehension of Saki.[12]

Spears seems curiously blind to the non-realist nature of Saki's fiction, and to the possibility that while the Pan-figures are not precisely symbolic, neither need they represent actual demi-gods or spirits in the 'real' world. Like Sredni Vashtar, they are metonyms or distillations of nature; of the animal world red in tooth and claw, indifferent and ruthless, which Saki offers as preferable to the human world of greed, hypocrisy, the intentional infliction of pain and death for anything other than survival, and simple unkindness. In 'The Wolves of Cernogratz', wolves both provide a chilly Eastern European atmosphere and enable Saki to make a connection between aristocracy and the indigenous wild when wolves come out of the forest to howl at the passing of the last member of a 'true' ancient bloodline, but would disdain to notice the death of the mercantile arrivistes who now own her ancestral home. These wolves have much in common with the 'children of the night' whose music is appreciated by the Count in Stoker's *Dracula*.

'They have come from far and wide to sing the death-music of my family. It is beautiful that they have come; I am the last von Cernograntz that will die in our old castle, and they have come to sing to me. Hark, how loud they are calling!'
   The cry of the wolves rose on the still winter air and floated round the castle walls.   (*Toys*, 45–6)

It is characteristic of Saki that having set up wolves, stags, and wild boars to be signs of the wild sublime, in the next breath, or next story, or next collection, he makes them absurd. In 'The Elk', a fearsome horned beast kills a woman, but the gruesomeness of this is not the point of the story. A matchmaking mother, Mrs Yonelet, throws her daughter Dora at an eligible bachelor, Bertie Thropplestance, heir to his grandmother's fortune. She announces that Bertie's rescue of Dora from a near-lethal attack by an elk kept in the park has brought the young people together, and that they are clearly fated to marry. Bertie's domineering, wealthy grandmother has other ideas. She reveals that Dora is only the most recent in a succession of young women rescued by Bertie, and that if Bertie must marry anyone he rescues from the elk, the gardener's boy has precedence. Mrs Thropplestance's chosen bride for her grandson and replacement for herself is said to be the German governess of a local family, who is as fearless, outspoken, and domineering as she is. It is she whom the elk kills, off-stage. Mrs Thropplestance dies soon afterwards, and Dora, who had retreated in defeat, chucks her fiancé and marries Bertie (*Beasts*, 247–55). The story is almost an anticlimactic or inverted sequel to the denouement of 'The Music on the Hill', but it does remind readers that it is not wise to try to tame wild animals.

Saki twice juxtaposes his quintessence of the natural and wild with his quintessence of the urban and artificial by bringing wolves into the theatre. In 'Reginald's Drama', wolves are the stage dressing of a protracted flight of fantasy. It is not quite clear whether they stand for a debasement of the natural world or a 'whiff' of it that is not quite belitted.

'[. . .] it would commence with wolves worrying something on a lonely waste—you wouldn't see them, of course; but you would hear them snarling and scrunching, and I should arrange to have a wolfy fragrance suggested across the footlights. It would look so well on the programmes, "Wolves in the first act, by Jamrach" ' [. . .]
'And the wolves?'
'Oh, the wolves would be a sort of elusive undercurrent in the background that would never be satisfactorily explained. After all, life teems with things that have no earthly reason. And whenever the characters could think of nothing brilliant to say about marriage or the War Office, they could open a window and listen to the howling of the wolves. But that would be very seldom.' ('Reginald's Drama', *Reginald*, 82–6)

Since the wolfy fragrance is only to be suggested, and is to be wafted over the footlights, live wolves would perhaps not be necessary, or desirable, so why Jamrach would have supplied them is not explained, unless Reginald scorns imitation, and demands live howling, to order. This theatrical counterfeiting of wildness, and inversion of something which elsewhere is treated as sacred, or at least thrilling, is characteristic of Saki's double-vision of the wild.

The supplier of the present-or-not wolves, Jamrach, was Johann Christian Carl (Charles) Jamrach, a well-known importer and dealer in wild animals. He came to England in 1843 and opened a famous 'emporium' in what is now Pennington Street, with a repository for the larger animals in Betts Street. A contemporary memoir of the area describes the shop:

I suppose that there is no other place in the world where a domesticated parson could ring his bell and send his servant round the corner to buy a lion. Had I a domestic capable of discharging such an errand, and a proper receptacle in which to put the article when brought home, I could indulge the whim for a lion at five minutes' notice. My near neighbour, Mr. Jamrach, always keeps a stock of wild beasts on hand. Anyhow, if he happened to be out of lions, I should be sure of getting a wild beast of some sort at his store. A little time ago one of our clergy, who knows of almost everything going on in the parish, happened to remark to me that Mr. Jamrach's stock was low. He had just looked in, and the proprietor said he had nothing particularly fresh then, only four young elephants and a camelopard, beside the usual supply of monkeys, parrots, and such small deer [. . .] You must pay about £200 for a royal tiger, and £300 for an elephant, while I am informed you may possibly buy a lion for £70, and a lioness for less. But a first-rate lion sometimes runs to a high figure, say even £300. Ourang-outangs come to £20 each, but Barbary apes range from £3 to £4 apiece. Mr. Jamrach, however, keeps no priced catalogue of animals, but will supply a written list of their cost if needed. He does not, moreover, 'advertise,' so much as royally 'announce' his arrivals. Certain papers in London, Paris, Berlin, and Vienna, occasionally contain a bare statement that such and such beasts and birds are at 'Jamrach's,' no address being given. He has customers in all the Zoological Museums in Europe, and the Sultan has been one of the largest buyers of his tigers and parrots.[13]

One can see that Munro would have been attracted by the shop, and by the idea of sending a servant round the corner to buy a lion, as he had sent a servant up a tree to procure birds' eggs in Burma.

A commemorative plaque on the site of the shop gives a further description:

Over a hundred years ago on what was then called Ratcliffe Highway near to this spot stood Jamrach's Emporium. This unique shop sold not only the most varied collection of curiosities but also traded in wild animals such as alligators, tigers, elephants, monkeys and birds. Jamrach's was known to seafarers throughout the world who, when their ship docked in London, would bring artefacts from distant lands in the knowledge that Mr. Jamrach would be a willing purchaser. The animals were housed in iron cages and were well looked after until they were bought by zoological institutes and naturalist collectors.

The commemoration depicts a small boy leaning back in order to be able to look up at a large tiger who has raised one paw. Further lettering tells the story:

In the early years of the nineteenth century a full grown Bengal tiger, having just arrived at Jamrach's Emporium, burst open his wooden transit box and quietly trotted down the road. Everybody scattered except an eight year-old boy, who, having never seen such a large cat, went up to it with the intent of stroking its nose. A tap of the great soft paw stunned the boy and, picking him up by his jacket, the tiger walked down a side alley. Mr. Jamrach, having discovered the empty box, came running up and, thrusting his bare hands into the tiger's throat, forced the beast to let his captive go. The little boy was unscathed and the subdued tiger was led back to his cage. In memory of Jamrach's any money collected from the fountain [opposite] will be donated to the World Wildlife Fund.

The Reverend Harry Jones tells a slightly different story, however, in which Jamrach is not the hero, and which would probably have appealed to Munro much more than the official account.[14]

Once, some long time ago, a disastrous and distressing accident happened in connection with this store of wild beasts. One of the tigers in transit escaped from his cage in the neighbourhood of the Commercial Road. Finding himself free, he picked up a little boy and walked off with him, intending probably, when he found a convenient retreat, to eat him. Of course, the spectacle of a tiger walking quietly along with a little boy in his mouth (he had him only by the collar) attracted the notice of residents and wayfarers. Presently the bravest spectator, armed with a crowbar, approached the tiger, and striking vehemently and blindly at him, missed the beast and killed the boy. The tiger was then secured.

Jamrach died in 1891, some years before the Reginald story was published, but perhaps the story coupled in Munro's mind with another commemorated encounter with a tiger, 'The Death of Munrow'. He certainly remembered Jamrach's Emporium while he was in Burma, when he described the noise of his pet as heard by the elderly lady in the adjoining hotel room as 'Jamrach's evening hymn' (Munro, p. 48).

In *William*, a troupe of performing wolves is included in a West End variety show organized as part of the consolidation of the German victory over England and as an opportunity for Society to demonstrate its acceptance of the new order. We see the spectacle through the eyes of Murrey Yeovil, and here there is no ambiguity; this is a horror story.

Yeovil had encountered wolves in North African deserts and in Siberian forest and wold, he had seen them at twilight stealing like dark shadows across the snow, and heard their long whimpering howl in the darkness amid the pines; he could well understand how a magic lore had grown up round them through the ages among the peoples of four continents, how their name had passed into a hundred strange sayings and inspired a hundred traditions. And now he saw them ride round the stage on tricycles, with grotesque ruffles round their necks and clown caps on their heads, their eyes blinking miserably in the blaze of the footlights. In response to the applause of the house a stout, atrociously smiling man in evening dress came forward and bowed; he had nothing to do either with the capture or the training of the animals, having bought them ready for use from a continental emporium where wild beasts were prepared for the music-hall market, but he continued bowing and smiling till the curtain fell.   (*William*, 137–8)

Yeovil's feeling for the wolves is almost a Sakian manifesto. Again here, wild and potentially lethal animals are as it were defanged and debased. The wolves could be a metaphor for the mighty of England, now performing the steps dictated by a Continental director, or could simply represent the crude bad taste of the new overlords. It is acceptable for Reginald to mix the wild with the cultivated, the Dionysian with the Apollonian, because he is presenting an ostended wild, a signifier of the wild, within a synthetic, man-made context. It is unacceptable for the real wild to be paraded in a man-made context which contains and debases it.

Even the great ferret-god Sredni Vashtar has a comic, absurd, and debased counterpart in 'Louis', a Toy Pomerian lapdog apparently adored and almost worshipped by Lena Strudwarden, and used by her to get her own way in everything, but because Lena is a grown woman with power rather than a small, powerless boy, Louis is anything but a creature of the wild.

'Look here', said Strudwarden, 'this eternal Louis business is getting to be a ridiculous nuisance. Nothing can be done, no plans can be made, without some veto connected with that animal's whims or convenience being imposed. If you were a priest in attendance on some African fetish you couldn't set up a more elaborate code of restrictions. I believe you'd ask the Government to put off a General Election if you thought it would interfere with Louis's comfort in any way.' ('Louis', *Toys*, 50–1)

Strudwarden is particularly outraged because his wife is not fond of animals in general or at all interested in wildlife.

'when we are down at Kerryfield you won't stir a step to take the house dogs out, even if they're dying for a run, and I don't think you've been in the stables twice in your life. You laugh at what you call the fuss that's being made over the extermination of plumage birds, and you are quite indignant with me if I interfere on behalf of an ill-treated, over-driven animal on the road. And yet you insist on every one's plans being made subservient to the convenience of that stupid little morsel of fur and selfishness.' (Ibid 51)

Where Sredni Vashtar is a death-dealer, Louis is the object of Strudwarden's plans for murder. Louis's inertia makes it difficult to make the death appear natural, but when a suitable method has been devised, the particular irony of 'Louis' is revealed; the toy Pomeranian really was a toy.

Though not a play, the setting for the presence of a wolf in the story 'The She-Wolf' is certainly theatrical. Clovis introduces one into a country-house party as part of a practical joke designed to snub Leonard Bilsiter, who has been boasting about his occult powers on the basis of an encounter at a station 'on the further side of Perm' during a railway strike. Although Clovis obtains a rather fine specimen of the North American timber-wolf, it is no amber lamp-eyed mythical grey shadow, but Louise, a she-wolf with an angelic temper, swapped by Lord Pabham for some arctic foxes. Leonard Bilsiter is duly duped and punished for his presumption. The story is Wildean or Cowardesque in its inversion of significance, its off-hand presentation of the serious or sensational, and *reductio ad absurdum*, but as with the elk, the object of the comedic inversion is something that Saki's narrative voices elsewhere hold dear. It seems that even the sacred had to be made profane; had to be cut down to size in the same manner as Leonard Bilsiter.[15]

The story opens with a description of Bilsiter as 'one of those people who have failed to find this world attractive or interesting, and who have sought compensation in an "unseen world" of their own experience or imagination—or invention' (*Beasts*, 1). On a first reading it is hard to tell which is the greater heresy, Bilsiter's trespass on Saki's sacred grounds, 'the unseen world' of imagination and the wild wolf-haunted forests, which should be reserved for children and men that wolves have sniffed at, or the existence of a tame timber-wolf in a private menagerie. Then one remembers that Munro was tempted to buy a wolf puppy which he would presumably have domesticated, and it is then difficult either to make the proper separation between author and character, or to reconcile the love of wild things and the desire to tame them. Munro, writing to his sister in 1901, when he was acting as her 'understudy' during her absence from their father's house, makes no objections to a travelling menagerie which kept both lions and wolves.

On Wednesday we drove to Bucks and met a menagerie, so with two other traps we turned into a field to let it pass. Bertie and I went in on both nights to see the beasts, and made friends with the young trainer, who was quite charming, and had sweet little lion cubs (born in the first coronation week) taken out of their cage and put into our arms, also seductive little wolf-puppies which you would have loved.   (Munro, 60)

A much-used device in the stories is the introduction of an animal into an unexpected setting. Some of these incongruous juxtapositions are engineered by children; in the case of small children, as a way of mitigating their extreme powerlessness. Anyone who has much to do with small children will know that they can represent as much an uncontainable force of nature as any wolf or lion, and more so, perhaps, when, like the Sakian children, they have been repressed; watched pots which when left boil over. Not all of these bring about acts of violence. Nicolas in 'The Lumber Room' only puts a frog in a bowl of bread-and-milk, so that he can be incontestably right for once (*Beasts*, p. 274). Matilda lets a boar-pig into the garden in 'The Boar-Pig' (ibid. p. 24) as a ruse to extort money from some gatecrashers to a garden party. Older children use animals for practical jokes or as part of what people might choose to interpret as kindly intentions. An alternative kind of 'unrest-cure' is organized by Vera, one of several girls ironically so named, who lodges a small black pig and a gamecock in a guest's bedroom during an imaginary flood ('The Lull', ibid. p. 75). Other animals arrive by chance to disrupt domestic order: a goat being devoured by a leopard in a guest room in 'The Guests' (*Toys*, p. 64) creates a spirit of Panic; an ox in a morning-room in 'The Stalled Ox' (*Beasts*, p. 225), inspires a further painting of havoc being created by animals in domestic spaces. All these are comic as well as Dionysian (the Dionysian ecstasy is felt by the perpetrator) or Panicking in effect, but the paintings in 'On Approval' (ibid. p. 305–11), of giraffe drinking at the fountain pools in Trafalgar Square, vultures attacking a dying camel in Upper Berkeley Street, hyenas asleep in Euston Station, and wolves and wapiti fighting on the steps of the Athenaeum Club, are apocalyptic. In fact the portentous turns to the ridiculous, as the pictures are revealed to be, if not a practical joke, at least neither prophetic nor good art (as defined commercially), and the purchasers realize that they have swindled themselves.

Saki was not, of course, the first or only author to juxtapose the sublime, Panic-inducing, or more straightforwardly frightening things with the mundane. The Augustan 'Age of Elegance' needed its safety-valve of the Gothic; Romanticism needed its dark side; men as well as women needed an outlet for all that repression. Saki's age, the late-Victorian and Edwardian periods, had its repressions, its secrets, and its straitjacket of social codes, and it too, had its Gothic. From the 1860s this was the Novel of Sensation (for example, *The Woman in White* (1859–60), *Lady Audley's Secret* (1862)); in the 1890s it was *fin de siècle* decadence (*The Yellow Book* (1894–7), *Salomé* (1891–4)); the 1900s had ghost stories such as M. R. James's *Ghost Stories of an Antiquary* (1904), Algernon Blackwood's *The Empty House* (1906) and Oliver Onions's *Widdershins* (1911). Some of Saki's work could be classified with these, and we might expect the once highly imaginative and oppressed child to be well able to recreate the 'stealthy linking of the joy of life with the terror of unseen things', but the object of the stories does not always seem to be the evocation of atmosphere or the frisson of terror, and still less is it the psychological penetration of Henry James. The sublime of nature is evoked in order to bring into being agents of retribution, and fear of the sharp-fanged and indifferent wild creature is the other side of the characters' erotic enjoyment of its/his beauty. In a number of stories supernatural events are narrated in spare language and a judicious deadpan tone which lacks the sensationalism of the novel of sensation. Like *Wuthering Heights*, Saki's terror stories of supernatural retribution have a powerful moral, even if that moral is not the conventional one.

Possible Freudian interpretations of some of Saki's stories are presented by Philip Stevick in 'Saki's Beasts', which focuses on the wolf in 'The She-Wolf', the pig in 'The Boar Pig', the trope of guilt in 'The Treasure Ship' and sexual symbolism in 'The Lumber Room' (all from *Beasts*).[16] Stevick concludes that the question of whether Saki was directly influenced by Freud's work cannot be determined, especially as the first English edition of *The Interpretation of Dreams* was published in 1913. 'But it is, in any case, entirely believable that the penetrating, critical, passionately honest imagination of Saki should have, at one level or another of his consciousness, played its little joke on his genteel, newspaper-reading public by surreptitiously dealing with a level of experience which no one has ever suspected of him.'[17] A more recent and in-depth psychological analysis of Saki's writing appears in Christopher Lane's *The Ruling Passion: British Colonial Allegory and The Paradox of Homosexual Desire*, which goes beyond the remit of this study in examining 'the precarious status of the "he" that desires in Munro's writing'.[18]

Langguth points out a martial strain in Fitzgerald's version of the *Rubáiyát*, a call to courage in the face of death (Langguth, p. 62), which would accord well with aspects of Munro's character, but an alternative interpretation was offered by the husband of one of Munro's nieces, the Reverend A. Aitken Crawshaw, who suggested that the name is a contraction of 'Sakya Muni', the Buddhist term for 'enlightened one' (Lambert, p. 27). There is also an assertion of immortality.

> And fear not lest existence closing your
> Account, and mine, should know the like no more;
>   The Eternal Saki from that Bowl has pour'd
> Millions of Bubbles like us, and will pour,
>
> When You and I behind the Veil are past,
> Oh, but the long, long while the World shall last
>   Which of our Coming and Departure heeds
> As the Sea's self should heed a pebble-cast.

This Saki is an immortal cupbearer who pours, it should be noted, bubbles. However strong the martial clarion, Saki did not depict war as it were at first hand in his fiction, even though he did give characters speeches in praise of the alleged romance of war. He did not write war or adventure stories. Of course, he did not write a lot of things, and there would be very little point in belabouring him for that. That he did not write certain kinds of fiction is, however, worth examining.

Munro was often hard up, as his frequent appeals to his publishers show. He wrote quickly and with an eye to commercial possibilities, as his letters also show. Had he wished to, he could have produced genre fiction. He was of the right class and outlook, and even had the right kind of first-hand experience to have written the kind of gung-ho, boys' own fiction produced by Rider Haggard and Rudyard Kipling at that time, but he did not. He never drew on his experiences in Burma, the Balkans, or Russia for stirring adventures in which cunning or savage foreigners threatening the Empire are thwarted in their dastardly intentions, and his war novel starts after the war. In spite of his many references to the wild and the wilderness, and his creation of the wonderful Saki archetype 'the man that wolves have sniffed at', he did not show his characters grappling with wolves, bears, or tigers. Reginald deplores the major who bores a Christmas party with 'a graphic account of a struggle he had with a wounded bear' and plaintively wishes that: 'the bears would win sometimes on these occasions; at least they wouldn't go vapouring about it afterwards' ('Reginald's Christmas Revel', *Reginald*, p. 100).

When a bad character (an interfering woman or an annoying man) encounters a wild beast accidentally and unwillingly, there is no competition. Those foredoomed by their attitude to nature, such as Sylvia Seltoun and Thirza Yealmton, cannot boast about their fight with the wild because they do not live to tell the tale. When an inadequate character attempts to pass him or herself off as a hunter, the consequences are grimly comic (as in 'Mrs Packleton's Tiger', *Clovis*, pp. 45–52). Characters do not have any hair-raisingly dangerous encounters in the stories; even the real hunters have theirs out of sight, in back-story, or in anticipation ('The Interlopers', *Toys*, pp. 119–28). When a bomb actually explodes in the time-frame of the story, we are spared much description of its effects ('The Easter Egg', *Clovis*, pp. 135–42). Though they hint at, presage, and follow ugly events, most of Saki's stories, like classical Greek drama, keep the goriness offstage. When children are involved, however, things are slightly different. (Discussion of this follows, below.)

In several Saki stories, then, Pan, or one of his animals, is an agent of revenge on the managing woman of the Thirza type discussed earlier. She is inevitably a crass and insensitive figure who appears to thwart and manipulate the male in her charge simply for the pleasure of exercising her power over him. As wife, she attempts to 'make something' of her husband, or order his life; as mother she withholds funds and adulthood; as sister, she tells tales and tries to reform her brother's morals. She is the antithesis of the young Dionysian or Pan-like figure,[19] a naiad of suburbia, who carries the hero away from a life of romance and adventure (whether wolves and Cossacks or duchess-baiting and choirboys) and commits him to a life sentence of dullness and routine. In 'Tea', the twin objects of horror for Saki, managing women and suburban life, coalesce in his depiction of the claustrophobia which overwhelms its protagonist James Cushat-Prinkly as he contemplates the numbing routine of domestic life as perpetuated by women.

Thousands of women, at this solemn afternoon hour, were sitting behind dainty porcelain and silver fittings, with their voices tinkling pleasantly in a cascade of solicitous little questions. Cushat-Prinkly detested the whole system of afternoon tea. According to his theory of life a woman should lie on a divan or couch, talking with incomparable charm or looking unutterable thoughts, or merely silent as a thing to be looked on, and from behind a silken curtain a small Nubian page should silently bring in a tray with cups and dainties, to be accepted silently, as a matter of course, without drawn-out chatter about cream and sugar and hot water.

If one's soul was really enslaved at one's mistress's feet, how could one talk coherently about weakened tea? (*Toys*, 24)

Cushat-Prinkly postpones proposing to the woman he is expected to marry, and avoids encountering her over the tea-tray, by visiting a remote cousin, Rhoda Ellam. He finds Rhoda surrounded by the impedimenta of her work, taking a picnic meal. Beyond pointing out where the caviar and teapot are, and telling him to find himself a cup, she makes no other allusions to food. She produces red pepper and sliced lemons 'where so many women would merely have produced reasons and regrets for not having any' and does not tinkle. Cushat-Prinkly enjoys having the luxuries of domestic pleasures supplied without the parade of domestic trivia and impedimenta, and finds that 'he was enjoying an excellent tea without having to answer as many questions about it as a Minister of Agriculture might be called on to reply to during an outbreak of cattle plague'. He proposes. After the honeymoon:

Cushat-Prinkly came into the drawing-room of his new house in Granchester Square. Rhoda was seated at a low table, behind a service of dainty porcelain and gleaming silver. There was a pleasant tinkling note in her voice as she handed him a cup.

'You like it weaker than that, don't you? Shall I put some more hot water to it? No?' (ibid. 28)

The liberated and liberating woman transforms into the fiendish gaoler whose instruments of torture are a tea-service and a tinkling voice. Another Saki story ends with Hell in sight. Cushat-Prinkly is back in the Hell of childhood: boredom; routine; containment; stultification. Is he a fool for falling into the trap of marriage, particularly for not expecting a free spirit to devolve into a Wife immediately after marriage, or does the reader blame the woman? Are his fantasies of accomplished beauties reclining on couches laughably commonplace, or indicative of a higher, aesthetic nature which deserves better than to be saddled with a pourer of tea? Cushat-Prinkly's fantasies are of an *Arabian Nights* kind: Nubian slave; reclining beauty; delicacies presented on a tray. While he despises and fears the dainty, the polished, and the tinkling when associated with the feminine world of enclosure and routine, he is happy to enjoy in fantasy similar luxury items (even 'dainties') which have escaped that connotation. The eroticism of softness, silken surfaces, warmth, and colour is conventionally associated with the feminine, and opposed to the hard, cold, outdoors eroticism of the male, including many Saki males. This makes Gabriel-Ernest's ambiguity, or amphibiousness, the more interesting. He sprawls outside and in; across a rock at the edge of a pool in a wood; across an ottoman (debased Western suburban version of Oriental furnishing) in a drawing room. The exposed brown body is arrestingly incongruous in its pose across and in front of the colours and textures of draped fabric, and reminiscent of Victorian paintings of harem women. Cunningham's gaze momentarily conventionally effeminizes Gabriel-Ernest, and Cunningham's sister emasculates him by treating him as a pet, but Saki restores him to the 'maleness' threatened by erroneous equations of a beautiful male object of male desire with 'femininity' by sending him into the woods again to hunt, and of course to kill. The suffocating perfumed sensuality of the imagined Orient with which Wilde's stories are sometimes laden is in Saki blown away by a chill wind from a more northerly east. Saki's men can successfully inhabit both rock and ottoman.

While woman is not overtly accused of bringing about the awful fate of 'Judkin of the Parcels' (an unending sameness of fetching and carrying unimportant packages) (*Reginald in Russia*, pp. 42–6); a wife is lurking darkly in the wings, and Saki brings all his upper-middle-class contempt for the drudge of trade to the story, and all his lower-upper-middle-class horror of being sucked into its maw through economic necessity to the depiction of its victim.

The play *The Watched Pot*, on which Charles Maude collaborated with Saki, contains one of the most ferocious female domestic tyrants, Hortensia Bavvel, thanks to whom the family home, Briony, has nothing in the way of diversion; no gambling, dancing, music; no Halma or chess on Sundays, 'for fear of setting a bad example to the servants' (*The Watched Pot, Square Egg*, p. 196). She is described as a Catherine the Second of Russia without any of her redeeming vices, who has done:

everything that had to be done in the management of a large estate—and a great deal that might have been left undone: she engaged and dismissed gardeners, decided which of the under-gardeners might marry and how much gooseberry jam should be made in a given year, regulated the speed at which perambulators might be driven through the village street and the number of candles which might be lighted in church on dark afternoons without suspicion of Popery. (ibid. 195)

Like other Saki managing women, she has sucked out the life and joy from a household, and before his death reduced her husband, Edward, to a nonentity. Another character, Ludovic, makes a telling reflection on this kind of Sakian marriage: 'Edward [...] used to declare that marriage was a lottery. Like most popular sayings, that simile breaks down on application. In a lottery there are prizes and blanks; no one who knew her would think of describing Hortensia as either a prize or a blank' (p. 194).

Saki represents another kind of conjugal hell in 'The Reticence of Lady Anne' (*Reginald in Russia*, pp. 7–12), and an early example of the death of a woman providing the man's escape from hell. Down-trodden Egbert is so accustomed to his wife's sustained maintenance of frigid silence as evidence of her displeasure that he makes futile and self-abasing attempts at conciliation and appeasement throughout a whole afternoon, unaware that she has been dead for two hours.

The death of the wife in 'The Seventh Pullet' is initially far less welcome, since John Blenkinthrope is fond of her, but it is extremely convenient, as he has been longing for something extraordinary to happen to provide him with matter for an interesting anecdote. Blenkinthrope inhabits the pallid limbo of every down-trodden middle-aged drudge.

'It's not the daily grind that I complain of', said Blenkinthrope resentfully; 'it's the dull grey sameness of my life outside of office hours. Nothing of interest comes my way, nothing remarkable or out of the common. Even the little things that I do try to find some interest in don't seem to interest other people' (*Beasts*, pp. 92). As the things he offers other people include his growing of a potato which weighs just under two pounds, this is not surprising. His friend Gorworth gives Blenkinthrope advice which could perhaps have been followed by Saki himself. He points out that the men Blenkinthrope would like to entertain and astound have lives as dull and unrelieved as his own:

and they certainly are not going to wax enthusiastic over the commonplace events in other men's lives. Tell them something startling, dramatic, piquant, that has happened to yourself or to some one in your family, and you will capture their interest at once. They will talk about you with a certain pride to all their acquaintances. 'Man I know intimately, fellow called Blenkinthrope, lives down my way, had two of his fingers clawed clean off by a lobster he was carrying home to supper. Doctor says entire hand may have to come off.' Now that is conversation of a very high order. But imagine walking into a tennis club with the remark: 'I know a man who has grown a potato weighing two and a quarter pounds.'   (ibid. 94)

Blenkinthrope of course complains that nothing remarkable ever happens to him, and Gorworth of course replies: 'Invent something.' Blenkinthrope is at first reluctant, but a taste of the pleasures of having centre stage in a commuter train carriage quickly makes him realize 'how safe and easy depravity can seem once one has the courage to begin' and 'how little the loss of one's self-respect affects one when one has gained the esteem of the world' (p. 95). He is accepted as the Munchausen of his circle, and regales his fellowcommuters with ingenious stories. 'And then one day came Nemesis.' He comes home to find his wife playing 'Death's Head Patience'. She remarks that she would be rather frightened if she were to complete the game, since her mother's great aunt died of excitement on finishing it, and her mother, thus made afraid of the game, was convinced that she would die if she were to get it out, and duly did. A little later, she is given 'such a turn' when she almost gets it out, held up only by a five of diamonds. Blenkinthrope points out that with a small rearrangement of cards she can do it. His wife makes the suggested move, and 'Then she followed the example of her mother and great-grand-aunt' (p. 96). That sentence is a perfect example of Saki's ruling-out of all inessentials and distractions, such as specification or emotion, from the humorous connection he wishes to make. The death is not the Nemesis, however. 'Something sensational and real had at last come into his life; no longer was it a grey, colourless record,' and Blenkinthrope cannot resist the temptation to see it as headline material. He writes it up for the press, but he is like the little boy who cried 'Wolf', and his friends consider it poor taste to be 'Munchausening' about such an event. Nemesis takes the form of the reduction of the romancer to one who bores chance acquaintances with the prowess in whistling of his canary or the dimensions of a beetroot. The Nemesis that overtakes so many Saki characters, when it is not a vengeance effected by one of the youths, is the inescapable horror of the daily, endless, ever-repeated sameness.

In spite of the brief flurry of excitement caused by her sending two men to their deaths in an attempt to rescue a portrait of a daughter who never existed, and which is anyway not in the house, Mrs Gramplain finds the old dull sameness descending upon her at the end of 'The East Wing', when 'it will all begin over again now, the old life, the old unsatisfying weariness, the old monotony; nothing will be changed' ('The East Wing', *Complete Short Stories*, p. 718).

Robert Drake concludes that 'there is in many ways, little to choose between Saki's stories of laughter and his stories of terror; they differ more in degree than in kind. It is but a short step from Reginald and Clovis to Sredni Vashtar and the Hounds of Fate: they are all Terrors of a sort who bring enlightenment and sometimes destruction to the arrogant, the smug, and the willfully blind.'[20] The Saki youths can be revenged on domesticating or bullying women by inflicting social embarrassment, extortion (especially if the women play cards), or petty blackmail, but the younger boys are more vulnerable, and the worst of the female villains are the older female relations and guardians who trammel the boys' freedom of movement and attempt to trammel their imaginations. Those merit the more terrifying forms of revenge. In this context, perhaps we should remember Ellen Moers's remark about Decadence appearing in 'the complicated awe of woman as the stronger sex'.[21]

The tormentor of 'The Lumber Room', the aunt of the young hero's cousins, is 'the soi-disant aunt' and 'alleged aunt'. That is, she usurps the power and prerogatives of, and by virtue of her malignity is worthy of, the name of 'aunt', a dire title in Saki's work. Nicholas, the child hero, has his defences against the domestic tyrant, and his *soi-disant* aunt's come-uppance is merely to be confined to a rain-water tank for thirty-five minutes; in other stories, however, the neglected, unloved boy exacts a more violent and extreme revenge. The anarchic force of nature which manifests as post-pubescent boys in both Gabriel-Ernest and the laughing Pan-boy with the flute is aligned with the oppressed pre-pubescent children, and perhaps called into being by them, as in 'Sredni Vashtar'. 'Conradin hated her with a desperate sincerity which he was perfectly able to mask [...] from the realm of his imagination she was locked out—an unclean thing which should find no entrance' (*Clovis*, 94). Conradin has two beloved pets, acquired with great difficulty and smuggled into a toolshed, a Houdan hen and a polecat-ferret:

a secret and fearful joy, to be kept scrupulously from the knowledge of the Woman, as he privately dubbed his cousin. And one day, out of Heaven knows what material, he spun the beast a wonderful name, and from that moment it grew into a god and a religion. [... I]n the dim and musty silence of the tool-shed, he worshipped with mystic and elaborate ceremonial before the wooden hutch where dwelt Sredni Vashtar, the great ferret.   (ibid. 95–6)

The Woman finds the hen and has it taken away. Suspecting the existence of another concealed animal, she ransacks Conradin's room, finds the key to the shed, and descends on the shed with the single-minded juggernaut quality of all these Saki women.

And Conradin fervently breathed his prayer for the last time. But he knew as he prayed that he did not believe. He knew that the Woman would come out presently with that pursed smile he loathed so well on her face, and that in an hour or two the gardener would carry away his wonderful god, a god no longer, but a simple brown ferret in a hutch. And he knew that the Woman would triumph always as she triumphed now, and that he would grow ever more sickly under her pestering and domineering and superior wisdom, and the doctor would be proved right. And in the sting and misery of his defeat, he began to chant loudly and defiantly the hymn of his threatened idol:

> Sredni Vashtar went forth,
> His thoughts were red thoughts and his teeth were white.
> His enemies called for peace, but he brought them death.
> Sredni Vashtar the Beautiful.   (ibid. 99–100)

Conradin watches. Finally, 'out through the doorway came a long, yellow-and-brown beast, with eyes a-blink at the waning daylight, and dark wet stains around the fur of jaws and throat' (pp. 101–2) While the maids have hysterics, and wonder who is to break the news to the frail child, Conrad calmly consumes buttered toast.

Latent violence hangs over the stories, but does not always happen. 'Sredni Vashar' has his revenge. There is death, and actual blood on the animal's mouth, but the reader doesn't see the giant polecat-ferret eat the wicked woman because Conradin, whose perspective we have, doesn't see it. This precludes the possibly comic effect of a hugely enlarged small rodent, and provides a wonderfully deadpan ending in which Conradin proves to be a suitably unshaken, conscienceless Saki hero. ' "Whoever will break it to the poor child? I couldn't for the life of me!" exclaimed a shrill voice. And while they were debating the matter among themselves, Conradin made himself another piece of toast' (p. 102). This image is beautifully judged. It could have fallen over into silliness: the great benefit brought about by bloody murder proves to be restitution to a deprived child—of buttered toast. It doesn't because of the attention paid to Conradin's careful and deliberated preparation and consumption; a luxury in that he will enjoy eating it, and in that there is no one to tell him not to go near the fire.

> And while the maid went to summon her mistress to tea, Conradin fished a toasting fork out of the sideboard drawer and proceeded to toast himself a piece of bread. And during the toasting of it and the buttering of it with much butter and the slow enjoyment of it, Conradin listened to the noises and silences which fell in quick spasms beyond the dining-room door.   (ibid. 101)

The sentence beginning 'And during' keeps pace with Conradin's ritualistic feast; his first, synecdochal, breaking of the ten-year fast from all gratification that The Woman has imposed on him, and there is a world of newly asserted autonomy in his taking, probably for the first time ever, a second slice.

'Sredni Vashtar' is a wonderfully accomplished story; elegantly compressed in language and incident. The 'buttering of it with much butter' is so much better than 'buttered it thickly' would have been, while 'the noises and silences which fell in quick spasms beyond the dining-room door' is vividly and economically realized. Whilst rigorously unsentimental, and blackly gruesome, the story is extremely poignant, and tends to leave even the most forgiving and charitable readers applauding the murder. Ethel Munro asserts that Mrs de Ropp is a portrait of Augusta (Munro, p. 7), the more fearsome of the two Aunts, and mentions that her brother said that he would not write about Charlotte (Aunt Tom) until after her death. She died in 1915, while he was training, and Ethel asserts that she appeared 'only sketchily' in his writing, apart from 'The Sex that Doesn't Shop', which 'is chiefly about her' (Munro, pp. 63–4).

In a letter to his brother, written after Aunt Tom's funeral, Munro was to suggest that Charles, Ethel, and he might feel 'some pride' in reflecting that the Aunts 'at the end of their lives came to see that we were likable and loveable' (Langguth, p. 256). To say this of the women who had brought up the three from infancy, and had clearly never made them feel that children do not need to prove their likeable- or loveable-ness, is to damn with faint praise indeed.

Older women, then, women In Charge, stand for domesticity, constraint, and repression; they are guardians of everything utilitarian, hide-bound, rule-bound, costive, and established; everything a Saki hero would want to rebel against. The matron of the suburbs is demonized as the antithesis of the wild, untrammelled, male animal, whether sleek, beautiful ferret or sleek beautiful boy, or, as in Gabriel-Ernest, something that is both. The very young boy has no defences of his own, but is attached in some way to a sublime force of nature which may come to his defence. That force of nature that is entirely wild and separate from the young boys merges with them as they become fully sexualized, and they become, literally or metaphorically, nature-spirits or animals. Nature provides revenge on behalf of a few older men also, for example in 'The East Wing' and 'The Music on the Hill', but only when it is also taking revenge on its own behalf. It is an agent of surrogate revenge only for a certain kind of child. Without such intervention, the men have to hope for the intervention of fate, as in the amnesia which rids a husband and children of Crispina Umberleigh for eight blissful years in another wish-fulfilment story, later made into a play ('The Disappearance of Crispina Umberleigh', *Toys*, pp. 29–38).

For Joseph S. Salemi, animals and the violent acts of animals are the manifestations of the cold-blooded detachment which, he writes, has prompted many readers to call Saki cruel or inhuman. Salemi sees the beasts as 'symbols of a psychological nemesis that dishes out retribution, with mechanical impartiality'.[22] The animals rarely attack arbitrarily, however. Robert Drake points out that though death is often treated flippantly in Saki's stories, when it is treated seriously, as a bitterly ironic fate, animals are often the agents of Nemesis, and though characters often bring about their own downfall, it is often with the help of an animal.[23] Drake acknowledges, however, that animals are not the only such mechanism for ironic fate in the stories. He refers to the agency of fate which brings characters who have been narrow-minded about themselves or the world to a realization of the truth—just before they are destroyed. In 'The Music on the Hill' it is a deer, in 'Sredni Vashtar' a polecat-ferret, but in 'The Hounds of Fate' the hounds are metaphorical, and the killer is a man.[24] This follows from Drake's suggestion in 'The Sauce for the Asparagus' that 'the characters of the Nut and Flapper serve as a set of beyond-norms, who attempt to bring the pompous, self-deceived people to a reconciliation with the real norms of honesty and good sense'.[25] In their ridiculing of others, he argues, these characters act as a corrective influence. Drake makes the point that in one Saki story the beyond-norm is an animal, the Tobermory of the story of that name.[26] Perhaps Tobermory should be seen as a cross between the characters who act as correctives, though he simply tells the truth rather than playing a practical joke, and the animals whose correctives leave the corrected too dead to change their ways. It may be significant that the presence of Clovis in 'Tobermory' as an addition to Bertie van Tahn was inserted when the story was prepared for inclusion in *The Chronicles of Clovis*, since in the original *Westminster Gazette* version Tobermory does not share centre stage.[27]

Saki's 'correctives' (practical jokes which make a point or the infliction of lighter punishments) are different, then, from his revenges (the infliction of death). Death is sometimes inflicted on those who would not and could not change, such as the Sheep (see below), and sometimes on those who have had the epiphany which would make them change ('The Hounds of Fate', *Clovis*, pp. 219–32). 'The Interlopers' (*Toys*, pp. 119–28) seems to be an exception. The two protagonists, each of whom believes he has the right to a piece of land and is willing to kill the other for trespassing on it, undergo the trauma (a tree falling which pins them to the ground) which corrects their behaviour; they agree to abandon the old feud; but they are killed anyway. The wolves who materialize from the darkness of the forest do not kill one of the men because they are agents of his desire for revenge on a trespasser, or to correct the quarrelsomeness of both, they kill both men because both are interlopers and disturbers of the wild.

'Saki's Ironic Stories' considers the example of 'The Sheep',[28] in which a fatuous, bumbling, and inept, yet self-satisfied character (the Sheep) is drowned because a young dog prevents the central character, Rupert (who dreads the Sheep's forthcoming marriage to his sister), from reaching a ladder in time to get across a frozen lake and pull him out (*Toys*, pp. 245–54). The dog is chained up. Though excited, it is not wild. It barks furiously and growls, but does not injure Rupert or even prevent him from reaching the ladder, though it does delay him long enough for the Sheep to disappear under the ice. Rather than one of the sublime, unstoppable agents of Nemesis that coalesce from the wild and / or from the psyches of the young boys they rescue, it seems to be a much more tame projection from a correspondingly less wild source, Rupert. At the end of the story, the dog appears as Rupert's inseparable, familiar-like companion. Rupert is not a dandy or Nut, nor a fierce, repressed little boy, so it is no surprise that his alter ego (or Pullmanesque daemon) is an animal associated with steadiness and reliability, and usually kept as guardian of domestic order. The Sheep is not an evil, abusive woman, so his drowning does seem a little extreme, but he played cards badly, which for Saki seems sufficient cause. The way a person plays bridge is often indicative of his or her character, and is taken very seriously. The Sheep does not learn from his mistakes. Having lost a rubber he should easily have won through the ineptitude of his partner, the Sheep, Rupert knows that '[i]f a similar situation had arisen in a subsequent hand he would have blundered just as certainly, and he would have been just as irritatingly apologetic' (ibid. pp. 245–6).

This does not immediately damn the Sheep. Rupert reflects that many men 'who have good brains for business do not possess the rudiments of a card-brain, and Rupert would not have judged and condemned his prospective brother-in-law on the evidence of his bridge-play alone', but: '[t]he tragic part of it was that he smiled and fumbled through life just as fatuously and apologetically as he did at the card-table. And behind the defensive smile and the well-worn expressions of regret there shone a scarcely believable but quite obvious self-satisfaction' (ibid. p. 246). This does damn the Sheep, and entitles Rupert to join the other Saki men who are both jury and judge. He is not enough of a Sakian dandy-youth (he has a sister, for one thing) to be the beyond-norm and thus executioner as well, which is why he needs the help of a less morally trammelled being.

If some of the pranks and practical jokes are for revenge or to administer a lesson, others seem to be conducted purely for entertainment or profit. Clovis spins an elaborate and highly unlikely story in order to realize a prediction in an almanack produced by another Vera not much given to veracity.[29] At first, his only motive for causing the suggestion that 'the hunting-field was not a safe place' for Jocelyn Vanner during November and December seems to be to help Vera make a profit or to amuse himself, since Jocelyn, though accident-prone, is a danger only to herself. It becomes clear, however, that both the direct and the indirect victims of the deception are culpable under Saki's law. Jocelyn makes the mistake of trying to be captivating to Clovis: ' "Scent is poor, and there's an interminable amount of cover," grumbled Clovis from his saddle; "we shall be here for hours before we get a fox away." "All the more time for you to talk to me," said Jocelyn archly' ('The Almanack', *Stories* pp. 2, 81). The other purchasers of the bogus almanack are eager for a second (extortionately priced) edition because their vanity has been carefully stoked. Mrs Duff 'easily recognized an allusion to herself as one of the best mistresses of the neighbourhood',

Mrs Openshaw recognizes hers as the garden which 'has long been the admiration of the neighbourhood for its magnificent flowers', and 'the forecast of servant troubles and unmerited bad luck on the golf links received ample confirmation in the annals of the home and the club' (*Stories* pp. 2, 80).

Not all women, even managing women, are vilified by the norms of Saki's narratives and/or killed by wild animals. In 'The Hen' (*Beasts*, pp. 40–9), the quarrelsomeness of women is pilloried, and their juggernaut tendencies are ridiculed in 'The Schwartz-Metterklume Method' (pp. 97–105), but neither of the annoying women characters is more than a comic stock type; they have no small boys to abuse. In 'Shock Tactics' (*Toys*, pp. 217–27) the mother of Bertie Heasant has kept a young man infantilized and in thrall longer than he or Clovis think decent, but though her attempts to monitor and trammel Bertie's life are deplorable, they are not as malicious as the acts of Mrs De Ropp, nor is Bertie as vulnerable as Conradin, so Mrs Heasant's punishment is only a fright and embarrassment, not death.

'The Schwartz-Metterklume Method' even has a managing woman character of whom the narrative voice evidently approves (she is kind to animals and rescues misused horses from ignorant carters) and who functions to demonstrate the superiority of the female aristocrat to the pretentious female *bourgeoise*. Saki was capable of producing more subtle characterization, however, and of attempting representation in free indirect style of a woman's train of thought. Jocantha Bessbury, in 'The Philanthropist and the Happy Cat' (*Beasts*, pp. 294–302), is a prototype Francesca Bassington in that her life revolves around the contents of her Chelsea house, and she complacently congratulates herself on the pleasantness and completeness of her situation. She decides to carry out an act of philanthropy, and becomes excited as she dwells on the imaginary image of herself performing the deed. The recipient she selects is a young man, another Bertie, she sees in a teashop:

in appearance a few years younger than herself, very much better looking than Gregory, rather better looking, in fact, than any of the young men of her set [. . .] The boy was distinctly presentable; he knew how to brush his hair, which was possibly an imitative faculty; he knew what colour of tie suited him, which might be intuition; he was exactly the type that Jocantha admired, which of course was accident.   (ibid. 298–9)

Jocantha presents her desire to herself as a philanthropic impulse, but it is made clear to the reader. The theatre tickets she had decided to give to a working girl are reassigned to the young man, and she resolves to return to the tea-shop to ask how he liked the play. 'If he was a nice boy and improved on acquaintance he could be given more theatre tickets and perhaps asked to come one Sunday to tea in Chelsea' (p. 300). She looks for an opportunity to address the young man, but he is absorbed in a book.

The laws of tea-shop etiquette forbid that you should offer theatre tickets to a stranger without having first caught the stranger's eye. It is even better if you can ask to have a sugar basin passed to you, having previously concealed the fact that you have a large and well-filled sugar basin on your own table; this is not difficult to manage, as the printed menu is generally nearly as large as the table, and can be made to stand on end. Jocantha set to work hopefully; she had a long and rather high-pitched discussion with the waitress concerning alleged defects in an altogether blameless muffin, she made loud and plaintive inquiries about the tube service to some impossibly remote suburb, she talked with brilliant insincerity to the tea-shop kitten, and as a last resort she upset a milk-jug and swore at it daintily. Altogether she attracted a good deal of attention, but never for a moment did she attract the attention of the boy with the beautifully brushed hair.   (Beasts, 300–1)

The young man, a dutiful son of Empire, remains absorbed in his book: Sepoy and Sahib, a Tale of the Great Mutiny, and Jocantha returns to her Chelsea house 'which struck her for the first time as looking dull and over-furnished. She had a resentful conviction that Gregory would be uninteresting at dinner, and that the play would be stupid after dinner' (p. 301). Jocantha's likeness and yet unlikeness to her cat is now made explicit, as, though the contrast between the animal's throbbing purr and languor and her frustration is the absence of the sexual 'kill' she had had in mind. 'On the whole her frame of mind showed a marked divergence from the purring complacency of Attab, who was once again curled up in his corner of the divan with a great peace radiating from every curve of his body. But then he had killed his sparrow' (p. 302). This is an interesting take on the trope of woman as predator. The cat is predatory by nature and does not offer itself as anything else, therefore its killing is acceptable, but Jocantha disguises her predation as benevolence, even to herself, and Saki is as ruthless towards the self-deceived as he is towards the hypocrite. The title of the book in which the young man is absorbed is also interesting in that it is almost certainly imperialist and of the 'gung-ho boys' own adventures fighting against brutal natives' kind. It is not hard to imagine Munro under his neatly parted and brush-polished hair envisaging himself so absorbed in that world of imperialist men as to be oblivious to Chelsea women and their theatre-ticket blandishments.

Young boys may be in the power of the Aunt, and husbands are almost invariably hen-pecked, but some Saki males manage to control the managing woman or even use her to their advantage. In 'Excepting Mrs Pentherby' (*Toys*, pp. 157–66), a woman is hired to be the secret official quarreller at a sort of perpetual house-party. Her irritating habits draw the fire of all the other women guests and unite them in hatred of her. The presence of a common enemy prevents the quarrels, bickering, and side-taking which are presented as inevitable in any party which includes a number of women. In 'The Threat', from the same collection, suffragettes buy up land near every major highway and landmark, and threaten to build replicas of the Victoria monument all over Britain (pp. 149–56). A typically clever, inventive, and urbane Saki man thwarts them by drafting an Act making it an offence to erect commemorative statuary anywhere within three miles of a public highway. The tone of the story is of casual and completely confident contempt for the women's movement.

The crime of the women is not that they beat or otherwise physically abuse the children, nor is the crime of the wives that they physically assault or humiliate their husbands. The great crime is that they condemn the children or men to lives of dullness, sameness, boredom, and futility, as the Munro Aunts did the children given into their care. The children long for an exciting event to relieve the seemingly endless vista of sameness; the men yearn for a change to routine; and both finally get it, in the form of bloody revenge, or terrible humiliation, or death.

Drake sees Saki's writing as presenting the world as 'a disordered, terrifying chaos' and as suggesting that 'all one can do in the face of this disorder is to follow the code, to practice an aristocratic, lonely virtue', a discipline such as Saki's, which is 'rigorous and ascetic'.[30] Yet surely, though Munro, in London at least, had a narrow routine, Saki embraced chaos as curative? Brian Gibson argues that Saki's fiction 'chafed against the stifling mundanity and routine of the Edwardian era' and finds that Saki's characters 'blackmail, lie, employ hoaxes or violence, and carry out other perverse or subversive acts in order to break the monotony of their bourgeois lives'.[31] In this, Gibson echoes one of V. S. Pritchett's reviews of Saki's work for the *New Statesman*. Pritchett characterized Saki as belonging 'to the early period of the sadistic revival in English comic and satirical writing—the movement suggested by Stevenson, Wilde, Beerbohm, Firbank, and Evelyn Waugh—the early period when the chief target was the cult of convention'.[32] Pritchett asserts that Saki 'writes like an enemy' and that '[s]ociety has bored him to the point of murder'.[33] In a later piece, Pritchett referred to this as 'the tamest and most laming period of English upper middle class life', adding: 'hence [Saki's] fancy for the paw-marks of the ferret, the great cats and the wolf; his dream, on the Mappin Terrace of the earlier nineteen-hundreds, of the bloodier excitements of the private hunt'.[34]

Gibson focuses on 'The East Wing', a story written for *Lucas' Annual* and not included in any collection or the uniform volumes until it was 'discovered' in 1946, and included in the 1948 reprint of the 1930 Bodley Head edition of the stories.[35] Using 'The East Wing' as his main example, Gibson characterizes Saki's satirical stance as 'dependent dissidence', which is rebellion from within rather than against the dominant order, and suggests that this mode of writing enabled Saki to advance a set of subversive propositions.[36] He writes:

Saki's tales seem to present a straightforward series of one-liners and exaggerated reactions to offbeat or fantastic situations [. . .] but in fact Saki's dependent dissidence primarily results from a series of opposing themes or binaries, developed throughout each story and Saki's oeuvre more generally, that offer such subversive conclusions as: homosexuality is preferable to marriage; the stifling routine and dullness of life necessitate violence, hoaxes, and self-delusions; and imagination must often conquer reality in order to make existence more bearable.[37]

This would explain the rare 'lapses into veracity' of characters such as Reginald, their predilection for protracted flights of fantasy, and their love of dressing-up for games, theatricals, or disguise. It would also explain Munro's persona of 'a man that wolves have sniffed at', and his cherished fantasy (never more cherished than when he was on a London street or a muddy Flanders ditch) of the Siberian farm he would have, and of the wilderness that was always on his (imagination's) doorstep.

Gibson does acknowledge in a footnote that 'The East Wing', whose subtitle is 'A Tragedy in the Manner of the Discursive Dramatists', is a skit on Bernard Shaw's drama, but he analyses the play as straight-faced rather than as playful or satirical. The play echoes Bernard Shaw's tendency to create characters who can seem to represent positions rather than personalities and who discourse at length on philosophical or moral issues. It also, like Shaw's drama, makes reference, but adds a twist, to contemporary events such as Suffragette protests, and includes paradoxical statements and actions, complex rhetoric, sophistry, and prolix self-justification. 'The East Wing' is a comic tragicomedy, exaggerating both the comic and tragic elements in order to satirize something that Saki accuses of pretentiousness and pomposity. The attitude of Saki's characters at least to Shaw's writing is made clear in *Bassington*, in a speech by Lady Caroline Benaresque, a self-proclaimed Socialist who monopolizes caviar sandwiches, as a put-down to the Reverend Poltimore Varden during a conversation about the exclusivity of art.

'Time is just as exclusive in its way as Art,' said Lady Caroline.

'In what way?' said the Reverend Poltimore.

'Your pleasantries about religion would have sounded quite clever and advanced in the 'nineties. Today they have a dreadfully warmed-up flavour. That is the great delusion of you would-be advanced satirists; you imagine you can sit down comfortably for a couple of decades saying daring and startling things about the age you live in, which, whatever other defects it may have, is certainly not standing still. The whole of the Sherard Blaw school of discursive drama suggests, to my mind, Early Victorian furniture in a travelling circus. However, you will always have relays of people from the suburbs to listen to the Mocking Bird of yesterday, and sincerely imagine it is the harbinger of something new and revolutionizing.' (*Bassington*, 176)

The image of Shaw's allegedly revolutionary and shocking ideas as a collection of shabby and cumbersome Chesterfields, sideboards, and what-nots being hawked around the countryside in a gaudy wagon is damning, but possibly less so than the suggestion that his audience, and his mind, are suburban.

Gibson reads the first character introduced in 'The East Wing', Lucien Wattleskeat, as a Saki dandy, but his name indicates that he is not. He has the narcissism and apparent languidness of Reginald and Clovis, but there are differences. For the youths, languor and ennui are affectations and side-effects of the company they are forced to keep, to be replaced by surprising energy when a hoax is underway. Lucien's laziness comes from his detachment and his detachment comes from his self-preoccupation. He is a more complete narcissist than Reginald or Clovis. He finds nothing nearly as interesting or nearly as valuable as himself. ' "I don't think I can risk my life to save someone I've never met or even heard about. You see, my life is not only wonderful and beautiful to myself, but if my life goes, nothing else really matters—to me" ' (*The Bodley Head Saki* (1963), p. 716). This seems like vanity and self-regard, and the reader prepares him or herself for a witty speech ingeniously defending self-interest. What follows, however, is not a manifesto of outrageous solipsism but a statement of fact.

'I don't suppose you can realize that, to me, the whole world as it exists today, the Ulster problem, the Albanian tangle, the Kikuyu controversy, the wide field of social reform and Antarctic exploration, the realms of finance, and research and international armaments, all this varied and crowded and complex world, all comes to a complete and absolute end, the moment my life is finished. Eva might be snatched from the flames and live to be the grandmother of brilliant and charming men and women, but as far as I should be concerned she and they would no more exist than a vanished puff of cigarette smoke or a dissolved soda-water bubble.' (ibid. 716)

This is surely a satirical subversion of Bernard Shaw's moral dialectic?

Notwithstanding the quibble about the status of 'The East Wing' as satire, Gibson's characterization of Saki's work provides a useful insight into both the stories and the novels. When twenty-first-century readers encounter Saki's *enfants terribles*, they are perhaps surprised to find that the bad behaviour of some of the younger boys is not, as we would expect today, an expression of rebellion against the values and beliefs of their parents' generation. We might expect the young son of Conservative parents in a small county town to dye his hair pink and profess Communism, or at least to lock himself into his bedroom, play loud music, and refuse to attend the declaration when his father stands for election. Saki's Edwardian boys are far less rebellious, if worse behaved. Their terrible behaviour is in support of their parents' beliefs and way of life.

Is it possible to extend the dependent dissidence of Saki's characters to Saki's writing as a whole? The fiction (and some of the political journalism) contains social critique and comedy. Which social changes, if any, the fiction advocates, however, is difficult to determine, since the victims of pranks and more extreme forms of revenge are usually punished for character faults and personal misdemeanours. Perhaps hypocrisy is the crime most often deprecated as ingrained at a social level, especially hypocrisy in relation to children. As the epigraph to Comus acknowledges, however, no remedy is offered, neither radical change nor social reform, only individual punishment. Eric Blair's dissidence produced the radical prophetic satire of George Orwell; that of Munro, whose background was so superficially similar to Blair's, produced only outrage and amusement.

The child victim, confined in the women's world of interiors and kept out of the wild is different from the *enfant terrible* who is an embryonic Clovis or, worse, Comus. Victor in 'Morlvera' is neither as frail as Conradin nor possessed of a mother up to the task of victimizing him (*Toys*, p. 209–18). All he does is throw a doll under the wheels of a carriage. Hyacinth, in the story of that name in the same collection, is a little horror who threatens to have three small children eaten by an enraged sow, but his threat is to be carried out if the children's father wins a local election and his loses. He is a (very) Young Conservative. Although his mother is hopelessly optimistic about his likely behaviour: ' "All that happened when he was eight; he's older now and knows better" ', he has an Aunt with no illusions or sentimentality about children. ' "Children with Hyacinth's temperament don't know better as they grow older; they merely know more." ' ('Hyacinth', *Toys*, p. 267). Like Hector as a small boy, Hyacinth looks angelic in his sailor suit and is described as 'a delightful child' but with 'a strain of unbridled pugnacity in him that breaks out at times in a really alarming fashion' (pp. 265–6; this is reminiscent of the young Hector Munro). Whether or not he will develop the sartorial and gourmandizing habits of the older Saki youths, he will certainly believe himself to be a superman. He is a dependent dissident who contravenes the codes governing social behaviour not because he seeks radical social change but in order to uphold the social structure.

Not all the children are dandies in the making; some of them are even girls. Where the boys are destructive or aggressive, the girls tend to rely on the weapon of their imagination for their practical jokes and hoaxes. Vera, in 'The Open Window' (*Beasts*, pp. 50–5), is typical of this kind of Saki character, her name again deeply ironic considering her unblushing employment of anything but the truth in the romances she embroiders at short notice. Her invention of a triple tragedy, which leads a nervous young man to believe he has seen ghosts, produces no more harm than a shock to the victim's (Framton's) already frayed nerves, but she is not seeking revenge, only entertainment.

So we have in 'The Open Window' a powerful, clever child in opposition to a weak, neurotic, suggestible adult [. . .] Vera's romance is a clever practical joke of the highest calibre—without wires, strings, or mechanical contraptions. If, once we are initiated, the story appeals to us, if we laugh or feel any satisfaction at Framton Nuttel's hasty exodus, we are most likely participating in a fantasy that is peculiar to the mind of a child, and particularly a frustrated child, who is powerless to resist the encroachments or dictates of a cruel or boring adult world.[38]

This entertainment comes at the expense of an adult and, as Janet Overmyer says, is a form of revenge enacted by a child not against the adult who abuses or imprisons them (if only in boredom), the adult with power over them, but against the adult they can overpower.[39] Stahl finds wish-fulfilment fantasies and practical jokes widespread in fiction, and sees them as symptomatic of 'a fascination with the domination of the adult world by a preternaturally powerful child'. The *enfants terribles* of whom Saki's narratives approve have the power of imagination, articulacy, and confidence, but above all they have the luck to encounter a less powerful adult. Other characters, whether abused boy such as Conradin or henpecked man such as Mortimer Seltoun, who do not have a convenient fool at hand to gull or whose abuse goes too far for such diversion to suffice as relief, have another resource, a truly preternatural power.

Part of the strength of revenge stories such as 'The Lumberroom' is the ironic distance Saki maintains between the language of the narrative, which is the language of the adults, and the narrator's sympathies, which are clearly with the child.

Nicholas was not to be of the party; he was in disgrace. Only that morning he had refused to eat his wholesome bread-and-milk on the seemingly frivolous ground that there was a frog in it. Older and wiser and better people had told him that there could not possibly be a frog in his bread-and-milk and that he was not to talk nonsense; he continued, nevertheless, to talk what seemed the veriest nonsense, and described with much detail the colouration and markings of the alleged frog.   (*Beasts*, 274)

Saki conveys the satisfaction felt by a child in being right for once together with the self-defeating need to point out the fact to adults who feel that their infallibility should be unquestioned by small boys, and who have the power of unjust and unjustified reprisal.

The dramatic part of the incident was that there really was a frog in Nicholas' bowl of bread-and-milk; he had put it there himself, so he felt entitled to know something about it. The sin of taking a frog from the garden and putting it into a bowl of wholesome bread-and-milk was enlarged on at great length, but the fact that stood out clearest in the whole affair, as it presented itself to the mind of Nicholas, was that the older, wiser and better people had been proved to be profoundly in error on matters about which they had expressed the utmost assurance.

'You said there couldn't possibly be a frog in my bread-and-milk; there was a frog in my bread-and-milk,' he repeated, with the insistence of a skilled tactician who does not intend to shift from favourable ground. (ibid. 274–5)

Nicholas is a more robust child than Conradin, and more aware of his ability to be combative and to stage-manage combat, as the words 'dramatic' and 'tactician' suggest. When his adversary further abuses her power to conceal the failings of her arguments and herself, she is thoroughly established as an Aunt and a Beast (as opposed to creature). She organizes an expedition to Jugborough Cove for the other children of the house merely to debar Nicholas from it, and informs him that the other children will have a wonderful afternoon racing over the sands. Nicholas replies that one of the children won't enjoy racing, because his boots are too tight (later we learn that the tide was in, so there was no sand to run on). ' "Why didn't he tell me they were hurting?" asked the aunt with some asperity. "He told you twice, but you weren't listening. You often don't listen when we tell you important things." "You are not to go into the gooseberry garden," said the aunt, changing the subject' (p. 276). Nicholas is far too well-versed in the ways of adults to see this as a non-sequitur. His request for a reason gets the 'because-I-said-so' kind of reply that children detest, and which he meets with child-like and Sakian logic. ' "Because you are in disgrace," said the aunt loftily. Nicholas did not admit the flawlessness of the reasoning. He felt perfectly capable of being in disgrace and in a gooseberry garden at the same moment.'

The frog incident is mirrored when the aunt is imprisoned in the rain-water tank. Nicholas does not make an improbable statement which only he knows is true, he asks a question to which he knows the answer but about which he knows that the aunt has lied. He uses adults' sanctimonious attempts to instil a sense of guilt in children, and adults' desire that children should believe what they are told to believe only when it suits the adult, against the adult.

'Fetch the little ladder from under the cherry tree—'

'I was told not to go into the gooseberry garden,' said Nicholas promptly.

'I told you not to, and now I tell you that you may,' came the voice from the rain-water tank rather impatiently.

'Your voice doesn't sound like aunt's,' objected Nicholas; 'you may be the Evil One tempting me to be disobedient. Aunt often tells me that the Evil One tempts me and that I always yield [. . .]'

'Don't talk nonsense,' said the prisoner in the tank; 'go and fetch the ladder.'

'Will there be strawberry jam for tea?' asked Nicholas innocently.

'Certainly there will be,' said the aunt, privately resolving that Nicholas should have none of it.

'Now I know that you are the Evil One and not aunt,' shouted Nicholas gleefully; 'when we asked aunt for strawberry jam yesterday she said there wasn't any. I know there are four jars of it in the store cupboard, because I looked, and of course you know it's there, but *she* doesn't, because she said there wasn't any. Oh, Devil, you *have* sold yourself!' (ibid. 282–3)

Nicholas's pleasure in triumphing over the aunt, however temporarily, is manifest, but it is nothing compared to the almost sacramental joy he experiences earlier in the story when he finds his way into the lumber-room of the title. Worlds of contempt are contained in the information that the 'aunt-by-assertion' is one of those who thinks 'that things spoil by use and consign them to dust and damp by way of preserving them' (p. 279). For a child starved of colour, texture, and taste, for whom the luxury of any kind of sensory pleasure, even strawberry jam, is severely rationed, and who is kept to parts of the house which are 'rather bare and cheerless', the lumber-room is 'a storehouse of unimagined treasures'. Cathedral-like, it is large and dimly lit, with one high window. It contains everything a Saki child could want, apart from live animals; that is, as well as wonderfully coloured hangings and a fascinating tapestry, it contains representations, in default of the real thing, of things the child would like to see or to have: 'quaint twisted candlesticks in the shape of snakes, and a teapot fashioned like a china duck [. . .] a carved sandal-wood box packed tight with aromatic cotton-wool, and between the layers [. . .] little brass figures, hump-necked bulls, and peacocks and goblins, delightful to see and to handle' (p. 280). There is also a picture book.

Nicholas peeped into it and, behold, it was full of coloured pictures of birds. And such birds! In the garden, and in the lanes when he went for a walk, Nicholas came across a few birds, of which the largest were an occasional magpie or wood-pigeon; here were herons and bustards, kites, toucans, tiger-bitterns, brush turkeys, ibises, golden pheasants, a whole portrait gallery of undreamed-of creatures. (ibid. 280–1).

This representation of nature in default of nature itself stimulates the boy's imagination rather in the way that Bewick's *History of British Birds* (edns. 1797–1847) did for Jane Eyre, who did not enjoy walks in cold weather. Nicholas is deep in assigning a life history to a mandarin duck when he hears his aunt's voice from the gooseberry garden, where she hopes to catch him trespassing. Best of all the treasures in the room is the tapestry, to Nicholas 'a living breathing story' of a hunt, and a representation of a more savage wild than those in the picture book. Nicholas, as a true Sakian child, immediately detects the wolves coming towards the huntsman, and immediately constructs a narrative.

There might be more than four of them hidden behind the trees, and in any case would the man and his dogs be able to cope with the four wolves if they made an attack? The man had only two arrows left in his quiver, and he might miss with one or both of them; all one knew about his skill in shooting was that he could hit a large stag at a ridiculously short range. Nicholas sat for many golden moments revolving the possibilities of the scene; he was inclined to think that there were more than four wolves and that the man and his dogs were in a tight corner. (ibid. 279–80)

This imagined narrative becomes a revenge fantasy against a representation of an adult surrogate rather like the practical jokes of the empowered children. On second thought, however, after his desire for revenge has been appeased by his aunt's imprisonment in the water tank, Nicholas is more merciful: 'it was just possible, he considered, that the huntsman would escape with his hounds while the wolves feasted on the stricken stag' (p. 284).

Nicholas's response to the signification of the natural world in spite of the incongruity of its domestic setting is akin to Reginald's suggestion that a wolfy fragrance wafted across the footlights of a stage would function as an ostension of wolves and of the wild, in spite of the synthetic setting, in 'Reginald's Drama' (discussed above). There are similar incursions from one world into the other in two stories already touched on, 'The Stalled Ox' and 'On Approval', also from *Beasts*. In the former, the presence of an ox in a morning-room is painted by the artist, Eshley, and that representation of a real incongruous juxtaposition inspires him to represent imagined ones. This marks a turning-point in his career. Earlier, Eshley had not found a market for his depictions of nature red in tooth and claw ('Turtle Doves alarmed by Sparrow-hawk' and 'Wolves on the Roman Campagna'), and had had to '[climb] back into grace and the public gaze' with representations of unthreatening, farmed animals ('A Shaded Nook where Drowsy Milkers Dream'; 'Where the Gad-Flies Cease from Troubling'; 'The Haven of the Herd') (p. 221). His new painting, 'Ox in a Morning-room, late Autumn', showing a farm animal bringing chaos to a domestic interior leads to representations of wild animals bringing chaos to other ordered domestic spaces. Two years later, the Royal Academy is 'thankful [. . .] to give a conspicuous position on its walls to his large canvas "Barbary Apes Wrecking a Boudoir" ' (p. 228). Why the public will buy sentimental paintings of farm animals chewing cud in picturesque farmland, will not buy paintings of predators hunting for prey in the wild, but will buy paintings of wild animals in domestic interiors is not explained in the story. Presumably the public likes its wildness well diluted; at the remove of artistic representation and away from its natural setting. Though the apes are destructive, they are not killing or eating anything or anybody.

Rather than providing a window into a colourful and exciting world for a confined child, these representations provide a regular healthy profit for a commercially minded and popular English painter ('The Stalled Ox') and (through the misunderstanding and cupidity of his customers) £1. 15s. for a Pomeranian swine-herd ('On Approval'). The incongruous habitat for animals in

Knofpschrank's sketches and painting in the latter story is London, but a London 'denuded of its human population' and left to 'a wild fauna, which from its wealth of exotic species, must have originally escaped from Zoological Gardens and travelling beast shows' (*Beasts*, p. 306). Both predators and prey are present in 'Giraffes drinking at the fountain Pools, Trafalgar Square', 'Vultures attacking dying camel in Upper Berkeley Street', and 'Hyaenas asleep in Euston Station'. These apocalyptic and desolate scenes are less popular than the interiors of Eshley's work, even though they suggest an incursion of the wild long after its presence would threaten or discommode humankind, and Eshley's paintings show animals causing considerable disruption and inconvenience. The point seems to be that Knofpschrank's animals are neither anthropomorphized nor made comical, and that he represents a vision of the wild's revenge on or ultimate triumph over humanity in its escape from the unnatural cages in which humankind has confined it, and its reclamation of the landscapes humankind has similarly confined in concrete.

These are all of course representations of representations, but the wolfy fragrance and the wolves attacking wapiti on the steps of the Athenaeum Club clearly function as signifiers of the wild, and indicate in their removedness a relationship obstructed or perverted which in the 'man that wolves have sniffed at' remains pure and direct. To watch performing wolves in a circus-show is appalling; to encounter lion and wolf cubs in a zoo or a travelling menagerie is acceptable, but not ideal; to have pet tiger-kittens and wolf cubs is second-best; to hunt and be hunted is best of all.

As well as solitary child victim and solitary *enfant terrible*, of whom Nicholas is a relatively mild example, there is a further variation on the disempowered/empowered child in Saki's writing: the team. Three children are far more effective, and far more daring both in the things they perpetrate and the things they demand, than the single child, but the device is used sparingly; most of the children who need to exact vengeance have been vulnerable from the fact that they are alone. The team in 'The Penance' (*Toys*, pp. 67–77) exercise power over Octavian Ruttle because he has a conscience and can empathize with the feelings of children, rather than believing that they shouldn't have any not specified by an elder. Since the team consists of two boys and a girl who have parents in India, and the crime which Ruttle expiates (thus becoming in the eyes of the children an 'Unbeast') is the killing of a pet, perhaps this is a wish-fulfilment story based on what could have happened had the Munro Aunts been kinder or more sensitive. It is significant that the penitent is neither an aunt nor a woman.

Not all children in Saki's stories are or call into being agents of the wild and/or Nemesis; some who might well have been victims of repression and abuse are also victims of the wild, such as the Toop child in 'Gabriel-Ernest' and the Gypsy child in 'Esmé', both of whom are consigned to the jaws of a wild animal (or animal-boy) without a narrative backward glance. As part of the homogenized mass of the working-class in Saki's work, they are uninteresting, undifferentiated, and insubstantial; mere (narrative and literal) fodder.

Saki was no more sentimental about his fellow artists than he was about animals and children. In addition to condemning Shaw's work, in the persona of Lady Caroline, Saki openly mocks Bernard Shaw himself.

A buzz of recognition came from the front row of the pit [. . .] It heralded the arrival of Sherard Blaw, the dramatist who had discovered himself, and who had given so ungrudgingly of his discovery to the world [. . .]

'They say the poor man is haunted by the fear that he will die during a general election, and that his obituary notices will be seriously curtailed by the space taken up by the election results.' (*Bassington*, 230–1)

One of a series of 'Heart-to-Heart Talks' in the *Bystander* (in July 1912) was ostensibly a conversation between Shaw and the German ambassador, except that the ambassador doesn't get a word in. The piece is taken up with a monologue on the theme of Shaw's fear that he will suffer the same fate as Shakespeare: 'My works will live for all time, but I, physically speaking, am mortal; fifty or sixty years after my death who knows but that a school of critics may arise, in America and in your country, and perhaps here in England, who will attribute all my plays to Arthur Balfour?'[40] Munro even envisages Shaw as having a special place in hell waiting for him which will torture him by frustrating his vanity, and incidentally prevent him from finding out whether his work does come to be attributed to someone else. In 'The Infernal Parliament', Bidderdale, who is just passing through Hell because of an error, and being given a tour by an urbane Fiend, is shown a room in which devils are pasting into a book hundreds of clippings of theatrical reviews. The book is to be the only reading matter available for the room's intended occupant. The visitor can't see anything very terrible in that, until he is told that the letter 'S' will be missing. 'For the first time Bidderdale realised that he was in Hell' ('The Infernal Parliament', *Square Egg*, p. 148).

There are no similar swipes at Wilde, who, born sixteen years before Saki and dying sixteen years before him, is the figure to whom Saki is most often compared. Wilde was a much more successful dramatist, and Munro admired and learned from him, but Wilde was not a better writer of short stories, dialogue, and epigrams. Many of Saki's epigrams have a Wildean ring: 'Scandal is merely the compassionate allowance which the gay make to the humdrum' ('Reginald at the Carlton', *Reginald*, p. 66). Some lines of dialogue cover familiar Wildean territory: 'This suit I've got on was paid for last month, so you may judge how old it is' (*The Watched Pot*, *Square Egg*, p. 220). At least one Aunt resembles Lady Bracknell. In 'The Secret Sin of Septimus Brope', the Aunt of Clovis, who, unusually among Clovis's family members, is given a name, Mrs Troyle (Troy, as in a stony, proud citadel? Toil, perhaps combined with trouble, as in *Macbeth*'s witches' chant? Royal, as in imperious?), has some wonderfully magisterial Wildean lines in an exchange with Mrs Riversedge.

'Dullness I could overlook,' said the aunt of Clovis: 'what I cannot forgive is his making love to my maid.'

'My dear Mrs Troyle,' gasped the hostess, 'what an extraordinary idea! I assure you Mr Brope would not dream of doing such a thing.'

'His dreams are a matter of indifference to me; for all I care his slumbers may be one long indiscretion of unsuitable erotic advances, in which the entire servants' hall may be involved. But in his waking hours he shall not make love to my maid. It's no use arguing about it, I'm firm on the point.'

'But you must be mistaken,' persisted Mrs Riversedge; 'Mr Brope would be the last person to do such a thing.'

'He is the first person to do such a thing, as far as my information goes, and if I have any voice in the matter he certainly shall be the last.'[. . .]

'I regard one's hair as I regard husbands: as long as one is seen together in public one's private divergences don't matter.'   ('The Secret Sin of Septimus Brope', *Clovis*, 251–7)

Saki characters' repartee and one-liners are matchless, however.

MRS. V. Harvest thanksgiving?
CLARE. Yes, it's one of our rural institutions. We get our corn and most of our fruit from abroad, but we always assemble the local farmers and tenantry to give thanks for the harvest. So broad-minded of us. It shows such a nice spirit for a Somersetshire farmer to be duly thankful for the ripening of a Carlsbad plum.   (*Watched Pot, Square Egg*, 204)

(Also see the lengthy extended remarks about Agatha's flower (dead leaf, brambles, gorse prickles . . .) arrangements, ibid. p. 206–13.)

The aestheticism which was presented as a daring and radical position in Wilde's work has become a fashionable pose and self-conscious affectation in Saki's. While Saki's writing shows an interest in eastern Europe and the exoticism of Russia, and even China, it is not as heavily inflected with Orientalism as Wilde's fiction and criticism, nor does it often adopt the cadences and syntax of pseudo-Arabic. Though his visual imagery is sometimes reminiscent of Aubrey Beardsley's illustrations (see the extract from 'Tea' above), it is hard to imagine Saki writing the whimsical and sentimental 'The Happy Prince' with a straight face, nor sustaining the semi-mystical, Arabian Nights quality of *A House of Pomegranates*. One feels that he might have enjoyed the 'The Canterville Ghost', but that he would have made the ghost's performances more theatrical and blood-curdling, and have given a different twist to the happy ending.

Rather than Wilde, the source of the occasional Orientalism in the stories may have been the late-Victorian and Edwardian fashion for Middle and Far Eastern exoticism which created another kind of coterie, and could more specifically have been supplied by James Elroy Flecker's *The Golden Journey to Samarkand*, which Ethel Munro gives as a special favourite of her brother's, though she said that he loved Persian poetry and Eastern stories in general (Munro, 91). It is not immediately obvious why the title poem of *The Golden Journey* would inspire anyone, though Saki makes it a pleasant diversion from a rainy October day for the Club Liar in 'A Defensive Diamond' (*Beasts*, p. 239).

> At the Gate of the Sun, Bagdad [*sic*], in olden time.
>
> THE MERCHANTS (together)
> Away, for we are ready to a man!
>   Our camels sniff the air and are glad.
> Lead on, O master of the Caravan:
>   Lead on the Merchant-Princes of Bagdad.
>
> THE CHIEF DRAPER
> Have we not Indian carpets dark as wine,
>   Turbans and sashes, gowns and bows and veils,
> And broideries of intricate design,
>   And printed hangings in enormous bales?
>
> We have rose-candy, we have spikenard,
>   Mastic and terebinth and oil and spice,
> And such sweet jams meticulously jarred
>   As God's own Prophet eats in Paradise.[41]

Where in, for example, *The Eve of St Agnes* or *Goblin Market*, the piling up of lush, succulent, and perfumed objects produces a sense of abundance and excess, or an atmosphere of oriental otherliness, in the 'Golden Journey' it reads like the inventory of one of Ben Travers's Bond Street shops. It is as if the author expected the concept of a 'golden' journey to a far away and exotic place to be sufficiently evocative in itself, so that the reader would fill in the textural detail.

As in Saki's stories, a woman's voice here calls the men away from adventure and travel to mundanity.

> THE PILGRIMS
> We are the Pilgrims, master; we shall go
>   Always a little further: it may be
> Beyond the last blue mountain barred with snow,
>   Across that angry or that glimmering sea,
>
> White on a throne or guarded in a cave
>   There lives a prophet who can understand
> Why men were born: but surely we are brave,
>   Who make the golden journey to Samarkand.
>
> THE CHIEF MERCHANT
> We gnaw the nail of hurry. Master, away!
>
> ONE OF THE WOMEN
> O turn your eyes to where your children stand.
> Is not Bagdad the beautiful? O stay!
> THE MERCHANTS (in chorus)
> We take the Golden Road to Samarkand.[42]

The poem comes from a play, however, *Hassan: The Story of How Hassan Made the Golden Journey to Samarkand*, whose themes seem to chime better with the darker side of Saki's writing. A woman who scorns a humble confectioner offers herself to him when he obtains the favour of the Caliph; two lovers forced to choose between one day of love followed by an agonizing death, or lifelong separation and forcible marriage for the woman, seem to choose love over life; having chosen their day together, the lovers are tortured to death while the man who begs mercy for them is forced to watch. Although the play was clearly written during Munro's lifetime, since Flecker died in 1915, Munro could not have seen it, because following publication in 1922 it was first performed in 1923. By then, Saki had gone on his final journey, towards Beaumont-Hamel.

8

The Unbearable Bassington

IT has been suggested that *Bassington* was not Saki's first but his second novel. In *The Galanty Show*, Montague Summers refers to *Mrs Elmsley* by Hector Munro, published by Constable in 1911, as by Saki, and the scholar and playwright Michael Connor published an article in the *TLS* putting the case for *Mrs Elmsley* as 'Saki's lost novel'.[1]

If *Mrs Elmsley* is by Saki, it is an aberration, since it is dull, melodramatic, sentimental, and a love story. The theme, lexicon, dialogue, and characterization do not seem at all like his characteristic style. In his *Bodleian* interview, published in December 1911, Munro refers to his first novel, which he 'hopes to have ready in five or six weeks' time' (though that of course may not have been true).[2] There are, however, two points which should be taken into consideration. The first is the hero's name, Colin Liddel, which has an obvious connection to the *Alice* stories which had influenced Saki in the past. The second is that when Munro was sharing lodgings with Albert Tocke at 1 Middle Temple Lane, a stone's throw away at 3 Pump Court, and on the same page of the 1901 census register, was a William Elmsley.[3] Nice though it would be to confirm the attribution through extratextual evidence, both points could of course be the products of chance; coincidences whose resulting confusion Munro might have enjoyed; and the textual evidence supports the view that Saki did not write it. The reference to the works of Shaw alone would seem to disqualify him, unless he was taking great pains to disguise himself (in which case he could have adopted a pseudonym), since Saki generally missed no opportunity to denigrate Shaw, and here his work forms part of the library one would expect of 'an advanced, educated woman'.[4]

Comus Bassington is too self-centred to be much of a dissident. He does not care enough for any system to protest or criticize or rebel against its principles, only against any infringement of his pleasures. His critique of society is only that he is not at its apex, and his breaking of rules is opportunistic and expedient rather than critical. He feels entitled to break rules that others must keep because he has the indelible sense of superiority of the Saki dandy, and because doing so is diverting. As a prefect caning another boy, he was upholding the values of the public school system by taking part in its system of corporal punishment. That he enjoys the caning for his own reasons makes him unpleasant, but not a rebel. Once he is away from England, in a place with no 'society' (in his terms) and no social life, Comus realizes how attached he was to a system and society, and the reader recognizes that he is a product of that system and society. With society had gone the opportunity to scandalize it and to keep tedium at bay. Without it, life shrinks to sameness. Surrounded by miles of unexplored land and countless unknowns, Comus is yet, in his terms, as Mappined as the animals at the zoo, and it kills him.

Where the covers of the short story collections have 'Saki (H. H. Munro)' the novels have 'H. H. Munro (Saki)', as though to indicate a shift of emphasis. Both of Saki's novels represent a break from the story collections, but in different ways. Both contain familir Saki archetypes and situations, but the anti-hero of *Bassington* is a twisted version of his type, and the hero of *William* is curiously diluted. In *Bassington*, while the Sakian (northern European) wild still exists intact, 'abroad' also features in two forms: sophisticated cities in which the more cosmopolitan English dawdle, and a steamy, unhealthy colony where those deemed worthless at home can be put in charge. In *William*, 'abroad' comes to England and threatens to engulf it.

Comus Bassington is less witty and far more cruel than Reginald or Clovis, but in some ways he has more depth of characterization, at least in part because he is allowed a relationship with a woman, his mother. Though the women in Saki's novels come off better than those in his short stories, and the female characters of *William* come off considerably better than most of the males, Francesca Bassington is guilty of the worst crime in the Saki canon: she is more attached to material possessions than to her son. Comus only very belatedly recognizes that he has some feeling for her, but as another young Pan figure he is exempt from the usual human attachments and obligations.

In appearance he exactly fitted his fanciful Pagan name. His large green-grey eyes seemed for ever asparkle with goblin mischief and the joy of revelry, and the curved lips might have been those of some wickedly-laughing faun; one almost expected to see embryo horns fretting the smoothness of his sleek dark hair. (*Bassington*, 30)

He is one of Saki's lords of life:

one of those untameable lords of misrule that frolic and chafe themselves through nursery and preparatory and public-school days with the utmost allowance of storm and dust and dislocation and the least possible amount of collar work, and come somehow with a laugh through a series of catastrophes that has reduced every one else concerned to tears or Cassandra-like forebodings. (*Bassington*, 19–20)

Maurice Baring, introducing Saki's novels for the Bodley Head *Complete Novels and Plays of Saki*, reports that 'an acute critic' wrote to him: 'Bassington is what Saki might have become and mysteriously didn't.'[5] Perhaps he is more like what Saki wished he was, or imagined he had been. The masters at Thaleby, Comus's school, think of him in terms of storm and wind. 'A man who has been trained to cope with storms, to foresee their coming, and to minimize their consequences, may be pardoned if he feels a certain reluctance to measure himself against a tornado' (*Bassington*, p. 32). When a form-master asserts that he could tame the boy, the housemaster exclaims: '"Heaven forbid that I should try," [. . .] 'But why?' asked the reformer. 'Because Nature hates any interference with her own arrangements, and if you start in to tame the obviously untameable you are taking a fearful responsibility on yourself"' (p. 33). Comus is thus clearly labelled as a product and force of Nature; powerful, amoral, inhuman, and beautiful. One of the masters mentions the name of a contemporary fictional character who might seem to be a touchstone for Comus and the other Saki youths, but is swiftly disabused.

> 'But what happens to them when they grow up?'
> 'They never do grow up,' said the housemaster; 'that is their tragedy. Bassington will certainly never grow out of his present stage.'
> 'Now you are talking in the language of Peter Pan,' said the form-master.
> 'I am not thinking in the manner of Peter Pan,' said the other. 'With all reverence for the author of that masterpiece I should say he had a wonderful and tender insight into the child mind and knew nothing whatever about boys. To make only one criticism on that particular work, can you imagine a lot of British boys, or boys of any country that one knows of, who would stay contentedly playing children's games in an underground cave when there were wolves and pirates and Red Indians to be had for the asking on the other side of the trap-door?'[6]
> The form-master laughed. 'You evidently think that the "Boy who would not grow up" must have been written by a "grown-up who could never have been a boy". Perhaps that is the meaning of the "Never-never land" [. . .]'[7] (*Bassington*, 34–5)

Saki's criticism of J. M. Barrie's *Peter Pan* is telling, since the *Pan* texts contain the sentimentality (especially in relation to mothers), whimsicality, and incipient heterosexual stirrings of tenderness for the female that Saki's stories avoid. The distinction between child and boy is also significant. Munro seems to have felt that he was a grown-up who had been and perhaps still was a boy, but that neither he nor Comus had many conventionally childlike attributes. 'An Old Love', written in 1915, perhaps describes his conception of real boyhood, which involves both play and actual fighting, together with a fascination with the 'romance' of war, but by the time that piece was published he was no longer offering Comus as an ideal real boy.

The narrative voice of *Bassington* dwells on Comus's athleticism and beauty, but the physical prowess is used for show and brutality, and the beauty is coldly inhuman. The boy seems the quintessence of youth; laughing and vivid; but unlike that of Gabriel-Ernest or the Pan-boy at Yessney, it is a youth doomed and damned.

The chin was firm, but one looked in vain for a redeeming touch of ill-temper in the handsome, half-mocking, half-petulant face. With a strain of ill-temper in him Comus might have leavened into something creative and masterful; fate had fashioned him with a certain whimsical charm, and left him all unequipped for the greater purposes of life. Perhaps no one would have called him a lovable character, but in many respects he was adorable; in all respects he was certainly damned.   (ibid. 30–1)

Comus might be named for a deity in a seventeenth-century masque, look like Pan, and behave like a force of nature, but he is human. As a central protagonist he cannot be a lightly sketched and elusive presence, and in a full-length novel Saki could not sustain a story about a faun or nature-spirit or transmogrifier without being relegated to children's reading. Without the supernatural power of Gabriel-Ernest and the Pan-boy, Comus will not stay young, beautiful, and removed from the necessity of social relations, but he is inhuman enough to have the arrogant solipsism which divides him from human love. Like Narcissus, he is a lovely boy adoring his own reflection, and that his reflection does not show horns fretting the smoothness of his sleek, dark hair only points up their absence. He lacks the generous friends provided for Saki's earlier narcissist, Reginald. No rich or fairy godfather or mother whisks him away to Paris or the Ritz, or Tir na nÓg, rather, an unmagical uncle ships him off to colonial Africa; the world of mortals, where he withers and dies. In a sense, Comus is another amphibian or dual character, but his natural side is corrupted, perhaps by the failure of the mother who made him like this either to adore him as a Pan or to love him as a person. Reginald's character owes something to the dandyism of decadence and the *fin de siècle*; he regards himself as a work of art which is worthy of the lavishing of endless time and money. Comus has more harmful pursuits than fashion.

We should remember that Milton's Comus is a prideful magician who uses his 'orient liquor' to try to tempt the Lady to join his life of idle sensuality and dissipation. In her *Milton's Puritan Masque*, Maryann McGuire suggests that Comus reflects 'the Puritan sense that the upper classes, because of their obsession with comfort and position, failed to fulfil either their specific callings as traditional governors or their general callings as God's righteous people'.[8] In Saki's novel, this is more true of Comus's mother.

In his description of Comus, Saki makes a distinction between loveable, which would be the product of character, and adorable, with its suggestion of *jeunesse d'orée*, which is the product of looks, vitality, and youthful arrogance. Comus may be foredoomed by fate, but he is also damned by the consequences of human actions; he is damned because his mother does not love him enough. Francesca's real love is reserved for her house (in which she has a life interest until its heiress, Emmeline Chetrof, marries) and its furnishings. Comus's vanity and self-interest, we infer, have grown out of his being aware that he is a commodity, once of entertainment and currently of decorative value, but valued at less than a Dresden figurine or an oil painting.

Given two opportunities to secure Francesca's possessions simply by allowing two women to find him loveable, Comus wilfully and perversely throws them away. Told to be kind to Emmeline Chetrof's younger brother, Comus beats the boy in a scene of particular viciousness. Encouraged to woo an heiress, Elaine de Frey, he behaves like a spoilt child. Elaine might have adored Comus, but when he constantly pesters her for money she ceases

to think she could love him. Francesca sees her home and possessions slipping away, and when she suspects that Comus expects
her to sell her most treasured possession, a battle-scene painted
by 'Van der Meulen', to support their way of life, she is horrified
beyond words. She allows her brother to find Comus a post in
a conveniently remote corner of the Empire. Utterly unfitted for
the job, without company, debilitated by the climate, out of his
proper habitat, Comus sickens. As his vivacity drains away, he
finally makes a human connection, or recalls that he once had one:

One person in the whole world had cared for him [. . .] But a wall of ice
had mounted up between him and her, and across it there blew that cold
breath that chills or kills affection.
    The words of a well-known old song, the wistful cry of a lost cause,
rang with insistent mockery through his brain:
    'Better loved you canna be,
    Will ye ne'er come back again?'
    If it was love that was to bring him back he must be an exile forever.
(*Bassington*, 299–300)

Incredibly, Saki manages to get the reader, or at least many readers,
on Comus's side, to the extent of willing him to win the heiress and
escape exile from his natural urban habitat. It seems that beautiful
boys are beyond reproach, and all should be forgiven any child
raised by an unloving and materialistic guardian.

    The London of the novel is both the only place where one
would not be bored to death, and a bleak, brittle world of
surfaces: loveless marriages; false friendships; rapacious women;
malicious-tongued old men; avaricious young ones; all fuelled by
gossip. Comus is the quintessence of London society except that
he lacks the hypocrisy of the other characters, which may be
his only redeeming characteristic. His mother personifies society's
materialism. 'Francesca herself, if pressed in an unguarded moment
to describe her soul, would probably have described her drawing-
room' (p. 10), a fitting setting for the possessions which have
become everything to her. She is surrounded and defined by

material objects. As well as a 'Pantheon of cherished household gods' (p. 15), her possessions are 'the embodied results of her successes, economies, good luck, good management or good taste' (p. 12). The military register suggests that she regards them as properly fought for and hard won; they are 'trophies'; though '[t]he battle had more than once gone against her' she had 'somehow always contrived to save her baggage train, and her complacent gaze could roam over object after object that represented the spoils of victory or the salvage of honourable defeat' (ibid.). That the most prized treasure represents a battle-scene accords with this, and we are told that the painting has come from Francesca's father's house as part of her dowry, which further reinforces our sense that she too has been a commodity bought and sold.

The narrative voice makes an inventory of Francesca's precious objects, and notes that Francesca is amused to think of 'the bygone craftsmen and artificers who had hammered and wrought and woven in far distant countries and ages, to produce the wonderful and beautiful things that had come, one way and another, into her possession' (p. 13).

Francesca's objects of desire are all handmade, and part of her pleasure in their possession is the idea of herself sitting in her exquisite room and receiving the exquisite products of many hours of (other people's) skilled labour. David Trotter finds Francesca Bassington the closest female equivalent to Soames Forsyte, who is similarly both obsessed by and identified with the material,[9] but while Soames includes his wife Irene with his possessions, he at least values her as one of them. Francesca Bassington fails to appreciate Comus even aesthetically. In a strange scene in which she rushes to the bathroom to scold Comus, she retreats hastily, embarrassed and clearly unwilling to see too much of him.

'You wicked boy, what have you done?' she cried reproachfully.
'Me washee,' came a cheerful shout; 'me washee from the neck all the way down to the merrythought, and now washee down from the merrythought to—'

'You have ruined your future. *The Times* has printed that miserable letter with your signature.'

A loud squeal of joy came from the bath. 'Oh, Mummy! Let me see!'

There were hasty sounds as of a sprawling dripping body clambering hastily out of the bath. Francesca fled. One cannot effectively scold a moist nineteen-year-old boy clad only in a bath-towel and a cloud of steam.   (ibid. 54–5)

Perhaps Munro could not scold a moist 19-year-old boy clad in a bath-towel and steam, but few mothers would have any difficulty with it. Comus's reversion to the nursery name in his cry: 'Oh, Mummy!', shows him caught out by his pleasure in hearing that his name is in print, so that, for once, he responds spontaneously and like a younger boy, but his mother still retreats as though he were an older stranger. Perhaps Francesca's inability to confront, still less appreciate, Comus's nude beauty is a sign of her Philistinism and a suggestion that her appreciation of her possessions is not aesthetic, but perhaps Munro simply could not imagine an adult woman in an intimate but non-sexual relationship with a young man. That Van Cheele in 'Gabriel-Ernest' is flustered by, and his sister must be protected from, Gabriel-Ernest's nakedness is similarly a sign of their deeply conventional bourgeois outlook.

The Bassingtons' social habitat is as strewn with the material as they are materialistic, or at least as materialistic as Francesca is, since Comus, though he borrows and spends freely, is less hedged about with objects than his mother. He lights on a silver bread-and-butter basket like a child suddenly enamoured of a glittery object useless to it, but he is not weighted and trammelled by things. Francesca is part of the world of 'getting and spending'. As Trotter points out, money, actual coin as well as wealth, is an important sign in Edwardian fiction and is used both literally and metaphorically. 'If the British race resembled a currency, then the most valuable members of the race ought to resemble its most valuable coin.'[10] 'Sterling value' connotes unfluctuating genuineness, but characters associated with small coins are often represented as having small souls. Francesca and her bridge cronies telling over the shillings and pence clearly reveal their characters and their relationships.

Lady Caroline's special achievement was to harass and demoralize partner and opponents alike.

'Weak and weak,' she announced in her gentle voice, as she cut her hostess for a partner; 'I suppose we had better play only five shillings a hundred.'

Francesca wondered at the old woman's moderate assessment of the stake, knowing her fondness for highish play and her usual luck in card holding.

'I don't mind what we play,' said Ada Spelvixit, with an incautious parade of elegant indifference; as a matter of fact she was inwardly relieved and rejoicing at the reasonable figure proposed by Lady Caroline, and she would certainly have demurred if a higher stake had been suggested. She was not as a rule a successful player, and money lost at cards was always a poignant bereavement to her.

'Then as you don't mind we'll make it ten shillings a hundred,' said Lady Caroline [. . .]' (ibid. 119–20)

The phrase 'poignant bereavement', associating loss of coins with loss of loved ones is particularly telling. Francesca occasionally gives away a coin, not to benefit the recipient, but rather as she might use a convenient tree to touch wood.

Francesca always gave a penny to the first crossing-sweeper or match-seller she chanced across after a successful sitting at bridge. This afternoon she had come out of the fray some fifteen shillings to the bad, but she gave two shillings to a crossing-sweeper at the north-west corner of Berkeley Square as a sort of thank-offering to the gods. (ibid. 135 6)

One of Comus's supreme acts of folly in his supposed courting of Elaine is to demand a silver sandwich basket belonging to her in greedy, transparently disingenuous terms.

'Swans were very pleased', he cried gaily, 'and said they hoped I would keep the bread-and-butter dish as a souvenir of a happy tea party. I may really have it, mayn't I?' he continued in an anxious voice: 'it will do to keep studs and things in. You don't want it.'

'It's got the family crest on it,' said Elaine. Some of the happiness had died out of her eyes.

'I'll have that scratched off and my own put on,' said Comus.

'It's been in the family for generations,' protested Elaine, who did not share Comus' view that because you were rich your lesser possessions could have no value in your eyes.

'I want it dreadfully,' said Comus sulkily, 'and you've heaps of other things to put bread-and-butter in.'

For the moment he was possessed by an overmastering desire to keep the dish at all costs; a look of greedy determination dominated his face and he had not for an instant relaxed his grip of the coveted object. [. . .]

'I know you don't really want it, so I'm going to keep it,' persisted Comus. (ibid. 105–6)

On hearing of Elaine's engagement to his rival, Comus returns the basket as a wedding present, with a jokey but dignified, face-saving note, and comes closer to the 'sterling worth' of the silver in his resigning than in his appropriation of it (pp. 204–5).

As has been seen, many of the encounters in Saki's fiction between the youths and other people are transactional and involve avarice and acquisition. The youths seem to cry: 'If you love me give me [the diamond tie-pie/dinner at the Ritz/a holiday in Biarritz].' That a mother should encourage her son to equate love with material generosity would be deplorable, but Francesca's refusing to exchange her precious Van de Meulen oil for Comus's keep (literally) is a transaction which should not have been made.

The society which the Bassingtons inhabit is, as Comus knows, 'an animal world, and a fiercely competitive animal world at that' (p. 59). When he is sent to a country where he is in close proximity to a world of real fierce animals, he does not fear and seems scarcely to notice them. They represent no threat to him because they could scarcely kill him more quickly or more miserably than his transplantation is killing him.

Comus is defeated by those aspects of Empire which the colonizer had been unable to subdue, climate and disease. He fails to be a Tarzan, a hybrid lord of the apes and the manor,[11] or even an effective civil servant. He might have been expected to have exercised the same gleefully sadistic power over those under his control in the colony as he did over those in his power at school, but the story, compressing his time abroad to one short section, has no reference to such episodes. Broken and dispirited, he seems to have lost his Nietzschean or Darwinian supremacy with his physical dominance over his subordinates and victims, and become instead a victim, of heat, sickness and the imperialist machine, but chiefly of abandonment.

In spite of everything, Comus achieves pathos. We pity him, sympathize with his loneliness and misery, and look for a reprieve. None comes, sentimentality is again avoided, and the narrative voice turns relentlessly to the agent of Comus's death. Francesca begins to dwell on the image of Comus, reprising the opposition of love/adore:

> the warm, living, breathing thing that had been hers to love, and she had turned her eyes from that youthful comely figure to adore a few feet of painted canvas, a musty relic of a long-departed craftsman. And now he was gone from her sight [. . .] and those things of canvas and pigment and wrought metal would stay with her. They were her soul. And what shall it profit a man if he save his soul and slay his heart in torment? (ibid. 311–12)

The woman who fails to love a fatherless male child is again the demon of the piece. Francesca, not Comus, is the unbearable Bassington. The final ironic blow, delivered by Francesca's voluble brother just as she has read the telegram announcing Comus's death, is that her precious Van der Meulen is a fake.

George James Spears would probably have disagreed violently with the suggestion that Saki achieved pathos for Comus and made his mother detestable, since in his 1963 study he not only put Comus beyond sympathy but also suggested that Saki was unable to create characters for whom anyone could feel sympathy.

> Munro can elicit indignation and raucous amusement but never empathy or sympathy. We may be terrified by his hero-villains and moved with a fascination akin to fear by their Iago-like machinations. Yet for their

victims, if we do not pour on the author's contempt, we feel only indifference . . . the over-all effect of his humour is one of disillusioned negation and embittered dissatisfaction.[12]

The victims of the youths' practical jokes are always barely sketched-in types and always, in the eyes of their victimizers, deserving of their fate, but the child-victims of unloving adults surely elicit sympathy, and the youths themselves, including Comus, as child-victims who have survived. Spears's suggestion that: 'we feel that at no time does Francesca deserve condemnation' and that to the reader 'she is much more sympathetic than Comus' seems to read against the sympathies and judgement of the narrative voice.[13] Yet C. H. Gillen, writing six years later, concurs. He finds Francesca a far more fully drawn characterization and as a character more to be pitied than condemned. He sees her moments of bleak loneliness in the park when she realizes how much she misses her son as a convincing and authentic representation of mother love, but surely the narrative voice indicates that this is too little, too late?[14]

Langguth suggests that the ending of *Bassington* is weak since it depends on a twist which might have been appropriate for a short story but which is too slight and contrived to be justified in a novel (Langguth, 208). Some contemporary critics, however, found the ending the book's greatest strength. Among the quotations from reviews featured on the end-pages of the 1924 reprint of the novel is the *Observer*'s declaration that it is one of 'the wittiest books [. . .] of the decade' and that it has 'a deepening humanity towards the end that comes to a climax of really disturbing pathos'. Also included was an extract from a review published in *Outlook*, a Tory magazine for which Saki was by then writing, which declared *Bassington* 'a great book', and declared that the review could not remember 'any book which has left us more saddened and more obsessed by a sense of dreary intolerable pain'.

Evelyn Waugh offers a longer and more judicious commentary in his introduction to a 1947 edition of the novel. For him,

Bassington has faults of structure not present in the short stories but characteristic of a first novel.[15] He regards the opening chapters as a false start. They should presage a series of episodes in which an *enfant terrible* would upset the plans of his mother in various ways, but of course that does not happen, and, for Waugh, the story really begins in chapter 4. He astutely remarks that the 'life of the book is lived within conventions more of the stage than of letters and already antiquated in 1912—the complete exclusion of sex, for instance'.[16] The world of Saki's writing is theatrical in that it is even more highly selective and focused than most other fiction. The focus is not on *minutiae* which could not be seen from the back of the stalls, as it were; any object in a town house described in detail is sure to be significant either for characterization or plot, and the descriptions of the countryside function as atmospheric backdrops. The novels do focus on characters' physical attributes to an extent, but the descriptions of figure and facial appearance are sketchy; more attention is paid to the things characters accrue; things needed for immediate gratification (waistcoats, oysters, paintings, tiepins, *marrons glacés*), and to dialogue. The stories shift from scene to scene like plays; the reader does not follow anyone from room to room or house to house; anything between the scenes is ignored or left to be imagined. Almost everything not significant within the scenes is also excluded. The stories echo their protagonists' sublime indifference to quotidian things, and Saki continues to employ that technique in *Bassington*. In spite of this assumed weakness, Waugh finds: 'its virtues are abundant and delectable'. Primarily, he praises the wit, which is

continuous and almost unfailing; there are phrases on every page which are as fresh and brilliant after thirty-four years (most cruel of all periods) as on the day they were written. 'Saki' has attempted and achieved a *tour de force* in limiting himself to the most commonplace material in its most commonplace aspect, in eschewing all the eccentrics which come so easily to English humorists, and the strong passions which are foundations of satire, and producing a work that is wholly brilliant.[17]

Langguth finds Comus without any redeeming virtue, even of degeneracy or interesting wickedness; he is simply irritating and self-centred. One brief episode, however, suggests that Comus can love, or could have loved. At an exhibition he comes upon a portrait of his mother. The artist has shown her with an expression in her eyes Comus has not seen for a long time.

It was the expression of a woman who had forgotten for one short moment to be absorbed in the small cares and excitements of her life, the money worries and little social plannings, and had found time to send a look of half-wistful friendliness to some sympathetic companion. Comus could recall that look, fitful and fleeting, in his mother's eyes when she had been a few years younger, before her world had grown to be such a committee-room of ways and means. (ibid. 182)

That Comus has seen the look as 'half-wistful', and only in 'fitful and fleeting' moments suggests that his early relationship with his mother was as a suitor and supplicant rather than a child secure in the knowledge of a parent's constant love. He mentally dates the portrait as capturing a look from a time when his mother was a few years younger rather than when he was younger, yet he is reminded that there was a time when he had thought of his mother as 'a "rather good sort" more ready to see the laughable side of a piece of mischief than to labour forth a reproof'. He reflects that their good fellowship has gone, but hopes that the old friendliness is still under the surface, 'ready to show itself again if he willed it'. Perhaps intending to take up the role of mischievous but not costly child which will again elicit his mother's affection, Comus feels 'that he very much wanted things to be back on their earlier footing, and to see again on his mother's face the look that the artist had caught' (ibid. p. 183). He resolves to marry Elaine and thus remove the cause of his mother's estrangement from him, and even to 'find some occupation that would remove from himself the reproach of being a waster and idler'. This is a large step for the self-centred youth so far represented. He reassures himself that there might yet be 'jolly times' ahead and, associating

Francesca's happiness with material things, promises himself that she 'would have her share of the good things that were going'. Almost immediately afterwards, he hears the news that dooms him, of Elaine's engagement to Courtney Youghal.

If Comus is the degenerate youth of the drawing room, Courtenay Youghal represents the degeneracy of the political sphere. The young MP is neither corrupt nor wicked; he is even good-looking and intelligent; he is simply a consummate politician; constantly self-promoting, ambitious rather than committed, self-confident, amoral, heartless. Perhaps a superman for his times. Well-groomed without being vain, single-mindedly self-seeking without being actively unkind, Machiavellian without being entirely devoid of sincerity, Youghal is an elusive character and a puzzle to Elaine, whom he pursues in rivalry with Comus. Trotter contrasts the character of Youghal with a heroine of a slightly earlier novel, who has 'a soul made of sincerity as a sovereign is made of gold' where Youghal 'does not possess the character or the convictions which would give his counsels a "sterling value" '.[18]

Bassington also contains another Saki archetype, the amphibious urban dandy/wild man. Tom Keriway appears almost out of nowhere, wrapped in two kinds of Saki glamour, that of the witty, accomplished sophisticate, and that of the lone hunter, and he functions as a model against whom Elaine should measure each of her suitors and find them wanting. He is the achievement of boyish dreams, his life boyhood games made real.

Tom Keriway had been a man to be looked upon with a certain awe and envy; indeed the glamour of his roving career would have fired the imagination, and wistful desire to do likewise, of many young Englishmen. It seemed to be the grown-up realization of the games played in dark rooms in winter firelit evenings, and the dreams dreamed over favourite books of adventure. (ibid. 141–2)

He has lived in Vienna, but also rambled through the Near and Middle East as leisurely and thoroughly 'as tamer souls might explore Paris'.

He had wandered through Hungarian horse-fairs, hunted shy crafty beasts on lonely Balkan hillsides, dropped himself pebble-wise into the stagnant human pool of some Bulgarian monastery, threaded his way through the strange racial mosaic of Salonika, listened with amused politeness to the shallow ultra modern opinions of a voluble editor or lawyer in some wayside Russian town, or learned wisdom from a chance tavern companion, one of the atoms of the busy ant-stream of men and merchandise that moves untiringly round the shores of the Black Sea [. . .] He seldom talked of his travels, but it might be said that his travels talked of him; there was an air about him that a German diplomat once summed up in a phrase: 'a man that wolves have sniffed at'.   (ibid. 142–3)

That phrase is crucial to Saki's representation of masculinity.

Like Saki, Keriway is fond of and uses horses, but is associated with wolves. He has been an adventurer akin to Richard Hannay (in John Buchan's *The Thirty-Nine Steps*, 1915) or Allan Quartermain (hero of a series of books by Rider Haggard published between 1885 and 1927), but those have happened in the back-story of the novel. When we meet him, even more than Yeovil, the central protagonist of *William*, he has been crippled by modern life. Illness and financial disaster have shaken 'half the life and all the energy' out of him and 'with something perhaps of the impulse which drives a stricken animal away from its kind', he has withdrawn to a secluded farm. Elaine meets him when a travelling wild-beast show, an echo of the menagerie which Munro and his friend Bertie had similarly met more than ten years before,[19] frightens her horse and sends her through a farm gate by which he is standing. Immediately he is associated with creatures which belong in the wild. The procession is loathsome because it tames the wild and blends it with the suburban. They watch: 'a string of lumbering vans and great striding beasts that seemed to link the vast silences of the desert with the noises and sights and smells, the naptha-flares and advertisement hoardings and trampled orange-peel, of an endless succession of towns' (pp. 144–5).

Keriway gives Elaine a lesson in the real nature of the country-side. She unthinkingly describes the farm as 'a charming little nook'

[. . .] which is 'utterly charming and peaceful'. Keriway replies that it may be charming but it is 'too full of the stress of its own little life to be peaceful' (pp. 144–5). Even the life of the poultry is epic:

their feuds and jealousies, and carefully maintained prerogatives, their unsparing tyrannies and persecutions, their calculated courage and bravado or sedulously hidden cowardice, it might all be some human chapter from the annals of the old Rhineland, or mediaeval Italy. And then, outside their own bickering wars and hates, the grim enemies that come up against them from the woodlands; the hawk that dashes among the coops like a moss-trooper raiding the border, knowing well that a charge of shot may tear him to bits at any moment. And the stoat, a creeping slip of brown fur a few inches long, intently and unstayably out for blood. And the hunger-taught master of craft, the red fox, who has waited perhaps half the afternoon for his chance while the fowls were dusting themselves under the hedge, and just as they were turning supper-ward to the yard one has stopped a moment to give her feathers a final shake and found death springing upon her.   (ibid. 146–7)

Keriway tells Elaine that no tragedy in literature has so affected him as one that he spelled out in words of one syllable, and three letters: 'the bad fox has got the red hen'. The line acted powerfully on him and he imagined the incident in a way both natural and artificial; a simple killing for food but also a 'tragedy'; an everyday part of country life and a dramatized, staged scene.

There was something so dramatically complete about it; the badness of the fox, added to all the traditional guile of his race, seemed to heighten the horror of the hen's fate, and there was such a suggestion of masterful malice about the word 'got'. One felt that a countryside in arms would not get that hen away from the bad fox.   (ibid. 148).

The reader might feel that the boy dwelt on the imagined picture to a morbid extent. 'I used to sit and picture to myself the red hen, with its wings beating helplessly, screeching in terrified protest, or perhaps, if he had got it by the neck, with beak wide agape and silent, and eyes staring, as it left the farmyard for ever.' He remarks that he has seen 'blood-spilling and down-crushings and abject defeat here and there in my time, but the red hen has remained in my mind as the type of helpless tragedy'. Perhaps Munro, usually all for the fox, was remembering a picture book from which he learned to read, or perhaps he was thinking of his pet Houdan hen, killed by order of the Aunts so many years before. Though Keriway as a boy empathizes with the hen, there is no doubt that he is also transfixed by the mastery of the kill of the hawk, stoat, and fox.

Elaine asks Keriway to tell her more about the farm, and his reply is given indirectly, alluding, suggesting, and leaving gaps where detail would have killed the magical otherness it seeks to evoke stone dead. The otherness is that of the land beyond the farm at Yessney, the wood on Van Cheele's property, and the habitats of the two old ladies in 'The Feud of Toad-Water'.

And he told her of a whole world, or rather of several intermingled worlds, set apart in this sleepy hollow in the hills, of beast lore and wood lore and farm craft, at times touching almost the border of witchcraft—passing lightly here, not with the probing eagerness of those who know nothing, but with the averted glance of those who fear to see too much. He told her of those things that slept and those that prowled when the dusk fell, of strange hunting cats, of the yard swine and the stalled cattle, of the farm folk themselves, as curious and remote in their way, in their ideas and fears and wants and tragedies, as the brutes and feathered stock that they tended.   (ibid. 149)

Keriway is reticent about mysteries he knows in the approved manner rather than voluble about things he does not understand as the foolish Leonard Bilsiter in 'The She-Wolf'. Though what he describes is neither a pastoral idyll nor a wilderness promising adventure, it is presented as somewhere magical and apart, and as somewhere and something appreciated in childhood but lost to adults. 'It seemed to Elaine as if a musty store of old-world children's books had been fetched down from some cob-webbed room and brought to life.' Keriway, having in spite of his years and physical condition retained the boy in himself, appreciates the countryside in which he lives, and sees its magic as well as the 'undercurrent of reality beneath its magic' (p. 152). Elaine thinks that he is content with his present and has put away desire for the excitement and adventure of his past in a far wilder landscape, but she is mistaken.

'You are a person to be envied,' she said to Keriway; 'you have created a fairyland, and you are living in it yourself.'

'Envied?'

He shot the question out with sudden bitterness. She looked down and saw the wistful misery that had come into his face.

'Once,' he said to her, 'in a German paper I read a short story about a tame crippled crane that lived in the park of some small town. I forget what happened in the story, but there was one line that I shall always remember: "it was lame, that was why it was tame".'

He had created a fairyland, but assuredly he was not living in it (p. 152).

Again, Keriway finds deep significance in a piece of childish language. The pathos of the second story is punctured by the triteness of the rhyme, which would have been similar in German (*lahm* and *zahm*), but the point is made: farmed land is better than town, but wilderness is better than farmed land. For this kind of Saki male, life after the wolf is a half-life. The turn from the wild to the domestic, or from youth to middle age, is a tragedy that leaves the once heroic figure crippled, tamed, trammelled, or wing-clipped. In the stories ('Judkin of the Parcels', *Reginald in Russia*, pp. 42–6, and 'Cross Currents', ibid. pp. 94–105), he is tragic-comic. In the novels he is just tragic. We are told that Judkin's story is the same as that of many others

who are from time to time pointed out as having been aforetime in crack cavalry regiments and noted performers in the saddle; men who have breathed into their lungs the wonder of the East, have romped through life as through a cotillion, have had a thrust perhaps at the Viceroy's Cup, and done fantastic horsefleshy things around the Gulf of Aden. And then a golden stream has dried up, the sunlight has faded suddenly out of things, and the gods have nodded 'Go' [. . .] And that man has known what it was to coax the fret of a thoroughbred, to soothe its toss and sweat as it danced beneath him in the glee and chafe of its pulses and the glory of its thews. He has been in the raw places of the earth, where the desert beasts have whimpered their unthinkable psalmody, and their eyes have shone back the reflex of the midnight stars [. . .] (ibid. 43–5)

This paean to Life as represented by the mastery of the speed and strength of horses could be Keriway's story, and in spite of the archness of the language of 'Judkin' there is an echo from '[h]e has been in the raw places of the earth, where the desert beasts have whimpered . . . ' to the wild places of the earth visited by Keriway and Yeovil, the men whom wolves have sniffed at.

'Cross Currents' opens on Vanessa Pennington, a woman with 'a strong natural bias towards respectability', which damns her, and who further, 'would have preferred to have been respectable in smarter surroundings, where her example would have done more good. To be beyond reproach was one thing, but it would have been nicer to have been nearer to the Park' (p. 96). Vanessa is another despised urban woman. This is a comic story and her admirer, Alaric Clyde, is to an extent a comic character, but he is a version of the Saki wilderness man, and in Saki's descriptions of the Wild seriousness creeps in even amid the comedy. Clyde's sense of honour compels him to stay away from Vanessa while she is married, and he is seduced by 'a more alluring mistress', the wild (p. 94). Clyde 'fancied that his continued shunning of the haunts of men was a self-imposed exile, but his heart was caught in the spell of the Wilderness, and the Wilderness was kind and beautiful to him' (p. 94). The description of Clyde's activities is a paean of the same kind as that in 'Judkin', except that it is a paean to a life currently lived rather than to nostalgia for one that is over. It could stand for Saki's Nirvana.

As an active and free young man, Clyde is far from being a broken exile like Judkin, but though there is no reason for him to suppose that he will ever have to give up this more exciting and fulfilling mistress, a chill wind blows across the description of his Eden.

When one is young and strong and unfettered the wild earth can be very kind and very beautiful. Witness the legion of men who were once young and unfettered and now eat out their souls in dustbins, because, having erstwhile known and loved the Wilderness, they broke from her thrall and turned aside into beaten paths.   (ibid. 94–5)

Unusually for an adult Saki male, Clyde survives marriage to the widowed Vanessa more or less intact. He manages it more through benign neglect than intent; he is simply too preoccupied to allow her to become important. He does not allow her to suck him into Surrey and the West End; he remains faithful to the wilderness, and she is induced to run off with another man. The comedy comes when they are all captured by the same Kurdish brigands. Clyde is poorly guarded, and 'his wilder, truer love was calling to him with a hundred voices from beyond the village bounds', so he slips away and resumes his love-affair with the Wilderness in the 'congenial solitudes of the Gobi Desert' (pp. 104–5). The wild always comes before women in Saki's writing. Clyde leaves Vanessa to notoriety, release, and a job as a cook in a West End club which, she reflects, is at least near the Park.

Jonathan Rutherford suggests that '[w]hite, English masculinity is in deep confusion over its history and identity. The legacy of Victorian public life and civic virtue has been reduced to detritus . . . but we still cling to its imperial myths; preserving in stone and memory its homoerotic, martial fantasies of an English manliness which once bestrode the globe.'[20] Saki's homoerotic martial fantasies seem to begin from the point at which this 'manliness' is faltering in its confidence.

Having stirred Elaine's imagination and her sensuality, Keriway vanishes from *Bassington*. Evelyn Waugh regarded the section as a fault in the novel's construction: 'an inexplicable interlude in chapter eight which only serves to arouse unfulfilled expectations in chapter fifteen. (Surely the mysterious Keriway will reappear in Vienna? But no.)'[21] Had this been a conventional, heterosexual romance, perhaps Keriway would have reappeared as the true love who would save Elaine from a society marriage. Had it been a conventional novel of Empire, perhaps he would have appeared as the true hero who would teach Comus how to hunt and shoot and kill, and have exciting homoerotic adventures. But *Bassington* is neither, and Keriway disappears.

Saki depicts men whom wolves have sniffed at, but neither he nor his characters seem entirely at home in the wilderness any more than they are entirely at home in the West End. Characters, like Munro himself, contemplate having wild animals as pets; the countryside is not described minutely, particularly, or very often as though the narrator were in it; none of the central human characters ever stays away from the city entirely and by choice (though Clyde leaves it as soon as possible), apart from the stereotypes of rustics, stuck in brooding, claustrophobic wolds and wealds. The 'real' countryside is present, but often it is of the mind, of the theatre, or of the zoo. Even more characteristic of a Saki man, perhaps, than Keriway is Mortimer Seldoun in 'The Music on the Hill': 'You will never get Mortimer to go [away from London]' his mother had said carpingly, 'but if he once goes he'll stay; Yessney throws almost as much a spell over him as Town does' ('The Music on the Hill', *Clovis*, p. 150). Seldoun's wife Sylvia watches 'the Jermyn-Street-look' fade from his eyes as they reach the country manor. He is a reverse amphibian, happy in neither habitat.

Evelyn Waugh's introduction to the Uniform Edition of *Bassington* sees it as prophetic of the war to come.

It is impossible in reading *The Unbearable Bassington* at this date to avoid a prophetic and allegorical interpretation which cannot have been consciously present to the author. It was 1912. Comus had only to wait two years to find full employment for all his talents. He was cannon-fodder in a time of peace. And it is impossible, now, not to see Francesca as a type of the English civilization which sends its sons to death for a home whose chief ornament turns out, too late, to be spurious.[22]

Like Comus, Saki had only to wait two years for employment and to send himself to death for his home, and only one year for a novel which made that point more explicitly.

9

When William Came

LIKE *Bassington, William* has its share of unhappy amphibians, and
its author was soon to be more than ever one of them. The book
was published a few weeks after Munro's reminder to his publisher
of the mortality of Kaisers, and in November received favourable
reviews and a letter of warm approbation from Field Marshal Earl
Roberts, which Munro copied and sent to John Lane. It is dated 8
January 1914.

Dear Sir

I have just now seen your book 'When William Came' and must tell you
how much interested I have been by it and how thoroughly I approve
the moral it teaches. I hope the book will be widely read and generally
appreciated as it deserves to be.

Yours very truly

Roberts[1]

The novel also received high praise of another kind; it was imitated,
by Noël Coward. 'The idea of England being occupied by Germany,
which I shamelessly borrowed for my play *Peace in Our Time* must
have been fairly startling to the upper-middle-class complacency
of 1912.'[2] Coward had fallen joyfully into Saki's writing at the
age of 15, in 1915, during a stay at the Rutland country house of
Mrs Astley Cooper. There, 'lying on a round table in the hall', he
found a copy of *Beasts and Super-Beasts*. He took the book up to
his bedroom, 'opened it casually and was unable to go to sleep
until I had finished it'.[3] Introducing the Penguin *Complete Saki* in

1967, Coward acknowledges that Saki was one of the two most significant influences on his career (the other was E. Nesbit),[4] and asserts that in the intervening fifty-two years neither Saki's 'verbal adroitness' nor 'the brilliance of his wit' had lost its appeal.

Many writers who raise youthful minds to a high pitch of enthusiasm are liable, when re-read in the cold remorseless light of middle age, to lose much of their original magic. The wit seems laboured and the language old-fashioned. Saki does not belong to this category. His stories and novels appear as delightful and, to use a much abused word, sophisticated, as they did when he first published them.[5]

William evidently also inspired the title of Martin Hawkins's *When Adolf Came* (1943), an imagined German occupation of the Second World War. Evelyn Waugh's depiction of upper- and upper-middle-class young men faced with war surely also owes something to *William?* Charles Ryder in *Brideshead Revisited* (1948) sets aside art and the enjoyment of privilege to fight for his country, though of course he has come to care about and to be willing to fight for the preservation of not just England but also religious faith. Ivor Claire, in *Officers and Gentlemen* (1955), on the other hand, remains true to his self-centred narcissism, and cracks.

Lambert called *William* a study in the decay of moral fibre. The *Morning Post* reviewer called it 'Mr Munro's first novel with a purpose', and, perhaps conflating Comus Bassington's cane with the symbol of comedy, announced that the author's 'jester's bauble has become a whip, and every stroke tells' (End-papers, *Bassington*; (repr. 1924)). Given that many of Saki's short stories centre on revenge or punishment; the cruel, unkind, fatuous, self-important, or self-aggrandizing getting their come-uppance, one would expect a war novel to depict the enemy as monstrous and evil, and the home nation as the agent of Nemesis. In *William*, however, the Germans, though bourgeois and philistine, are not evil, and the British have not initiated hostilities. The enemy is guilty only of invading and sequestrating British property (though of course that is represented as so appalling as to be almost unthinkable).

The purpose of the whip strokes appears to be to jolt the jester's countrymen from slumber.

This is unlike a number of the other war conspiracy and anti-German fictions of the time.[6] William Tufnell Le Queux (like Munro a foreign correspondent who reported on the Balkan troubles) produced numerous pulp fiction stories warning of the perfidy, sneakiness, cunning, and ruthlessness of the Germans, and, most famously, *The Invasion of 1910: With A Full Account of the Siege of London* (1906). In Robert Erskine Childers' *The Riddle of the Sands* (1903) and John Buchan's *The Thirty-Nine Steps* (1915) dark plots are afoot, and spies have deeply infiltrated British society. In Frances Hodgson Burnett's *The Head of the House of Coome* (1922) and its sequel *Robin* (1922) (both published after the First World War but set in the years before and during the war), Germans are brutal, ruthless, and evil. They disguise themselves as governesses and respectable gentlemen, and plot not only to invade the country, but to kidnap and rape its innocent girls. Invasion novels were common enough to spawn parodies, such as P. G. Wodehouse's *The Swoop! Or How Clarence Saved England: A Tale of the Great Invasion* (1909).

The novel opens on a vision of an England in which complacency and liberal thinking have diluted the qualities of the people who were once unquestioningly confident of their fitness to be rulers of half the world. English youth has become effete and apathetic, the absence of national service has robbed the nation of its gym and proper outlet for aggression, and what is left are 'men and women to whom the joys of a good gallop or the love of a stricken fatherland were as letters in an unknown alphabet' (*William*, 122). Long-standing peace and unshakeable belief in the invincibility of the Empire have led to the disbanding of the Royal Navy and a careless indifference to the growing power of Germany. The result is that the once-great Britain has become a colony of the Habsburg Empire. The author who had made Reginald say 'I forget what he was—something in the City, where the patriotism comes from' ('Reginald on Worries', *Reginald*, 52) had appointed himself patriot-in-chief.

Lorene Birden finds Germanophobia in Saki's writing, but whether this is specifically hatred of Germany or contempt for any nation not British and fear of any nation threatening Britishness is unclear.[7] Birden demonstrates that the apparently superficial story, 'A Matter of Sentiment', stages a house-party of gamblers trying to decide which horses to back in the Derby, and finding comical ways to conceal their betting from a disapproving hostess, to dramatize the English attitude towards Germany in 1911, the year the story was published.[8] It is therefore a kind of prelude to *William*, though the latter emphasizes that the public were not enough concerned about the threat of German invasion.

In 'A Matter of Sentiment' it is revealed that the censorious anti-gambling Lady Susan had not only made a bet but had won. She explains that she was tempted by the name of the horse, Sadowa. ' "You see, I was always mixed up with the Franco-German war; I was married on the day that the war was declared, and my eldest child was born the day that peace was signed, so anything connected with the war has always interested me" ' (*Clovis*, pp. 248–9). Birden suggests that Lady Susan 'marks the transition of Saki's perceptions from appreciation, to doubt, to alarm, an alarm for England's lack of preparation'.[9] That Lady Susan immediately notices the name 'Sadowa', which she explains was one of the battles of the Franco-German war,[10] though we infer that she does not take a great interest in world affairs generally, represents a British obsession. 'Just as Lady Susan's bet is "a matter of sentiment", swaying her from her usual judgments, so any rumor about Germany would sway popular sentiment or opinion at times, creating uproars and possibly influencing political decisions.'[11] Birden points out that in 1911 there were a number of distractions from 'the German question', including the Parliament Bill, national insurance, women's suffrage, and the Coronation, but that it was always an undercurrent.[12] 'Lady Susan's feeling of being "mixed up" with the Prussians is a microcosmic representation of the country's Germanic barometer. However, her connection with the [German] Empire is unequivocally positive: it is associated with marriage, family, and financial gain, three high Victorian values still enduring in the Edwardian age.' In spite of these positive associations, Birden argues that the inclusion of this connection marks the beginning of Saki's absorption with the German question, and reflects the 'real paranoia present in the English mind at the time'.

Britain (though Birden tends to use 'England') was not irrevocably aligned with France and against Germany in 1911; like the house-party guests, the country had a choice of nations it could back, any one of which might emerge as the winner. Though there was a notional Anglo-French alliance against Germany, Anglo-German negotiations continued until stopped by Agadir. Though Lloyd George was Germanophile, Sir Edward Grey was Germanophobic.[13] The countries' convoluted and secretive negotiations are mimicked in the story by the house-party guests each fancying a different runner, each receiving a tip through a chain of possibly unreliable sources, and all being furtively informed by the butler that there is a sure winner, which loses.

That Sadowa was not a battle in the Franco-Prussian war but part of the preceding Prussian war against Austria, Birden interprets in two ways. The first is artistic licence: 'because Sadowa was an easy victory for Prussia, and thus a presage of the growing might of this new power. Sadowa, more than the French conflict, can be considered the real source of British fear of the Germans'.[14] The second is Saki's habitual mockery of the ignorance of the upper classes, but even this has deeper implications. 'Given that Saki's main concern in the opposition of the two countries is England's lack of knowledge, foresight, and preparation, this shift and its implied accusation of ignorance constitute a subtler version of the criticism that is to come in *When William Came*.'

When Saki returns to the Derby in 'A Bread and Butter Miss' (*Toys*, 87–95) it is again an 'open' race with many contenders, and again a cast of Saki characters, including Bertie van Tahn, is gathered at a house-party, wondering where to place their respective bets. This time, the clue to the name of the winner is not a matter of sentiment but a dream. Lola Pevensey dreams on two consecutive nights that the winner is a horse called Bread and Butter, whose jockey's colours include lemon. Lola omits the detail that it is a brown horse, and her fellow guests' bets are consequently divided between Nursery Tea and Le Five O'Clock. When the omission is discovered, the dream is revealed to have been accurately prophetic, but its interpreter flawed. Typically, it is the Saki dandy youth who is awake to the signification of costume and colour.

'Merciful Heaven! Doesn't brown bread and butter with a sprinkling of lemon in the colours suggest anything to you?' raged Bertie (*Toys*, p. 95).

Lola retires to her room, unable to face the 'universal looks of reproach directed at her when Whitebait was announced winner at the comfortable price of fourteen to one' (ibid.).[15] Saki returns to a similar scenario and a similar cast of characters, but has no further need for embedded prophecy and social satire.

A number of characters in *William* are variations on the types of the stories. Ronnie Storre and to a lesser extent Tony Luton are members of a subgroup of the Saki *kouros* or ephebe found in 'Adrian', the attractive but ultimately treacherous working-class young man. In *William*, they represent the degeneracy of both the lower classes (ruthless users and social climbers) and the upper (society women use them to fill empty lives). Their energy (a Yeatsian passionate intensity) is contrasted with the vapidity and languor of the superannuated dandy, the exhaustion of the man whom wolves have sniffed at, and the self-exculpating inertia of the working-class masses. Langguth regards Percival Plarsey as a

Reginald who has committed the crime of reaching middle age. He suggests that where *Bassington* had killed the aspect of Munro that had generated his best work, in *William* 'Munro exhumes the corpse to defile it' (Langguth, p. 230). Plarsey is certainly vain, self-centred, and affected, but he is fatuous, commonplace, and boring; perhaps a *faux* rather than a faded Clovis. Equally at home in Vienna and Budapest as in the forests of Siberia, Yeovil is the apotheosis of the Saki amphibian, or would be if he were not enervated by long illness. As with all Saki heroes, while he is young and vigorous he is at his best in extremes; only after his vigour has been drained by illness does he sink into familiarity and comfort. The one place where he is not at home is the middle-class, middle way, the suburbs and 'Garden Cities' of middle England (see the scathing description of modern villas and their inhabitants in 'The Quest' (*Clovis*, pp. 119–528)). Yeovil is a fierce patriot whose opinion on the occupation of Britain by Germany, and of those who tolerate it, is clearly the approved response of the narrative voice.

In the tradition of imperial adventure stories, Yeovil, as alpha male, ought to be a Scarlet Pimpernel who will rescue the English ruling class from the German enemies, or better still, a Richard Hannay who will avert, or at least postpone the war, not by promoting pacifist ideals, but by pre-emptive action. He arrives too late, however, when the war is already over and his own physical and spiritual state almost mirrors that of his country; his *virtus* is all but lost. Nor is he alone in his inability to act. Faced with a *fait accompli*, debarred from military service, forbidden to bear arms, those who have not fled abroad seem ready to sink into acceptance or apathy. There is no want of patriotism. Intense love of the country is represented in the characters who, unable to fight for their nation, either retire to the fastnesses of their country estates or create a pocket of England abroad. In *William*, these are represented by women, the indomitable Eleanor, Dowager Lady Greymarten (said by Ethel Munro to be based on a living person admired by Saki (Munro, p. 90), possibly Lady St Helier, since

Saki was a member of her circle, or Lady Charnwood, wife of Godfrey Rathbone Benson, who had been created Baron in 1911 and who became a friend) and Mrs Kerrick, a cameo in an interlude unconnected to the rest of the plot.

Although the novel's subtitle suggests that its focus is the capital under the rule of the Hohenzollern dynasty, a number of crucial scenes take place in the countryside. Lady Greymarten lives on an estate which, like Keriway's farm and the house and land in 'The Holy War', represents Saki's dream-England, even its name, Torywood, suggesting an older landscape governed by old-fashioned values. A lengthy quotation is necessary here:

Tall grasses and meadow-weeds stood in deep shocks, field after field, between the leafy boundaries of hedge or coppice, thrusting themselves higher and higher till they touched the low sweeping branches of the trees that here and there overshadowed them. Broad streams, bordered with a heavy fringe of reed and sedge, went winding away into a green distance where woodland and meadowland seemed indefinitely prolonged; narrow streamlets, lost to view in the growth that they fostered, disclosed their presence merely by the water-weed that showed in a riband of rank verdure threading the mellower green of the fields. On the stream banks moorhens walked with jerky confident steps, in the easy boldness of those who had a couple of other elements at their disposal in an emergency; more timorous partridges raced away from the apparition of the train, looking all leg and neck, like little forest elves fleeing from human encounter. And in the distance, over the tree line, a heron or two flapped with slow measured wing-beats and an air of being bent on an immeasurably longer journey than the train that hurtled so frantically along the rails. Now and then the meadowland changed itself suddenly into orchard, with close-growing trees already showing the measure of their coming harvest, and then straw-yard and farm buildings would slide into view; heavy dairy cattle, roan and skewbald and dappled, stood near the gates, drowsily resentful of insect stings, and bunched-up companies of ducks halted in seeming irresolution between the charms of the horse-pond and the alluring neighbourhood of the farm kitchen. Away by the banks of some rushing mill-stream, in a setting of copse and cornfield, a village might be guessed at, just a hint of red roof, grey wreathed chimney and old church tower as seen from the windows of the passing train, and over it all brooded a happy, settled calm, like the dreaming murmur of a trout-stream and the faraway cawing of rooks.

It was a land where it seemed as if it must be always summer and generally afternoon, a land where bees hummed among the wild thyme and in the flower-beds of cottage-gardens, where the harvest-mice rustled amid the corn and nettles, and the mill-race flowed cooled and silent through water-weeds and dark tunnelled sluices, and made soft droning music with the wooden mill-wheel. And the music carried with it the wording of old undying rhymes, and sang of the jolly, uncaring, uncared-for miller, and the farmer who went riding upon his grey mare, of the mouse who lived beneath the merry mill-pin, of the sweet music on yonder green hill and the dancers all in yellow—the songs and fancies of a lingering olden time, when men took life as children take a long summer day, and went to bed at last with a simple trust in something they could not have explained.   (*William*, 195–9)

This is a reversion to the landscape of the picturesque rather than the sublime, described in painterly terms, with careful attention to foreground and background, low, middle, and upper height, light and shade. The eye travels from meadow and woodland to farmed land and orchard as though there were little difference between the two, and the buildings associated with a farming community are weathered and mellow, as if organic. The reference to 'little forest elves' could be horribly twee; one can only hope that these are Saki-esque rather than nursery-rhyme types. There are a number of elements of the folk revival, '*Vanishing England*' movement: the opposition of the movement of the heron and the train, setting up a characteristic early twentieth-century privileging of nature (if regulated nature) over industry; the summarized folk-songs with their archaisms; the description of countrymen whose lives in this paradise send them happy to bed like children, trusting in something they could not name. This is not the village and these are not the villagers of Saki's stories. The reference to the song about the sweet music is audacious considering what happened the last time a Saki character encountered music on a hill, and there are other echoes of the stories in *William*, but 'There is a young tutor living out in these woods' later in the novel (p. 269) is a bit of a disappointment after 'There's a wild beast in your woods' ('Gabriel-Ernest', *Reginald in Russia*, p. 47).

Yeovil hungrily devours this dream-England, and does not need his Hungarian fellow traveller to tell him that it is a country worth fighting for (*William*, p. 198). The stranger produces a *j'accuse* of the English nation in insulting terms which the narrative voice perhaps could not use:

'a great nation such as this was, one of the greatest nations in modern times, or of any time, carrying its flag and its language into all parts of the world, and now, after one short campaign, it is—'
And he shrugged his shoulders many times and made clucking noises at the roof of his voice, like a hen calling to a brood of roving chickens.
'They grew soft,' he resumed.   (ibid. 199–200)

The metaphorical softening of the steel in British backbones is aligned with the softening of supposedly hard muscle and the relaxing of firm political policies. The Hungarian traveller finds softness in body, attitude, and acumen; in religion as well as politics. There is a hint that, having abandoned a tough, muscular Christianity and Stoic *virtus* in favour of a vapid and empty Anglicanism, the English would have done better to have reconnected to their land by embracing a Sakian nature religion in groves and forests with blood sacrifices (a religion of virile men) rather than dutifully attending services in comfortable pews with embroidered cushions, and taking sherry with the vicar. The English have learned to look on Christ as

'a sort of amiable elder Brother, whose letters from abroad were worth reading. Then, when they had emptied all the divine mystery and wonder out of the faith naturally they grew tired of it, oh, but dreadfully tired of it. I know many English of the country parts, and they tell me they go to church once in each week to set the good example to the servants. They were tired of their faith, but they were not virile enough to become real

Pagans; their dancing fauns were good young men who tripped Morris dances and ate health foods and believed in a sort of Socialism which made for the greatest dullness of the greatest number.' (*William*, 201–2)

It may be useful to recall that in *Bassington*, Comus's chief flaw is not his enjoyment of the infliction of pain but his want of ill-temper. 'With a strain of sourness in him Comus might have leavened into something creative and masterful' (p. 31). Mildness, apathy, softness, and forbearance are deplored. Without righteous anger and the willingness to act upon it in pursuit of revenge and redress, England will no longer be 'masterful'.

The enemies, then, are a weakening of male virility and Tory values. The Hungarian voices an attack on the movement through whose symbolic values Yeovil (and perhaps we) have just been observing the land. The Hungarian accuses the English of an insular lack of insight in choosing to trust other countries, but seems to argue for the return of an earlier insular mistrust. His advocacy of xenophobia is unpleasant but it contains a delightful satirical picture of the established English way to tame, 'civilize', and befriend foreign powers.

'They grew soft in their political ideas,' continued the unsparing critic; 'for the old insular belief that all foreigners were devils and rogues they substituted another belief, equally grounded on insular lack of knowledge, that most foreigners were amiable, good fellows, who only needed to be talked to and patted on the back to become your friends and benefactors. They began to believe that a foreign Minister would relinquish long-cherished schemes of national policy and hostile expansion if he came over on a holiday and was asked down to country houses and shown the tennis court and the rock-garden and the younger children.' (ibid. 202)

As in many eighteenth- and nineteenth-century texts, Eleanor, Dowager Lady Greymarten is metonymically related to her house and lands, and Yeovil is as powerfully affected in his understanding and admiration of her by Greymarten as Elizabeth Bennet is in her understanding of Mr Darcy by her visit to Pemberley. (This does not of course involve a romantic or physical interest; the only specific as opposed to general physiological detail of another character Yeovil notes in this episode are the laughing brown eyes and friendly smile of a young groom (ibid. 211, 214). Since the head of the estate is likened to the head of state, Lady Greymarten represents a kind of idealized benevolent imperial power.

Eleanor, Dowager Lady Greymarten, had for more than half a century been the ruling spirit at Torywood. The affairs of the county had not sufficed for her untiring activities of mind and body; in the wider field of national and Imperial service she had worked and schemed and fought with an energy and a far-sightedness that came probably from the blend of caution and bold restlessness in her Scottish blood.

For many educated minds the arena of politics and public life is a weariness of dust and disgust, to others it is a fascinating study, to be watched from the comfortable seat of spectator. To her it was a home. (ibid. 215)

That Lady Greymarten, emblem of romantic patriotism, is part of an endangered landscape and endangered species, is made clear by her being made a tortured spectator, at long distance and second-hand, of the moral degeneracy of the younger generation, represented by her granddaughter, Gorla Mustelford.

As Yeovil, from the back of his gallery, watched Gorla running and ricocheting about the stage, looking rather like a wagtail in energetic pursuit of invisible gnats and midges [. . .] a bitterer tinge came to his thoughts as he saw the bouquets being handed up, thoughts of the brave old dowager down at Torywood, the woman who had worked and wrought so hard and so unsparingly in her day for the well-being of the State—the State that had fallen helpless into alien hands before her tired eyes. Her eldest son lived invalid-wise in the South of France, her second son lay fathoms deep in the North Sea, with the hulk of a broken battleship for a burial-vault, and now the granddaughter was standing here in the limelight, bowing her thanks for the patronage and favour meted out to her by this cosmopolitan company, with its lavish sprinkling of the uniforms of an alien army. (ibid. 144–5)

Like Yeovil, Lady Greymarten is accustomed to being one of the master-race and cannot get used to life as part of the conquered.

As members of the master-*class* of English society, they feel their subservience all the more, it is suggested, and, it is also suggested, are perhaps less to blame, though more likely to accept the blame, than the lower classes. In one of a series of conversations with minor characters which enable Yeovil to think and to articulate his arguments, a young clergyman answers a question about how 'the poorer classes of the community have taken the new order of things'.

'Badly', said the young cleric, 'badly, in more senses than one. They are helpless and they are bitter—bitter in the useless kind of way that produces no great resolutions. They look round for someone to blame for what has happened; they blame the politicians, they blame the leisured classes; in an indirect way I believe they blame the Church. Certainly, the national disaster has not drawn them towards religion in any form. One thing you may be sure of, they do not blame themselves. No true Londoner ever admits that fault lies at his door. "No, I never!" is an exclamation that is on his lips from earliest childhood, whenever he is charged with anything blameworthy or punishable. That is why school discipline was ever a thing repugnant to the schoolboard child and its parents; no schoolboard scholar ever deserved punishment. However obvious the fault might seem to a disciplinarian, "No, I never" exonerated it as something that did not happen. Public schoolboys and private schoolboys of the upper and middle class had their fling and took their thrashings, when they were found out, as a piece of bad luck, but "our Bert" and "our Sid" were of those for whom there is no condemnation [. . .] Naturally the grown-up generation of Berts and Sids, the voters and householders, do not realize, still less admit that it was they who called the tune to which the politicians danced.' (ibid. 180–1)

The clergyman, a man of God but not of peace, is of the kind of religion that the novel evidently approves. He and Yeovil agree that 'the cruel mockery of the whole thing' is that now military service, which could have saved the country, will be forced upon the working-class populace when they no longer have a country to fight for. In fact, as a humiliating irony, shortly afterwards comes an announcement from the new imperial regime that the British subjects, having 'habituated themselves as a people to the disuse of

arms and resolutely excluded military service and national training'
have been deemed unsuited to the bearing of arms (pp. 187–9).

The symbolic emasculation of the British (in terms of conventional or stereotypical masculine attributes) has both led to their
defeat and is a product of it. In his compelling psychoanalytic
study, Christopher Lane asserts that Saki establishes but cannot
sustain an antonym between 'effeminate' homosexuality and militarism: "Though significant traces of Saki's aesthetic rigidity and
stylized self-mastery recur in the figure of Munro, the political
journalism and militarism that he produced under his own name
sought to redeem through (hyper)masculinity the effeminate and
urbane excesses of his nom de plume'.[16] Lane further suggests that
Saki's 'fascistic version of masculinity' exchanges 'the effeminacy
of Munro's assiduous dandies [. . .] for the "glory" of military
combat', but are the dandies effeminate; are they in *William* any
more weakened by political inertia than the non-dandies? Neither
homosexuality nor lack of enthusiasm for combat must equate
to effeminacy, nor does dandyism necessarily entail softness of
any kind. It is important to distinguish between characters the
narrative voice clearly despises as degenerate dandies and those it
approves as retaining strength, a combative strain of ill-temper, or
attraction to violence. Examples of the former characters in the
fiction include *William's* Ronnie and in the journalism, the 'Boys
of the Lap-dog Breed' ('Pau-Puk Keewis', *The Fortnightly Gazette*,
10 May 1915, quoted in Langguth, p. 261) the 'variant from the red-
blooded type' ('An Old Love', *Morning Post*, 23 April 1915, quoted
in Reynolds, p. xix), and the would-be actor who had the temerity
to write asking for Munro's help in obtaining work in a London
theatre in a time of war (letter to Ethel Munro dated 5 March 1915,
Munro, p. 100). As Lane says, in Saki's work militarism, rallying to
the defence of the nation, both invests that nation with a symbolic
unifying force and offers a 'cure' for the social ill of weakness. The
desire for war is represented as part of human nature: 'it comes in
the first place from something too deep to be driven out' as well as

habitual: 'the magic region of the Low Countries is beckoning to us again, as it beckoned to our forefathers, who went campaigning there almost from force of habit' ('An Old Love', Reynolds, p. xix). Going to war to fight for one's country, then, is a return to a natural and proper state of mind and body both biologically and culturally; a return to health; but the sickness is not identified with homosexuality or so-called effeminacy, indeed, Saki is clear that the 'Lap-dog breed' is sexless:

It is inconceivable that these persons were ever boys, they have certainly not grown up into men; one cannot call them womanish—the women of our race are made of a different stuff. They belong to no sex and it seems a pity that they should belong to any nation; other nations probably have similar encumbrances, but we seem to have more of them than we either desire or deserve.   ('An Old Love', Reynolds, p. xx)

Munro could be investing English women with the status of honorary men, possessed of allegedly masculine characteristics such as courage, strength, and endurance, but his emphasis seems to be the 'lap-dogs' ' lack of a proper (bellicose) boyhood than their possession of stereotypically feminine attributes. To introduce a biographical element for a moment, we should perhaps remember that in his sister Munro had an example of a bellicose woman who declared herself interested in and excited by violence. 'And the last words I called out to him were: "Kill a good few for me!" ' (Munro, p. 109).

Saki's short stories are populated by youths who are or have been boys and who are proactive, at least in the play-acting of violent action ('The Unrest-Cure', 'The Feast of Nemesis'), and the protagonists of two of the plays have courage and resolution enough to commit suicide, even with insouciance (*The Death Trap*, *Karl-Ludwig's Window*). One of the most beautiful and desirable Saki youths, the werewolf Gabriel-Ernest, is far from conventionally weak or soft or effeminate, though he is both sensually languorous and drawling. It is not difficult to imagine his fighting for England, at least as an extension of his territory. The horned youth in 'The

Music on the Hill' is misogynistic and an object of male worship, but, Pan-like, organically associated with the land, and in his way fighting to defend it. The Nietzschean Superman aspect of the figures of male homoerotic desire precludes their being placed in the 'feminine' position of marginalized or excluded from aspects of masculine culture, rather, they could be leading it. One feels that they would have no difficulty in taking part in military action, but that they might have a problem with military discipline.

Rather than simply punishing and excluding the dandy, as Lane suggests, perhaps militarism in Saki's work finds a way to offer him greater inclusion, albeit entailing a stepping-down from the superior position. The youths of the short stories and *Bassington* make a virtue of self-sufficiency, but they need an admiring and/or gaping audience, and yet have no real intimate, bonded group of the kind the romanticized comradeship of war and the concepts of common nationhood and common cause provide. Munro joined the army as a private but made reference in his letters to offers of commissions, and clearly thought of himself as among, but ambivalently of, the troops. Paradoxically, this being part of, belonging, also allowed for apartness. Munro seems to have embraced military life and military discipline as a vocation; to have regarded it as a form of *pieta* which would not have been fulfilled by the life of an officer giving the orders. Perhaps to have joined as an officer, one of his 'own sort', would have entailed an impossible whole-hearted sublimation of persona and a loss of the sense of superiority as an older man of junior officer rank in a larger chain of command.

William is a novel of empire in that it represents and reinforces the image of England as the home country invested with symbolic power, and the image of English people as proper guardians of empire. (In *William*, the English race is described as dethroned.) It also expresses the colonizers' fear of being colonized by an other which here is not the colonized subject but a competing empire.

The novel's title reminds readers of an earlier William who came, and both conquered and colonized the country.

Where many authors of imperial adventure fiction constructed a masculine ideal to oppose the colonial other, Saki here offers women. Lady Greymarten has achieved the Sakian ideal; she is equally at home in a capital city, amid political and social bustle, and in the depths of the country, and she is powerful and influential in both.

> In her town house or down at Torywood, with her writing pad on her knee and the telephone at her elbow, or in personal counsel with some trusted colleague or persuasive argument with a halting adherent or half-convinced opponent, she had laboured on behalf of the poor and the ill-equipped, had fought for her idea of the Right, and above all, for the safety and sanity of her Fatherland.   (ibid. 215)

As a political commentator, Saki would have been alert to every rhetorical device. His lexical choices and the nuances of his prose are always worth examining. Although 'Right' here probably means correct, true, and proper, the definite article surely gives a whisper of the political Right, while the use of 'counsel' and 'trusted' with Lady Greymarten's colleague and 'halting' and 'half-convinced' with her opponents makes telling associations.

Lady Greymarten and Mrs Kerrick are not quite the first positive pictures of women in Saki's work. Lady Veula Croot, who talks to Comus Bassington about his coming exile, is sensible and sensitive without being sentimental, (*Bassington*, pp. 241–2). Saki's expressed opinion of the women of England appears to have risen as his opinion of the majority of men fell, and he saw in the women the martial spirit he felt was lacking in the men. Even his positive remarks about women are, however, at best essentialist and at worst silly, and are often produced simply to put the younger generation of men, similarly homogenized, in a poor light. Maurice Baring asserts that Saki 'understood the English character, especially the English female character, and best of all, the English of the county families, the well-to-do prosperous men and women who live in the Shires and hunt in the Midlands and play Bridge in Belgravia'.[17] Saki specialized in instant snapshot recognition of a type through characterizing foible, but they are types; the Munros believed in types. Though there is more to the women in the novels than in the stories even in *William* they remain types, and it is the concept of a national type that Baring subscribes to here.

William's Mrs Kerrick is a type of whom the narrative very evidently approves. The similarity of her name to that of Bassington's Keriway marks a family resemblance, but it is used only once after it introduces the chapter, otherwise, she is 'the hostess', 'this lady', 'the mother', and, most significantly, 'the Englishwoman'. She is Saki's idealization of all those things, but especially The English Woman, the woman who, when her men are dead, wounded, or fighting, preserves a vestige of her country for which the next generation will be reared to reverence and to be willing to die for. A French visitor presses her to explain why she chooses to live in a remote spot with hardly any amenities or society.

'In all this garden that you see,' said the Englishwoman, 'there is one tree that is sacred.'

'A tree?' said the Frenchman.

'A tree that we could not grow in England.'

The Frenchman followed the direction of her eyes and saw a tall, bare pole at the summit of the hillock. At the same moment, the sun came over the hill-tops in a deep, orange glow, and a new light stole like magic over the brown landscape. And, as if they had timed their arrival to that exact moment of sunburst, three brown-faced boys appeared under the straight, bare pole. A cord shivered and flapped, and something ran swiftly up into the air, and swung out in the breeze that blew across the hills—a blue flag with red and white crosses. The three boys bared their heads and the small girl stood rigidly to attention. Far away down the hill, a young man, cantering into view round a corner of the dusty road, removed his hat in loyal salutation.

'That is why we live out here,' said the Englishwoman quietly. (ibid. 273–4)

Unlike Mrs Kerrick, remaining in the occupied homeland, and in spite of Lady Greymarten's example of energetic action, Yeovil as an exhausted convalescent, falls back into country pursuits and a comfortable way of life as to a feather bed:

He had ceased to struggle against the fascination of his present surroundings. The slow, quiet comfort and interest of country life appealed with enervating force to the man whom death had half-conquered. The pleasures of the chase, well-provided for in every detail, and dovetailed in with the assured luxury of a well-ordered, well-staffed establishment, were exactly what he wanted and exactly what his life down here afforded him. (ibid. 289–90)

In this section of *William*, England is once again invested with earth-magic.

There was a charm, too, even for a tired man, in the eerie stillness of the lone twilight land through which he was passing, a grey shadow-hung land which seemed to have been emptied of all things that belonged to the daytime, and filled with a lurking, moving life of which one knew nothing beyond the sense that it was there. There and very near. If there had been wood-gods and wicked-eyed fauns in the sunlit groves and hillsides of old Hellas, surely there were watchful, living things of kindred mould in this dusk-hidden wilderness of field and hedge and coppice. (ibid. 288)

Both earth magic and the other dream-England of farming, hunting, and shooting, however, are opiates.

He was experiencing, too, that passionate recurring devotion to an old loved scene that comes at times to men who have travelled far and willingly up and down the world. [The invasion] seemed far away and inconsequent amid the hedgerows and woods and fallows of the East Wessex country. Horse and hound-craft, harvest, game broods, the planting and felling of timber, the rearing and selling of stock, the letting of grasslands, the care of fisheries, the upkeep of markets and fairs, they were things that immediately mattered. (290–1)

Yeovil acknowledges that those devoted to this England and the pleasures of English country life must leave them behind for a more active, engaged life in order to fight for, if not that way of life, since it does not appear to be threatened with the same changes that have overtaken London, the ownership of it.

And Yeovil saw himself, in moments of disgust and self-accusation, settling down into this life of rustic littleness, concerned over the late nesting of a partridge or the defective draining of a loose-box, hugely busy over affairs that the gardener's boy might grapple with, ignoring the struggle-cry that went up, low and bitter and wistful, from a dethroned disposed race, in whose glories he had gloried, in whose struggle he lent no hand. In what way, he asked himself in such moments, would his life be better than the life of that parody of manhood who upholstered his rooms with art hangings and rosewood furniture and babbled over the effect?   (ibid. 291)

Forced by etiquette to accept a lift from a German officer that evening, Yeovil cannot bring himself to lift his hat in his customary salutation to the graves of his ancestors. 'Murrey Yeovil had found the life that he wanted—and was accursed in his own eyes. He argued with himself, and palliated and explained, but he knew why he had turned his eyes away that evening from the little graveyard under the trees; one cannot explain things to the dead' (p. 303).

Although the union flag represents the United Kingdom, in the 'Englishwoman' section of *William* it seems to stand primarily for England, both the land and the lineage which Yeoville wants to rejoin, but from which he feels his inaction debars him. Always a symbol and rallying-point, the flag is invested with greater symbolic power, evidently not only representing the country and its freedom, but also in a sense being that country, as British embassies abroad are considered British territory. The flagpole is incorporated into the function of the flag. The organic register used to describe it ('tree' and 'grow') suggests that the organic life of England and the English continues and the English resistance will multiply, while the adjective 'sacred' can apply to both the symbol, the flag, and the thing it represents, the country. Where the sudden dropping of the sun behind a hill revealed the werewolf; the beast (however desirable) within in 'Gabriel-Ernest'; here the rising sun is a part of nature's elaborate staging, a spotlight to shine on the symbol of all that is noble.

The four children who unfurl and salute the flag show that there is hope for England in its (upper-class) younger generation, and are precursors of the young boys who at the end of the story will restore the nation's broken pride. Mrs Kerrick, like Lady Greymarten, is the 'True Blue' woman whom Munro had encountered as a small boy in the mythical England represented in *Puck of Pook's Hill*, *The Wind in the Willows*, and *Johnnykin*.

'Whenever there are blue eyes and blue skies in dear old England, and while the blue sea surrounds it. And while there are hay-fields, and while people think with love of quiet days of the olden time, and while fairy tales are written for children—there will be Little Boy Blue.'

As she said this, Johnnykin looked into *her* blue eyes and saw in them the same sweet look as in the little boy's, and felt that she was to him what the Little Boy Blue is to all children 'in Summer when the days are long'.[18]

Finally, it is the youth of Britain, a junior army of Boy Scouts who show the way, or at least make a symbolic act of defiance which might be a beginning. The young boy as object of desire is replaced, or supplemented, by the young boy as soldier and hope of the nation.

A rally has been organized as a show both of strength (that of the occupiers) and cooperation (that of the occupied). The climax is to be a march-past by the Scouts. If even a third of the Scouts show up, the event will have been a success; it will have demonstrated that the younger generation has accepted the *fait accompli*. Any miscarriage will be a serious embarrassment for the new regime. A character remarks that: 'nothing has been left undone to rally the Scouts to the new order of things. Special privileges have been showered on them [. . .]' (p. 309).

The Scouts are to march in at three o'clock. As the hour approaches, the crowd becomes restive, but is controlled by the ubiquitous police and plain-clothes detectives. The reader sees through the eyes of Yeovil, watching the show from the back of the crowd as he had earlier watched the variety show from the back of the theatre.

And now a dull flush crept into his grey face; a look that was partly new-born hope and resurrected pride, partly remorse and shame, burned in his eyes. Shame, the choking, searing shame of self-reproach that cannot be reasoned away, was dominant in his heart. *He* had laid down his arms — there were others who had never hoisted the flag of surrender. He had given up the fight and joined the ranks of the hopelessly subservient; in thousands of English homes throughout the land there were young hearts that had not forgotten, had not compounded, would not yield. The younger generation had barred the door.   (ibid. 321–2)

The final, strongly visual, scene uses a powerfully evocative image; one flag which evokes two others, neither present at the scene and one purely metaphorical. The imperial standard, from which Yeovil averted his eyes when he passed it flying triumphantly over Buckingham Palace, now impotently floating and flapping, becomes a banner of empty pageantry and ignoble humiliation. Behind it are the union flag just as in Mrs Kerrick's garden, potently running swiftly up its pole and springing out into the air, and the absent 'flag of surrender' that we are told the younger generation has not hoisted.

And in the pleasant May sunshine the Eagle standard floated and flapped, the black and yellow pennons shifted restlessly, Emperor and Princes, Generals and guards, sat stiffly in their saddles, and waited.
    And waited . . . ,(ibid. 322)

The hopes of England and *William's* narrator lie with the English Boy Scouts, or red-blooded, blue-eyed, true-blue English boys. This marks a revolution in Saki's writing. In the short stories brown skins and dark eyes are preferred, and the Scouts are derided. Their quasi-military training is mocked in 'The Unrest-Cure' when they are (allegedly) mobilized and show considerably more enthusiasm when they learn that they are to assist in a massacre. The kind of taxonomic interest in nature encouraged by scouting manuals is cited by Clovis as having cluttered his memory to the extent of pushing out the difference between right and wrong ('Clovis on Parental Responsibilities', *Beasts*, 207). The attempt to imbue lower-class boys with middle- and upper-class values though military-type drills and outdoor activity (not just in the Scouts, but also through the Fresh Air Fund, the Lads' Drill Association, the Boy's Brigade, and other organizations)[19] is parodied in 'Reginald's Choir Treat' (*Reginald*, 41–5).

The militarism of *William*, with its call to arms and deprecation of England's failure to provide its young men with military service, contrasts with the mockery of German and Russian worship of military uniforms in Saki's earlier journalism[20] and stories. In 'Ministers of Grace' by coining the verb 'to koepenick', he inserts a sly allusion to the alleged German indoctrinization of blind obedience to men in uniform. Koepenicking is the replacement of an authority-figure with 'a spurious imitation that would carry just as much weight for the moment as the displaced original' ('Ministers of Grace', *Clovis*, 268). This is a reference to the affair of the 'Captain of Koepenick' ('Hauptmann von Köpenick').[21] Koepenick, or Copenick, was a small town near Berlin later incorporated into a suburb of the city. In 1906, an ex-shoemaker and convicted forger, Wilhelm Voigt, newly released from prison, needed papers to get work, but was caught up in bureaucratic procedures. He bought a second-hand uniform and in the guise of a Prussian army captain, commandeered a group of soldiers. Under his command, the soldiers took over the City Hall, seized the treasury, arrested the mayor; and confiscated passports, the men unquestioningly obeying Voigt's, or rather the uniform's, commands. In Saki's story, the authority-figures are politicians and newspaper owners, their replacements are angels.

In *William*, Saki seems wholeheartedly to embrace military values of conformity and obedience to authority, and the message of Baden-Powell's *Scouting for Boys* that discipline, out-door activity, and hygiene will develop boys of the right character, honour, and healthful strength to produce 'national efficiency' and to defend their country and their country's possessions.[22]

Saki's writing frequently associates war with boys or boyishness, and the loss of the desire for war with a loss of proper youthful vigour and red-bloodedness. The clergyman with whom Yeovil has a consoling conversation in *William* describes the combative tendency of working-class youths as a saving grace, and going to war as a cure for social ills. Deploring the loss of military service, he says:

'Every now and then in the course of my work I have come across lads who were really drifting to the bad through the good qualities in them. A clean combative strain in their blood, and a natural turn for adventure, made the ordinary anaemic routine of a shop or warehouse or factory almost unbearable for them. What splendid little soldiers they would have made, and how grandly the discipline of a military training would have steadied them in after-life when steadiness was wanted. The only adventure that their surroundings offered them has been the adventure of practising mildly criminal misdeeds without getting landed in reformatories and prisons; those of them that have not been successful in keeping clear of detection are walking round and round prison yards, experiencing the operation of a discipline that breaks and does not build. They were merry-hearted boys once, with nothing of the criminal or ne'er-do-well in their natures, and now—have you ever seen a prison yard, with that walk round and round and round between grey walls under a blue sky?'

Yeovil nodded.

'It's good enough for criminals and imbeciles,' said the parson, 'but think of it for those boys, who might have been marching along to the tap of the drum, with a laugh on their lips instead of Hell in their hearts.' (*William*, 184–5)

The army is the healthy alternative to misery and degeneracy for working-class youths, and at the time Munro was writing *William*, Scouting was seen as providing an ideal training for entry into the army and for obedience to the officer class.

Baden-Powell's aim was to recruit Scouts from the much maligned East End and comparably degenerate working-class areas of the larger British cities. His main constituency, however, belonged to a slightly higher class fraction which traditionally sought to emulate those whom they knew to be their betters. As Michael Rosenthal states in his history of the phenomenal appeal of Scouting to the British boy:

> Locating the principles of admirable behaviour—patriotism, a sense of honour, self-sacrifice in an aristocratic, heroic (and highly mythologized) past far removed from the imaginative world of working-class lads, Baden-Powell conferred on Scouting an august tradition that emphasized the need for the lower classes to look to their betters for instruction and moral marching orders.[23]

[. . .] In addition, the state was taking an exceptionally close interest in boys' health and fitness for the army. In response to these cultural imperatives, Scouting went to remarkable lengths to devise schemes whereby boys could be led towards some useful goal and be duly rewarded for it.[24]

In 'An Old Love', published in the *Morning Post* of 23 April 1915, perhaps as a riposte to the article on 'peace toys' which had appeared the month before, and which he satirizes in 'The Toys of Peace',[25] Saki writes admiringly of a 'boy' of nineteen who has told him that in spite of its horrors war seems to have something in it 'different to anything else in the world, something a little bit finer'. War, the article suggests, is, quite properly, a boy's first love, and Saki elides smoothly between toy soldiers and war games, and real war.

Nearly every red-blooded human boy has had war, in some shape or form, for his first love; if his blood has remained red and he has kept some of his boyishness in after life, that first love will never have been forgotten. No one could really forget those wonderful leaden cavalry soldiers; the horses were as sleek and prancing as though they had never left the parade-ground, and the uniforms were correspondingly spick and span, but the amount of campaigning and fighting they got through was prodigious. There are other unforgettable memories for those who had brothers to play with and fight with, of sieges and ambushes and pitched encounters, of the slaying of an entire garrison without quarter, or of chivalrous, punctilious courtesy to a defeated enemy. Then there was the slow unfolding of the long romance of actual war, particularly of European war, ghastly, devastating, heartrending in its effect, and yet somehow captivating to the imagination. The Thirty Years' War was one of the most hideously cruel wars ever waged, but, in conjunction with the subsequent campaigns of the Great Louis, it throws a glamour over the scene of the present struggle. The thrill that those far-off things call forth in us may be ethically indefensible, but it comes in the first place from something too deep to be driven out; the magic region of the Low Countries is beckoning to us again, as it beckoned to our forefathers, who went campaigning there almost from force of habit. ('An Old Love', *Morning Post*, 23 April 1915)

The shifts in register and tone in this piece suggest a convergence of Munro the journalist, Munro the soldier, and Saki, who, following the journalist-soldier's recourse to personification and convenient mystifications (the 'magic region', 'beckoning'), injects a surprising and bathetic note of humour ('campaigning almost from force of habit'). Having scathingly dismissed the 'variant[s] from the red-blooded type' who have assured him that they are not in the least interested in war, and have announced ' "I'm not at all patriotic, you know" [. . .] as one might announce that one was not a vegetable or did not use a safety-razor', Saki takes comfort in the memory of an event reminiscent of the last scene of *William*, though here the boys are doing the very thing they refused to do in his novel. 'One remembers with some feeling of relief the spectacle last August of boys and youths marching and shouting through the streets in semi-disciplined mobs, waving the flags of France and Britain. There is perhaps nothing very patriotic in shouting and flag-waving, but it is the only way these youngsters had of showing their feelings' (*Morning Post*, 23 April 1915). That the boys are semi-disciplined rather than 'mafficking' makes their march acceptable. Disciplined mobs of young boys of martial habits and political ideals, have unfortunate connotations of the *Hitlerjugend* in our time, but in Saki's work they stand for the hopes of a nation not quite moribund. Saki appears to have come a long way since 'Reginald's Choir Treat'. There the boys are the butts of Reginald's wit and the vehicles for his whimsy. Habituated to the voice of Authority, they stolidly obey the command of their social superior, even though it is to march, naked, wet, miserable,

and self-conscious, through the village to the sound of a pipe.
(They literally march to Reginald's tune, and that it is played on
the pipes suggests that he is self-consciously playing Pan.) Perhaps
Saki might have gained more respect for boys *en masse* rather than
just for beautiful superman boys, or perhaps the boys who do not
march in *William* are marked as superior by their membership of
an organization run on military lines rather than one that produces
church music. Perhaps Yeovil imagines the boy scouts as an earlier
self, unfallen, before he was afflicted with exhaustion, illness, and
the wrong marriage, and as the England that has not capitulated; a
clean slate for the future and for the Saki male.

Spears writes almost patronizingly of Saki's supposed bellicosity as
a 'guise' in which he appealed more to his British reading public
than the guise of the stories' narrators.

To the British public, of course, the writer's infectious love of his country
is especially gratifying. The castigation of politics and politicians is never
offensive when it is designed to make for national unity and strength.
In fact, Saki, wearing the guise of a bellicose jingo and hymning with
fervor the glories of British imperialism and the delights of English hedges
and hunting fields, is probably, on the whole, more palatable to his
countrymen than Saki as Clovis ridiculing Gladstonian society.[26]

In fact, *William* has proved less popular and enduring than the
short stories by which Saki is chiefly known; it has remained in
print in the Penguin collected edition, but has not been through
the many different editions and reprints of the stories, while Saki's
willingness to fight and die for his country seems to have struck
many English readers as unexpected and out of character. The
novel is certainly bellicose: the young parson with the 'tenderness
for little devils' is clearly meant as a hero, and the reader is to
approve of his credo of war: ' "I have learned one thing in life,"
continued the young man, "and that is that peace is not for this
world. Peace is what God gives us when He takes us into His rest.
Beat your sword into a plough-share if you like, but beat your
enemy into smithereens first." ' (*William*, p. 183). Lambert sees

Munro's interest in warfare and desire to fight for his country as his antidote to the social change that his reactionary outlook feared and detested.

Not for him the plush and mahogany. Not for him, either, the hope in aristocracy and the Roman Catholic Church with which Evelyn Waugh has buttressed a similar revulsion; and still less the desperate clutch at communism with which another middle-class anarch, Brecht, was to ward off the void. Saki sought in romantic patriotism the splendour he could not find in society, in anaesthetizing dreams of battles long ago the gallantry he missed in civilization. Nursing a dream of chivalry, he could not suffer other people. Even the tributes of his friends (except perhaps those in the Army) seem to suggest the charming courtesy which is rooted in indifference. (Lambert, 61).

War did not remain a dream for Munro, and the war he was involved in was far from splendid or chivalric, but even from the trenches he wrote as though he still believed in those remote, impossible ideals, whilst organizing his daily life around the quest for mundane grails: tea for the men; food that could be scavenged; the energy to keep up with his duties. A piece written during the Balkan war articulates the fantasy of romantic warfare through a dialogue between two archetypal Saki characters, the Merchant, with small-minded mercantile interests, and the Wanderer, who displays both flippant cynicism and romantic idealism, but an idealism not about the nobility of war fought by chivalrous rules or for a just cause, but for war as exotic adventure; as other to the familiar. The Wanderer is nostalgic for the old, protracted kind of warfare.

> 'War is a cruelly destructive thing,' said the Wanderer [. . .]
> 'Ah, yes, indeed,' said the Merchant, responding readily to what seemed like a safe platitude; 'when one thinks of the loss of life and limb, the desolated homesteads, the ruined—'
> 'I wasn't thinking anything of the sort,' said the Wanderer; 'I was thinking of the tendency that modern war has to destroy and banish the very elements of picturesqueness that are its chief excuse and charm.' ('The Cupboard of the Yesterdays', *Toys*, 287)

The Wanderer argues that the end of the Balkan troubles will be a loss.

'The Balkans have long been the last surviving shred of happy hunting-ground for the adventurous, a playground for passions that are fast becoming atrophied for want of exercise. In old bygone days we had the wars in the Low Countries always at our doors, as it were; there was no need to go far afield into malaria-stricken wilds if one wanted a life of boot and saddle and licence to kill and be killed. Those who wished to see life had a decent opportunity for seeing death at the same time.'   (ibid. 288)

He advances the argument that 'old-time happy-go-lucky wars' have provided occupation and income for younger sons and that, more importantly, the Balkan wars stand for a vanishing period in European history. As a child his imagination was caught by the region, its geography, and its history through its battles. The problem with modern war is that it will be over quickly and will bring about a division and settlement of land; it will bring what for him are twin evils, modernity and uniformity. Something will remain, 'but the old atmosphere will have changed, and the glamour will have gone; the dust of formality and bureaucratic neatness will slowly settle down over the time-honoured landmarks' (p. 292).

An anecdote follows. Having been carefully brought up by Saki, unwilling to be one of those who cannot understand the sentiment of the gentleman-warrior, and to earn the disapproval of the narrative by siding with low mercantile interests, even so, the reader is painfully aware of its objectionable nature. The point of the story is to illustrate the Wanderer's point about the uncertainty and drama which give the Balkan countries their charm. He knew a man in Sofia whom he found unrelievedly nondescript, tiresome, and dull. One day he learned that some men turned up, murdered him in the street, and left as quietly as they had come. To the merchant he says: 'You will not understand it, but to me there was something rather piquant in the idea of such a thing happening to such a man; after his dullness and his long-winded small-talk it seemed a sort of brilliant *esprit d'escalier* on his part to meet with an end of such ruthlessly planned and executed violence' (p. 291). Glamour, excitement, danger, difference, a licence to kill; larky younger sons going off for a combination of the Grand Tour and a safari; Saki was writing of war in a way we might associate with James Bond stories, or the wilder satire of *Blackadder Goes Forth*, and yet the tone seems serious; however, he had been in the Balkans, he had seen revolution and bloodshed, and was to continue to write in something like this way even when he had participated in it. Perhaps the subject here is less the imagined death of a 'real' character than the narrative itself, a Saki denouement of ruthlessly planned and executed violent poetic justice.

In 1913, London continued as ever, and it was still necessary to make a living. John Lane had been selling Saki's stories to the USA, and they were well enough known there by 1913 for E. V. Lucas to suggest that Saki write something for the 1914 *Lucas' Annual*. Munro wrote on 9 December, agreeing to the suggestion, asking what length Lucas would like, and ending: 'also the important, if deplorable, mercenary aspect has not been touched on'.[27] The next month he sent the piece, with a terse, two-line covering letter.

Dear Mr Lucas

Herewith the story I promised you. It is a skit on the Bernard Shaw school.

Very sincerely Yours

H. H. Munro

The story was 'The East Wing'. Personal animosity and the delivering of correctives, especially to Shaw, went on, even during larger, national battles.

10

William and Lance-Sergeant Munro

SAKI rarely put sensible words in duchesses' mouths; most of
their speeches are there to be disagreed with or made ridiculous by
Reginald, Clovis, or the narrative voice. Reginald and 'the Duchess'
regard each other 'with mutual distrust, tempered by a scientific
interest' ('Reginald at the Theatre', *Reginald*, 27). In the course of
a conversation about 'Right and wrong, good conduct and moral
rectitude' in that story, the Duchess is given a set-down that would
have stunned a hippo. She is oblivious to it, but it shows Reginald
in an unusually compassionate light (or at least deploring a want
of active charity in the Duchess). In spite of this and other points
of violent (and perversely invented) disagreement, Reginald and
the Duchess do not diverge as much as we might expect on the
subject, particularly when they reach things: 'which I suppose are to
a certain extent sacred'. The Duchess lists 'Patriotism, for instance,
and Empire, and Imperial responsibility, and blood-is-thicker-
than-water, and all that sort of thing' (p. 28). Reginald, perhaps
surprisingly, replies: 'Of course I accept the Imperial idea and the
responsibility. After all, I would just as soon think in Continents as
anywhere else.' But he continues: 'And some day, when the season
is over and we have the time, you shall explain to me the exact
blood-brotherhood and all that sort of thing that exists between
a French Canadian and a mild Hindoo and a Yorkshireman, for

instance' (p. 29). To hear Reginald use the words 'accept' and 'responsibility' in the same sentence is surprising, since he has professed the almost professional irresponsibility of the dandy. However much he concedes that the white man has a burden of responsibility, however, he retains the imperial Englishman's sense of his empire as a set of colonies ruled by a master nation. It is clear that for him there is no blood-brotherhood and concomitant equality between the native Englishman and the native of a colonial country. He seems to be in favour of the British Empire continuing on its present lines, that is, of economic advantage to Britain. There is no sense of fraternal responsibility; none of this hypocritical pretence of brotherly love and Commonwealth. The Duchess resorts to another adage: 'Oh well, "dominion over palm and pine", you know,' quoted the Duchess hopefully; 'of course we mustn't forget that we're all part of the great Anglo-Saxon Empire' (p. 29). Reginald digresses into fatuous anti-Semitism, but gives the Duchess an opening for extolling the Empire's philanthropic activities of feeding the minds and bodies of its colonial inhabitants. Having made her demonstrate that she is unaware of the starvation under her own nose, Reginald continues:

> 'And even your philanthropy, practised in a world where everything is based on competition, must have a debit as well as a credit account. The young ravens cry for food.'
> 'And are fed.'
> 'Exactly. Which presupposes that something else is fed upon.'
> 'Oh, you're simply exasperating. You've been reading Nietzsche till you haven't got any sense of moral proportion left. May I ask if you are governed by *any* laws of conduct whatever?' (ibid. 30–1)

As if aware that the conversation has been in danger of becoming almost serious, Reginald deflects it into the flippantly snobbish again, and we end with Debrett as a sacred book, but he has made a point, and a stand. He believes in the British Empire and the 'responsibilities' that go with it, and since he feels no kinship with its inhabitants, it is as a possession that he views it; a possession to be husbanded, perhaps, but to be held on to, fought for, and perhaps killed for.

Munro's beliefs, including his patriotism, were evidently not always on view. G. K. Chesterton recalled that 'Saki was obviously very national in the fact that the very normal loyalties to which he was true were almost completely covered in public with a coat of mail of flippancy, at once as sparkling and impenetrable as the costume of a harlequin.'[1] The coat of mail was to come off once war had been declared.

Munro went with a friend to hear the speech in which Sir Edward Grey announced to the House that unless Germany capitulated, Britain would enter the war. He later told Reynolds that the strain of listening to the Minister's slow, deliberate speech was such that he found himself sweating. 'That night we dined at a chop-house in the Strand with two friends. On our way Munro insisted on walking at a tremendous pace, and at dinner, when he ordered cheese and the waiter asked whether he wanted butter, he said peremptorily: "Cheese, no butter; there's war on"' (Reynolds, p. xvi).

Munro's excitement and desire to broadcast that he was in the know seem almost schoolboy-like, yet he was 44, in theory too old to enlist. 'A day or two later he was condemning himself for the slackness of the years in London and hiring a horse to take exercise, to which he was little addicted, in the Park. He was determined to fight' (ibid.). Munro reported on the same speech himself in his 'Potted Parliament' column for the *Outlook* on 8 August 1914.

For one memorable and uncomfortable hour the House of Commons had the attention of the nation and most of the world concentrated on it. Grey's speech, when one looked back at it, was a statesman-like utterance, delivered in excellent manner, dignified and convincing. To sit listening to it, in uncertainty for a long time as to what line of policy it was going to announce, with all the accumulated doubts and suspicions of the previous forty-eight hours heavy on one's mind, was an experience that one would not care to repeat often in a lifetime [. . .] When the actual tenor of the speech became clear, and one knew beyond a doubt where we stood, there was only room for one feeling; the miserable tension of the past two days had been removed, and one discovered that one was slowly recapturing the lost sensation of being in a good temper. (quoted in Munro, 96)

It seems significant that the declaration of hostilities and the prospect of fighting should restore Munro to good temper, especially given his stipulation of ill-temper as a necessary leavening quality to Comus. Good temper did not extend to tolerance, at least of those who spoke against entering the war. His scathing denunciation of such people echoes *William* and anticipates his further broadsides from the trenches.

Of the men who rose in melancholy succession to counsel a standing aloof from the war, a desertion of France, a humble submission to the will of Potsdam in the matter of Belgium's neutrality, one wishes to speak fairly. Many of them are men who have gloatingly threatened us with class warfare in this country—warfare in which rifles and machine-guns should be used to settle industrial disputes; they have seemed to take a ghoulish pleasure in predicting a not-too-far-distant moment when Britons shall range themselves in organized combat, not against an aggressive foreign enemy, but against their own kith and kin. Never have they been more fluent with these hints and incitements than during the present Session; if a crop of violent armed outbreaks does not spring up one of these days in this country it will not be for lack of sowing of seed. Now these men read us lectures on the wickedness of war. (Munro, 96–7)

In a contribution to Ethel Munro's memoir, a friend from before the war who became a comrade in Munro's regiment, W. R. Spikesman, describes spending the afternoon and evening of Saturday, 2 August 1914[2] with Munro. They spent the afternoon swimming, walked in Green Park, then dined and visited Munro's Club, the Cocoa Tree. Afterwards, they passed the Geographical Society Club, which was holding a dinner in honour of the explorer Ernest Shackleton, who was about to leave for the South Pole. Munro was reminded of Yeovil in *William*, and felt that it was 'tragic' for

Shackleton, who was leaving England 'and civilization' for places where he would be out of touch with current events (Spikesman, Munro, pp. 110–11).

Horses had always been important to Munro and when he enlisted, on 25 August, it was as a trooper in the 2nd King Edward's Horse, which was mobilized on 9 August. 'He put on a trooper's uniform with the exaltation of a novice assuming the religious habit' (Reynolds, p. xxi). From the regimental training camp in Slough he wrote to his publisher, John Lane:

I am a trooper in the above force, and I've asked A.R. Reynolds (permanent address: National Liberal Club, Whitehall) to look after my literary affairs while I am on service. If anything 'conclusive' happens to me, my brother, C. A. Munro, Governor H.M. Prison, Mountjoy, Dublin, is my executor.

I hope to get out [carat insertion: to the front] in the course of a couple of months. It is only fitting that the author of 'When William Came' should go to meet William half way. I hope that things are going well with you. Very sincerely yours (Trooper) H. H. Munro.   (quoted in Langguth, 253)

Munro had brought forward his date of birth in order to enlist, but in spite of the last-minute exercise regime, his age and the more sedentary habits of the last few years made the life of a cavalry trooper too much for him. That September he transferred to the 22nd Royal Fusiliers. He was then reunited with Spikesman, who had been rejected by the army four times but had finally managed to enlist. Touchingly, Spikesman writes that from that time until Munro's death they were always together or knew where to find each other (quoted in Munro, p. 111). Spikesman initially had doubts about whether Munro would take to army life, in particular the discipline and early rising, but he never knew Munro to be late or to complain. He states that Munro intended to play a part in the war, and as big a part as he could (Spikesman, ibid. p. 111). Spikesman's use of the word 'part' probably denotes 'contribution' but it could also mean 'role', and for Munro his role in the army seems to have been consciously stage-managed and performed.

Langguth remarks that Munro did not join the army to maintain a smart appearance (p. 254); he seems to have shed his own interest in being well dressed and well groomed along with his interest in fictional characters who are too well dressed and well groomed, but the rugged, manly disorder of undress khakis could be as much a costume as the outfits of an Edwardian gentleman. A posed photograph of Munro in battledress shows him tidy enough, but a snapshot shows him in another pose, the antithesis of his former life. In crumpled kitchen fatigues: woolly hat, collarless shirt with sleeves rolled, braces on view, and dusty boots; he is every inch a hard-working NCO. He had grown a moustache, Langguth assumes to compensate for the upper teeth extracted by an army dentist, but perhaps simply for its military connotations.

In November 1914, Munro wrote to his sister from Horsham in Sussex that, like other German speakers, he had been allocated teaching duties. The Board of Education required the lessons to begin with German Grammar, but Munro and his fellow teachers refused, on the grounds that tired men would not pay attention to a lot of dry rules. He also reported that 'Lady C' (presumably Lady Charnwood) had sent him a lot of chocolates and acid drops which he was distributing, especially among the poorer men (letter to Ethel Munro dated 29 November 1914, quoted in Munro, p. 98).[3] The same letter asks Ethel whether she remembers a 'Capt C, of B.T.', now a Major in the Argyll and Sutherland Highlanders, who had written to ask if Munro would want a commission. Munro writes that he would not accept it because he should then have so much to learn that he might not see service at all. His three and half months' training, he says, will fit him to be a useful infantry soldier, but he should be a very indifferent officer. He adds, however, that it is nice to be asked (p. 99).

Spikesman recalls that Munro refused several offers of a commission, and gives as the reason that Munro felt he should be familiar with a soldier's duties before he was justified in expecting a soldier to obey his commands (Spikesman, ibid. p. 112). During the encampment and training at White City and Horsham Munro's friend recalled that he was 'like a fine, healthy boy, full of life, fun, and devilment' (quoted ibid. p. 122). In February 1915,[5] on leave from the camp to attend the funeral of Aunt Tom, who had died of a stroke, he wrote to Charlie from the Golden Lion in Barnstaple. As Executor, he had been going through Aunt Tom's letters, and had come across one from 'Uncle W.' (presumably Wellesley Munro) written in 1889. 'Besides some plain and salutary speaking to Aunt Tom about the aunts' indebtedness to the Gov. he alludes in scathing terms to a campaign of abuse which Aunt Augusta seems to have directed against us 3' (Letter to Charles Munro dated 13 February, quoted in Langguth, p. 256). In an unwontedly forgiving and even humble spirit, Munro added: 'All of that generation are dead now, so the letter may as well be destroyed when you have read it. I think Ethel and you and I may feel some pride in reflecting that the old folks at the end of their lives came to see that we were likable and loveable and they obviously greatly preferred us to our cousins' (ibid.).

Later that month, the battalion moved to Roffey, also in Sussex, then there was further training at Clipstone and Tidworth. During that spring, Munro wrote several letters to Ethel describing the 'fun' and 'rags' of camp life, and his duties as a hut orderly and, subsequently, as a Corporal. In March 1915, he reports that 'most of us find the life very jolly' and that they 'have a good deal of fun, with skirmishing raids at night with neighbouring huts, and friendly games of footer'. He adds significantly: 'it is like being boy and man at the same time' (letter to Ethel Munro dated 5 March 1915, quoted in Munro, pp. 99–100). A later letter mentions that he and his comrades 'have a lot of fun in our hut and never seem too tired to indulge in sport or ragging' (letter to Ethel Munro dated 2 April 1915, quoted ibid. p. 100). He writes as though his dream of romantic warfare played like a game by boys with 'clean combative' instincts is still intact. 'All the same I wish we could count on going away soon; it is a poor game to be waiting when others are bearing the brunt and tasting the excitement of real warfare' (letter to Ethel Munro dated 5 March 1915, quoted ibid.). Following a description of his trench-digging prowess, the same letter refers to 'the perfectly horrible reply' Munro had sent to '[a] youth I know, about 22, in the pink of health as far as I know', who had written to ask if Munro could use his influence 'to get him an engagement at Daly's or some other London theatre [. . .] as he wanted to study voice-production in Town and it was really rather important' (ibid.). In Munro's life as well as his art, devotion to his country had drawn ahead of devotion to youth and insouciant beauty.

An article in *The Bystander* of June 1915 humorously describing the duties of a Company Orderly Corporal (Munro's rank and function at the time) offers certain golden rules which should be observed 'by any C.O.C. who wishes to make a success of his job' (quoted ibid. p. 102). The first two of these might have applied to the narrative voice of Saki's stories: cultivate an indifference to human suffering and develop your imagination.

From Tidworth Camp in Hampshire, Munro wrote that there was some prospect of the battalion's being sent to Serbia. 'which I would like. I told one rather timorous youth that the forests there swarmed with wolves, which came and pounced on men on outpost duty' (letter to Ethel Munro dated 10 October 1915, quoted ibid. p. 104). He added that he hoped it wouldn't be Gallipoli. A few weeks later, the prospect of Serbia has retreated, but the prospect of at least moving out is assured. Munro writes of it as though it were a personal treat.

After the long months of preparation and waiting we are at last on the eve of departure and there is a good prospect of our getting away this week. It seems almost too good to be true that I am going to take an active part in a big European war. I fear it will be France, not the Balkans, but there is no knowing where one may find oneself before the war is over; anyhow I shall keep up my study of the Servian language. I expect at first we shall be billeted in some French town. (letter to Ethel Munro dated 7 November 1915, ibid. 104).

In France, Munro turned down another offer of a commission.

One day, so one of his comrades told me, Hector was washing potatoes when a General came along who had last met him in his own house at Bridge.
'What on earth are you doing here, Munro?' he asked, and tried to persuade him to accept another job, a softer one, but also farther from the front line. But he was genuinely attached to his comrades, and quite determined to get to close quarters with the Boche. (ibid. 104–5)

Spikesman's account depicts Munro as a model soldier and NCO. In their maiden trench visit in Vermelles in November 1915, Munro was one of the first to volunteer to form the Company's first wiring party (Spikesman, ibid. p. 112). He always thought of the men first, and gave his friend a 'slating' for having assumed that after a long march the company HQ rather than his men had first call on him. Though Munro could and did lose his temper, his friend reports that there the matter always ended, and there was never any littleness in anything he did or thought (Spikesman, ibid. pp. 113–14).

In December 1915, Munro was sent on a two-week mixed officers' and NCOs' course. He returned to the trenches in the New Year and in February was still evidently pleased to be at the front, describing 'a rather hot part of the line' as a place he enjoyed better than any other the regiment had been in. He also described a near-miss when, having made his bed (an overcoat and a waterproof sheet) on the fire-step of a parapet of the trench, he went on his round of the sentries. A bomb 'riddled the overcoat and sheet and slightly wounded a man sleeping on the other side of the trench. I assumed that no 2 bombs would fall on exactly the same spot, so remade the bed and had a good sleep' (letter to Ethel Munro dated 8 February 1916, ibid. p. 107). In March during 'a spasm between trenches' they were in a small village 'where I have found excellent Burgundy', to which they returned on two other occasions. This may have been Ham-en-Artois, where Spikesman records their having been in 'about April 1916'. He was still enjoying himself, and still describing his activities in the conventional off-the-shelf terms for letters home of jolly fun and adventure. He had, he reports, a 'boisterous welcome' from 'elderly farm-wives, yard-dogs and other friends'. 'I am in very good spirits; the fun and adventure of the whole thing and the good comradeship of some of one's companions make it jolly, and one attaches an enormous importance to little comforts such as a cup of hot tea at the right moment' (letter to Ethel Munro dated 20 May 1916, ibid. p. 108). Munro seems to have tried to impose the exclusivity and rule-boundness of a club on all possible occasions, even behind the lines. In Ham-en-Artois he managed to buy a joint of pork, and found a French epicerie-keeper willing to cook and serve it to a select few. In what sounds like a rather schoolboyish move, Munro declared the occasion the inauguration of the 'Back-Kitchen Club', for which he devised a set of rules. Spikesman remarks that it is needless to say that the rules were never broken during Munro's time (ibid. pp. 116–18).

While he was at the front, Munro continued to contribute to the *Bystander*, *Morning Post*, *Outlook*, and *Westminster Gazette*, as well as to a publication new to him, the *Fortnightly Gazette* of the 22nd Battalion Royal Fusiliers. One piece, which became the title story of the posthumously published collection *Square Egg*, is as good an account as any of what it was like to live in the trenches of the front line. Told in the first person, it seems to be a diary or 'letter from the front' piece concerned with observation and personal anecdote, which quickly moves away from the badger analogy which introduces it. Typically, it is not the fighting which appals the narrator, but '[p]arliament, taxes, social gatherings, economies, and expenditure, and all the thousand and one horrors of civilisation' which, fortunately the war has made seem 'immeasureably remote' ('The Square Egg: A Badger's-Eye View of the War, Mud in the Trenches', *Square Egg*, p. 121). Though the horrors of war are as remote as those of the civilization he has gratefully left behind, the discomforts of trench warfare are described as very much on Saki's mind; the discomforts and the possible relief to discomfort available at the *estaminets* of France. The description of the *estaminet* moves from the generic (an oasis of hot coffee and *vin ordinaire* in a dripping wilderness of unrelieved mud and sodden sandbags) to the specific of the Fortunate Rabbit, where the narrator meets a familiar Sakian character, the storyteller. This one is of the con-artist rather than the pure romancer or romancer-for-effect type, referred to here in appropriately military terms as a 'purse-sapper'. It is this character's tale of the (expensive) development of the conveniently shaped egg that gives the story and the collection their titles.

Munro also sent accounts of his time in the trenches to his niece, Charlie's elder daughter Felicia, who had shared his wolf fantasies during the holidays at Carrig Cnoc, and whom he addresses as 'little Wolf'.[5]

We went out on the march for three days this week and slept out in the open fields behind haystacks and hedges. A little black and white goat strayed away from some other regiment and marched at the head of our columns, but it did not know that we are the fastest marching regiment in this Division, and before the three days were over it was too tired to walk and had to be carried in one of our transport carts; it is resting now and will be quite fit again. Perhaps I may be going out to Serbia and may meet some wolves in the forests there, which will be fun. (letter to Felicia Munro, no date provided, possibly November 1915, quoted in Langguth, 263–4)

In February 1916, he wrote again, again making animals the focus of his attention. The life of a soldier enabled him to articulate his admiration for the feral, and act out the fantasy of being a predator.

It is nice being out here, except the marching which is tiring because we carry so much, but that cannot be helped. I think you would enjoy going out at night to mine the wire entanglements in front of our lines: You have to creep, creep like a prowling cat, and when the enemy sends up a flare light every few minutes, you have to press yourself flat on the ground and pretend to be a lump of earth. It reminded me of the times when you and I were wolves and used to go prowling after fat farmers' wives. At night lots of owls come to the trenches to catch the mice that swarm all over the place and they must have plenty of sport. Our kitchens are drawn by horses and mules and follow us wherever we go, and the cooks of our company have a jolly little tabby kitten that goes everywhere with them and is quite used to a travelling circus as it wont [sic] understand living in one place. (letter dated 8 February 1916, quoted in Langguth, 267–8)

Munro had been a bird-watcher and egg-collector from a boy, but though his letters to his sister and later his niece contain specific descriptions of local flora and fauna, he had never published the 'nature notes' kind of journalism, and in his fiction had tended to represent generic landscapes appropriate to Tory landowners or Pan-like shape-shifters. 'Birds on the Western Front', however, written for the *Westminster Gazette* and after his death collected in *Square Egg*, is both local and specific. Though it is written from and about north-eastern France, however, none of the birds mentioned is specific to France, and most are those most often associated with English gardens and meadows: the skylark and the chaffinch; or English countryside: the magpie, owl, crow, partridge, kestrel, and sparrow hawk. Even when Munro was at the front, Saki's writing dwelt on England and English country ways, and his last published article ends on a note of conservativism and continuity, as well as the familiar didacticism.

The English gamekeeper, whose knowledge of wild life usually runs on limited and perverted lines, has evolved a sort of religion as to the nervous debility of even the hardiest game birds; according to his beliefs a terrier trotting across a field in which a partridge is nesting, or a mouse-hawking kestrel hovering over the hedge, is sufficient cause to drive the distracted bird off its eggs and send it whirring into the next county.

The partridge of the war zone shows no signs of such sensitive nerves. The rattle and rumble of transport, the constant coming and going of bodies of troops, the incessant rattle of musketry and deafening explosions of artillery, the night-long flare and flicker of star-shells, have not sufficed to scare the local birds away from their chosen feeding grounds, and to all appearances they have not been deterred from raising their broods. Gamekeepers who are serving with the colours might seize the opportunity to indulge in a little useful nature study. (*Square Egg*, 136)

Had he lived, perhaps there would have been a Saki story in which an elaborate practical joke teaches a gamekeeper the error of his hawk- and terrier-killing ways.

In June 1916, Munro had a short leave which he spent with his brother and sister at the Richelieu Hotel (later the Dean Hotel) in London. His sister recalls that he showed signs of wear and tear, but was in great spirits, and that he told her: 'I could never settle down again to the tameness of London life.' He spoke of his plan for after the war; he and 'a friend' would buy land in Siberia and run a farm. Ethel assumed that she was included in the plan, and that she would provide the practical to Munro's romantic element. 'This idea appealed strongly to me—I saw myself bringing up the rear with all the things he would find on arrival he ought to have brought and had not. It would have been a remarkable life, wild animals beyond the dreams of avarice, at our very doors, and, before long, inside them' (Munro, pp. 108–9). It was this plan that prompted Reynolds to suggest that 'the dross' of Munro's London life had been 'burnt up in the flames of war' (Reynolds, p. xxiii). Perhaps Munro did think of himself at this stage as resembling Yeovil or Keriway or Judkin, a diminished version of a former self etiolated by years of being cooped up in town after turning his back on the wild. Apart from his year in Burma, however, he had hardly lived in the wild. He had crossed it during his time as a foreign correspondent, but had lived mostly in cities. Devon at the turn of the century and after was hardly wilderness, and the Munros were not farmers, so the fantasy of a farm in Siberia would have been a new life rather than a return to an old one. Back in 1911, in the *Bodleian* interview, he had suggested that he was slightly surprised to find himself living as bucolically as in a Caterham cottage.' "You are not staying in London now?" "No, I am living the simple life at Caterham. Perhaps I may develop, in time, a longing for three acres and a cow. Just now I am wildly excited at the prospect of dinner and a play afterwards. Since I have become a country cousin . . ."'[6] When his leave was up, Munro's brother and sister saw him off from Victoria Station. Ethel, recording her last words to her brother ('"Kill a good few for me!"'), adds that she believes he did, offering the thought as a consolation, since he had not had 'the satisfaction' of a bayonet charge, which, she reported, was his ambition (Munro, p. 108).

Spikesman's accounts of the period July–November 1916 are full of praise for Munro's dogged endurance, his dauntless bravery, and his leadership qualities. In August they were in the battered and desolate Delville Wood, in inadequate, shallow trenches with no definite line, among knots of soldiers who had become detached from the battalions, and many dead. Munro surprised even his friend, remaining calm and coolly giving orders or words of advice, organizing a strong section, and giving the isolated men a front to face (pp. 117–18).

In October, Munro had a reoccurrence of the malaria he had contracted in Burma, and he was ordered back to Base. For Spikesman, '[i]t was a big miss, and I felt just lonely and I know I was severely "told off" by my friends for being such a misery, but if I had seen the results of the next "do," I would have borne a longer miss' (p. 118). Getting wind of the coming big attack on Beaumont Hamel, though far from fit, Munro returned. Spikesman gives an account of that attack which I summarize here. On 15 November they were in position in front of Pendant Copse and the Quadrilateral, to the left of Beaumont Hamel, and stayed in position until the early hours of the next day, when they were ordered to flank out to the left of the advance line, because the marshy ground had made it impossible for the troops on that side to come up. They reached a trench from which a figure rose to shout a greeting to Captain Roscoe, the Company commander, and the two engaged in talk. A number of the soldiers took the opportunity to snatch a brief rest, and Munro found a shallow crater whose lip he could use as a back rest. Spikesman heard him shout: 'Put that bloody cigarette out,' then a rifle shot, followed immediately by a command to get into the trenches (p. 119).

Spikesman, like Munro, had been promoted to Corporal in France. After Munro's death, in 1917, he was commissioned Lieutenant. For a man, and perhaps more for an ex-officer of the British army, in the 1920s it would have been impolitic to publish something that could be construed as suggestive of homosexual relations with another man, whether or not the relationship actually had been sexual, yet he describes his friend in affectionate terms and ends his piece courageously. He recalls that it was about an hour later that someone came to him and said: 'So they got your friend.' He continues: '[m]y feelings then I cannot describe, but I knew I had lost something inestimable, the friendship of a man whose ideas and thoughts I tried to emulate, someone whom I loved for his being just "Saki" ' (Spikesman, ibid.).

Munro's death certificate gives his age as 42, though he was in fact a month short of his forty-fifth birthday, having reduced his age in order to enlist. Years later, Willie Mercer imaginatively relived the events of his cousin's enlistment and war experiences in the novel *Lower than Vermin*, which he dedicated 'in memory of that brilliant novelist "SAKI" (H. H. Munro) whose first cousin I had the honour to be'.[7]

An account of the formation of the 22nd Royal Fusiliers, their training, and their activities in France is provided by J. M. Greenslade, MM, in Major Christopher Stone's history of the battalion. Greenslade's 'Miscellanies' chapter recognizes the efficiency of 'Corpl. Munro' as a member of the Orderly Room Staff: 'an invaluable, overworked staff, struggling cheerfully through the avalanche of memos. and returns week after week—the prop and mainstay of successive adjutants'.[8] Concluding his account of the Battle of Ancre, Greenslade writes: 'Among the dead was Sgt. H. Munro ("Saki") a very gallant gentleman, who brought as much honour to the Battalion as that other self-effacing scholar, L. G. Russel-Davies [. . .]'[9]

Reynolds quotes, presumably from a letter, 'the officer in command of the 22nd Royal Fusiliers', perhaps Captain Roscoe, who was killed in 1917.

'Poor Saki! What an admiration we all had for him [. . .] I always quoted him as one of the heroes of the war. I saw daily the appalling discomforts he so cheerfully endured. He flatly refused to take a commission or in any way to allow me to try to make him more comfortable. General Vaughan told him that a brain like his was wasted as a private solder. He just smiled. He was absolutely splendid. What courage! The men simply loved him.' (quoted in Reynolds, p. xxiv)

His obituary in the *Morning Post* recalled his 'adventures' as a Special Correspondent, in all of which he 'displayed an undaunted courage and an enterprise that no discouragement of circumstance could quench. Again and again he took with a frolic welcome the gravest risks.'[10]

This self-effacing, secretive man of numerous acquaintances but few intimates, in some ways deeply unpleasant, in some ways admirable, achieved popularity and even love when he was endeavouring to be a killer. He was certainly capable of love, if for nothing else then for the place and ideal for which he fought and died.

ENDNOTES

INTRODUCTION

1. At Christie's Captains and Kilns Sale in New York. The figure came from the Hope McCormick collection.
2. For an account of the sale, see <http://www.maineantiquedigest.com/articles/mayo3/bc0503.htm>, accessed 11 Apr. 2007.
3. At 671.
4. *Scots Magazine* (July 1793), 360.
5. Langguth gives the source of this story as Mrs P. A. G. Bryan, née Munro, Saki's niece, whom Langguth interviewed at her home in Belfast. Langguth, 7.
6. Nancy Mitford, *Don't Tell Alfred* (Harmondsworth: Penguin, 1980), 154.
7. His maternal grandfather was a rear admiral.
8. A metamorphosis from the idle, card-playing, cynical foreign correspondent Hugh Blair, a fictionalized portrait of Munro in Roy Reynolds, *The Gondola* (London: Mills and Boon, 1913), 260–7.
9. Rothay Reynolds, 'Hector Hugh Munro', preface to Saki, *The Toys of Peace and Other Stories* (London: The Bodley Head, 1919), pp. ix–xxiv (hereafter Reynolds).
10. The possession of 'Scottish blood' is described as admirable and valuable in the case of one Saki character, Eleanor, Dowager Lady Greymarten, a heroine of *William*, and a young man in the same novel who has refused to live in England under foreign occupation has taken a position in a school in Scotland, suggesting that Scotland perhaps held out where England had fallen. Lord Charnwood attributes 'Gaelic' characteristics to Munro in his introduction to *Bassington* in the *Complete Novels and Plays of Saki* (London, 1933), 147–8.
11. H. W. Nevinson, introducing *Beasts* for the Bodley Head uniform edition, suggests that Saki's alleged cynicism and impatience with all enthusiasm are typically English characteristics and adds: 'Saki was entirely English.' Introduction, *Beasts and Super-Beasts*, Uniform Edition (London: The Bodley Head, 1926), p. vii.
12. Will Self, Introduction, Saki, *The Unrest-Cure and Other Beastly Tales* (London: Prion, 2000), pp. x–xi.
13. Nancy Mitford, *The Pursuit of Love* (Harmondsworth: Penguin, 1994), 113.

14. Valerie Shaw, *The Short Story: A Critical Introduction* (Harlow: Longman, 1983), 20.

15. Christopher Morley, Introduction, *The Complete Short Stories of Saki* (London: The Bodley Head, 1930), pp. vi–vii. (Hereafter Morley.)

16. Noël Coward, Introduction (1967), *The Complete Saki* (Harmondsworth: Penguin, 1982), p. xiii.

17. Alan Sinfield, *The Wilde Century: Effeminacy, Oscar Wilde and the Queer Moment* (New York: Cassell, 1994), p. vi.

18. Christopher Stone, *From Vimy Ridge to the Rhine: The Great war Letters of Christopher Stone*, eds G.D. Sheffield and G.I.S. Inglis. Marlborough: Crowood, 1989, 74–5.

CHAPTER I

1. Ethel Munro's suggestion that the sisters were fifteen years apart in age is contradicted by the 1881 census, which gives the age of Charlotte M. Munro as 50 and Augusta J. Munro as 39.

2. Saki's female characters are discussed in more detail later in Chs. 8 and 9.

3. The quotation is from P. G. Wodehouse, *The Inimitable Jeeves* (London: Herbert Jenkins, 1923).

4. E. M. Munro, letter to *The Spectator* (13 June 1952), 780.

5. Graham Greene, letter to *The Spectator* (20 June 1952), 811.

6. E. M. Munro, letter to *The Spectator* (27 June 1952), 856.

7. Charles G. Leland, *Johnnykin and the Goblin* (London: Macmillan, 1877).

8. 'The Mappined Life', *Toys*, 185–92. Briefly discussed in Ch. 5.

9. Leland, *Johnnykin*, 10.

10. Ibid. 22.

11. Ibid. 10–11.

12. Ibid. 17–18.

13. Ibid. 19.

14. Ibid. 23.

15. Ibid. 37–8.

16. Ibid. 77–8.

17. Ibid. 153–4.

18. Ibid. 181–2.

19. Ibid. 159–60.

20. Ibid. 53–4.

21. Carroll, *Alice's Adventures Through the Looking-Glass*, 205–13. Martin Gardiner notes: Roger Green thought Alice's dialogue with the pudding might have been suggested to Carroll by a cartoon in *Punch* (19 January 1861) showing

a plum pudding standing up and saying to a diner, 'Allow me to disagree with you', *The Annotated Alice* (Harmondsworth: Penguin, 2001), 276. It is possible that Saki's anthropomorphized food derives from Lewis Carroll or old numbers of *Punch*.

22. Leland, *Johnnykin*, 160–1.

23. Discussed in more detail in Ch. 8.

24. Leland, *Johnnykin*, 212.

25. Lewis Carroll, *Alice's Adventures in Wonderland* (London, 1870), 10.

26. Ibid. 12–13.

27. Ibid. 88–9.

28. See Lewis Carroll, *Sylvie and Bruno* (London: Macmillan, 1889).

29. Discussed in more detail in ch. 7.

30. Carroll, *Looking Glass*, 8.

31. Ibid. 5–6.

32. Ibid. 94.

33. Carroll, *Wonderland*, 120.

34. Ibid. 121.

35. William Empson, *Some Versions of Pastoral* (London: Chatto & Windus, 1935), 268–9.

36. Gardner, *Annotated Alice*, 13.

CHAPTER 2

1. The author is grateful to Mr John Sharman, Secretary of the Old Bedfordians for his scrutiny of the Old Bedfordians' records.

2. See the discussion of 'An Old Love', *Morning Post* (23 April 1915) in Ch. 9.

3. Letter to A. G. Dew-Smith from Hotel Belvedere, Davos, dated November 1880.

4. *The Fortnightly Review*, July 1878, 74–87.

5. As pointed out by Dr John Ballam in his forthcoming study of Symonds's work.

6. See Rictor Norton (compiler), *The John Addington Symonds pages*. Selection copyright 1997; updated 24 November 2000 <http://www.infopt.demon.co.uk/symindex.htm>, accessed 9 May 2007.

7. John Maddison Morton, *Box and Cox: A Romance of Real Life in One Act*. First performed in London in 1847. The play is a farce in which Box and Cox share rented rooms, one living there during the day, the other at night. The expression 'box and cox' came to mean taking turns.

ENDNOTES

CHAPTER 3

1. Whereas most currencies were based on the gold standard, Indian currency was based on the silver. The discovery of large quantities of silver in the US and elsewhere led to a fall in its price. Between 1871 and 1896, the value of the pound against the rupee increased from 10.8 to 16.6. For this and other economic factors in 'the fall of the rupee', see B. E. Dadachanji, *History of Indian Currency and Exchange*, 3rd edn. (Bombay: D. B. Taraporevala, 1934).

2. Charles H. Gillen, *H. H. Munro (Saki)* (New York: Twayne, 1969), 23.

3. A young Welsh girl who was forced to marry a rich industrialist instead of the local harper with whom she had fallen in love. The half-legendary story became the basis for R. D. Blackmore's novel *The Fair Maid of Sker* (1872). The novel is largely set in Heanton Court, the house taken by Colonel Munro on the family's return from Davos.

4. The Nats are not specifically the two brothers to whom Munro refers, but spirits, usually of those who have met a violent death, who if not placated can wreak mischief or worse on the living.

5. For Jamrach, see Ch. 7.

6. See Ch. 4.

7. Tim Carey, *Mountjoy: The Story of a Prison* (Wilton, Cork: Collins, 2000), 187.

8. Sean Milroy, *Memories of Mountjoy* (Dublin, 1917), 4 (cited by Carey). My omission.

9. Carey, *Mountjoy*, 187–8.

10. Ibid. 188–9.

11. Ibid 190.

12. J. Lewis May, *John Lane and the Nineties* (London: The Bodley Head, 1936), 194.

13. Ibid. 194–5

CHAPTER 4

1. Edward Garnett, 'Early Russian History', *The Bookman* (August 1900), 155.

2. *The Athenaeum*, 3779 (31 March 1900), 398.

3. Letter headed 'The Religion of the Slavs', signed 'H. H. Munro', *The Athenaeum*, 3781 (14 April 1900), 466.

4. J. A. Spender, foreword to *The Westminster Alice, Complete Novels and Plays*, 293.

5. Ibid.

6. *The Westminster Alice* (London, 1902), 2. Hereafter *Alice*.

7. Concentration camps at this time referred to the camps set up by the British during the South African Wars to intern the wives and children of Boers fighting against the British.

8. Hanging from the saddle is a book labelled '*Bloch, Is War Impossible?*'. J. A. Spender explains: 'Emile Bloch, the Belgian strategical writer, had lately written an elaborate book in eleven volumes to prove that modern warfare on any large scale would be extraordinarily different from what most of the General Staffs supposed it would be, and W. T. Stead in his lively way had peptonized the eleven volumes into one and issued it with the title, *Is War Impossible?* The appearance of "Alice in Pall Mall" with Stead's title in the cartoon moved M. Bloch to send me the whole eleven volumes to prove that he had said not that war was impossible, but something extremely different, and, as events proved, something extremely wise and prescient' (Spender, *Complete Novels and Plays*, 294).

9. When Clovis composes his 'Recessional' in a Turkish Bath, watched by Bertie van Tahn, the resulting story is rather less interesting. See 'The Recessional', *Clovis*, 233–41.

10. Rothay Reynolds gives the date of the first appearance of the pseudonym as 1890: 'when he published in the *Westminster Gazette* the second of the political satires [which became] Alice in Westminster', but this is an error. Munro was 20 in 1890, and still enjoying a prolonged adolescence. See Reynolds, 'A Memoir of H. H. Munro', *Toys*, p. x.

11. Joseph Bristow, *Empire Boys: Adventures in a Man's World*, Reading Popular Fiction Series (London: Harper Collins, 1991); Anonymous, 'England After War', *Fortnightly Review*, NS 72 (1902), 4. [Bristow's note.]

12. J. W. Lambert, Introduction, *The Bodley Head Saki* (London: Bodley Head, 1963), 34–5.

13. Montague Summers, *The Galanty Show* (London: Cecil Woolf, 1980), 239.

14. Ibid. 240.

15. Wilfred Hindle, *The* Morning Post *1772–1937* (London: Routledge, 1937), 2.

16. Ibid. 4–5.

17. Keith M. Wilson, *A Study in the History and Politics of The* Morning Post *1905–1926* (Lewiston, N.Y, and Lampeter: Edwin Mellen, 1990), 4.

18. Hindle, *Morning Post*, 2.

19. Ibid. 3.

20. Wilson, *History and Politics of the* Morning Post, 34–5.

21. Ibid. 52–3.

22. James R. Thrane traces Munro's movements as foreign correspondent in his introduction to two uncollected stories, 'Two New Stories by "Saki" (H. H. Munro)', *Modern Fiction Studies* 19/2 (Summer, 1973), 140–1.

23. For example, 'The Angel and the Lost Michael', *Morning Post* (16 November 1903), 'Spade Work out of Monmouth', *Morning Post* (30 November 1903), and 'The Coming of Nicholas', *Morning Post* (21 December 1903).

24. Munro was not the only English foreign correspondent employed there by the *Morning Post*. Thrane mentions 'one R. P. Mahaffy' as writing for the *Post* in January 1905 ('Two Stories', 140), and Maurice Baring, later to write an introduction to one of the anthologies of Saki's work in the Bodley Head uniform series, was a correspondent on Russian affairs in 1905 and became a St Petersburg correspondent from October 1906.

25. Introduction to *Beasts and Super-Beasts*, p. vii.

26. (London: Nisbet, 1925).

27. Ibid. 111–12.

28. 'Death of Mr. H. H. Munro. Lance-Sergeant "Saki"', *Morning Post* (25 November 1916), 4.

29. Thrane, 'Two New Stories', *Modern Fiction Studies* 19/2: 140.

30. *Morning Post*, 15 January 1906.

31. Ibid. 17 January 1906.

32. Ibid. 5 June 1906.

33. Ibid. 25 November 1916, 4.

CHAPTER 5

1. Hugh Walpole, Preface, *Reginald* and *Reginald in Russia*, Uniform Edition (London, Bodley Head, 1926), pp. viii–ix.

2. F. Anstey, *The Long Retrospect* (London: Oxford University Press, 1936), 338.

3. Ibid. 332.

4. Reynolds, Memoir, *Toys*, p. xv.

5. Letter sent from the Cocoa Tree Club, dated 15 February 1911, in the Harry Ransom Humanities Research Center, University of Texas at Austin.

6. Letter dated 18 March 1912, in The Harry Ransom Humanities Research Center, University of Texas, Austin.

7. See Thrane, 'Two Stories', 141 n. 5.

8. Death of 'Saki': Killed in the Battle for Beaumont Hamel', obituary, *Westminster Gazette* (24 November 1916), 5.

9. Christopher Lane, 'The Unrest Cure According to Lawrence, Saki, and Lewis', *Modernism/Modernity* 11/4 (November 2004), 783; see Philip Hoare, *Oscar Wilde's Last Stand: Decadence, Conspiracy, and the Most Outrageous Trial of the Century* (New York: Arcade, 1997), 1 and 41–63 (Lane's note).

10. See the letter to Ethel Munro dated 26 July 1893 in Munro, 40.

11. Ben Travers, *Vale of Laughter: An Autobiography* (London: Geoffrey Bles, 1957), 69–70.

12. Ibid. 70. The anecdote is repeated with slight variations in Travers, *A-Sitting on a Gate* (London: W. H. Allen, 1978), 46.

13. Travers, *A-Sitting on a Gate*, 46.

14. Ibid. 74.

15. Letter in the Harry Ransom Humanities Research Center, University of Texas, at Austin.

16. Letter dated 26 April 1911, in The Harry Ransom Humanities Research Center, University of Texas, Austin.

17. Letter dated 23 Oct. 1911, ibid.

18. Spears suggests that the name connotes someone without the benefit of the grace of the grail. George James Spears, *The Satire of Saki: A Study of the Satiric Art of H. H. Munro* (New York: Exposition 1963), 48.

19. Letters dated 9 and 19 June 1911, in The Harry Ransom Humanities Research Center, University of Texas, Austin.

20. Letter dated 5 July 1911, ibid.

21. Letter dated 13 August 1911, ibid.

22. Letter dated 24 August 1911, ibid.

23. *The Bodleian*, III/3 (December 1911), 330.

24. Ibid.

25. Ibid. 331.

26. Emil Otto Hoppé (1878–1972), originally from Germany, was at the time one of the best-known society photographers in England.

27. Francis Toye, who joined the staff of *The Bystander* in 1911 or 1912, recalled: 'We had some agreeable contributors, including that queer fish known as 'Saki', who remains in my memory as the author of one of the most pregnant sentences: "She was a good cook, and as good cooks go, she went" ', *For What We Have Received* (London: Heinemann, 1950), 93.

28. Travers, *Vale of Laughter*, 67–8.

29. Langguth, 209–10.

30. Geoffrey Alderman, *The Jewish Community in British Politics* (Oxford: Clarendon 1983), 66.

31. Antony Taylor, 'London Bombs and Alien Panics', *Chartist* (November 2005), <http://www.chartist.org.uk/articles/econsoc/nov05taylor.htm>

32. Alderman, *Jewish Community in British Politics* 66.

33. See ibid. 66–8.

34. Ibid. 69.

35. Quoted ibid. 187 n. 38.

36. The Right Hon. Arthur James Balfour, MP, *Decadence*: Henry Sidgwick Memorial Lecture. (Cambridge: Cambridge University Press, 1908).

37. Lane, 'The Unrest Cure', 784.

38. Leo Bersani, 'Is the Rectum a Grave?' in Douglas Crimp (ed.), *AIDS: Cultural Analysis/Cultural Activism* (Cambridge, Mass.: MIT, 1988), 222 and 218 (Lane's note).

39. Lane, 'The Unrest Cure', 786.

40. Letter dated 16 February 1914, in Lane collection 42.4, The Harry Ransom Humanities Research Center, University of Austin, Texas.

41. Letter dated 25 July 1913, ibid.

42. Letter dated 19 November 1913, ibid.

43. Letter dated 7 October 1913, in John Lane, 42.2, ibid.

44. Letter dated 16 May 1911, ibid.

45. Undated letter, ibid.

46. Letter dated 18 January 1912, ibid.

47. Note dated 8 August 1912, ibid.

48. Note dated 14 Aug. 1912, ibid.

49. Note dated 26 August 1912, ibid.

50. Letter dated 1 September 1912, ibid. Charles Garvice was a writer whose published work included novels with titles such as *With All Her Heart*, *Linked by Fate*, *She Loved Him*, and *A Wilful Maid*. He also wrote under the name Caroline Hart.

51. Letter dated 22 October 1912, ibid.

52. J. W. Lambert and Michael Ratcliffe, *The Bodley Head 1887–1987* (London: The Bodley Head, 1987), 147.

53. Letter dated 12 February 1912, in John Lane, 42.2, The Harry Ransom Humanities Research Center, University of Texas at Austin.

54. Undated letter, ibid.

55. Letter dated 23 July 1913, ibid.

56. Letter dated 25 July 1913, ibid.

57. Letter dated 14 July 1913, ibid. Aunt Augusta had died in 1900, but Aunt Tom was still living in Devonshire.

58. Letter dated 10 September 1913, ibid.

CHAPTER 6

1. 'Dogged', *St Paul's* (18 February 1899), 206; repr. Saki, *Stories 2*, selected and introduced by Peter Haining (London: Everyman, 1983), 1.

2. The child who in 'Sredni Vashtar' is not expected to live to adulthood. His name may have been suggested by that of the 'hapless boy in whose person the Hohenstauffen line came to a tragic and piteous end' when he was executed by a mechanical device that anticipated the Guillotine, as reported by Munro from Paris. See *Morning Post* (20 March 1907), 3. This Conradin, the son of Conrad IV, was born in 1252 and beheaded in 1268.

3. 'Dogged', *Stories 2*, 1.

4. Ibid. 2.

5. Ibid.

6. Walter Allen, *The Short Story in English* (Oxford: Clarendon, 1981), 86.

7. See Armine Kotin Mortimer, 'Second Stories', in Susan Lohafer and Jo Ellyn Clarey (eds.) *Short Story Theory at a Crossroads* (Baton Rouge: Louisiana State University Press, 1989), 277.

8. Lambert and Ratcliffe, *Bodley Head*, 87, 146. Though J. W. (Jack) Lambert, a journalist who wrote for the *Sunday Times*, knew Munro well, and was to write an introduction to the *Bodley Head Saki*, some of his recollections were evidently less than accurate, or were transmitted less than accurately. *The Bodley Head 1887–1984*, which describes Munro condescendingly as a 'saddened homosexual with a gift for a turn of phrase', suggests that he was a poet. His published poetry is strictly comic and satirical verse. Lambert and Ratcliffe, 91, 147. Like Lambert, Maurice Baring refers to Munro as a Corporal in his introduction to *Bassington*, and so does Lord Charnwood in his introduction to *William* in *Complete Novels and Plays*, probably because Lance Sergeant was an appointment rather than a rank. See introduction, *Bassington*, 10, and introduction, *William*, 149.

9. Lambert and Ratcliffe, *Bodley Head*, 146–7.

10. Richard Harter Fogle discusses the character of Lady Carlotta in 'Saki and Wodehouse', in Joseph M. Flora (ed.), *The English Short Story, 1880–1945: A Critical History* (Boston: Twayne, 1985), 90–2.

11. Miriam Quen Cheikin, 'Practical Jokes as a Clue to Comedy', *English Literature in Transition*, 21 (1978), 122.

12. Cheikin, 'Practical Jokes as a Clue to Comedy', 123.

13. Fogle, 'Saki and Wodehouse', 84.

14. Simon Stern, 'Saki's Attitude', *GLQ: A Journal of Lesbian and Gay Studies*, 13 (1994), 282.

15. Peter Raby, 'A Weekend in The Country: Coward, Wilde and Saki', in John Kaplan and Sheila Stowell (eds.), *Look Back in Pleasure: Noël Coward Reconsidered*, 137.

16. Robert Drake, 'The Sauce for the Asparagus: A Reappraisal of Saki', in John Hadfield (ed.), *The Saturday Book 20* (London: Hutchinson, 1960), 61–73.

17. 'Nautch' is an Anglicization of the Hindu word 'nach', meaning 'dance'. Nautch girls were professional dancers and singers who became popular among soldiers and other colonists in India in the eighteenth and nineteenth centuries. A comic opera, *The Nautch-Girl*, by George Dance and Frank Desprez, was performed by the D'Oyly Carte Company at the Savoy Theatre in 1891–2.

18. A. A. Milne, introduction to *The Chronicles of Clovis*, Uniform Edition (London: Bodley Head, 1926), p. xi.

19. Milne, introduction, *The Chronicles of Clovis*, p. xi.

20. S. B. Mais, *Books and Their Writers* (London: Grant Richards, 1920), 314.

21. Ibid.

22. Ibid. 317.

23. Ibid. 329.

24. William York Tindall, *Forces in British Literature: 1885–1946* (New York: Knopf, 1947), 136–7.

25. Gillen, *H. H. Munro*, 65–6.

26. Robert Drake, 'Saki: Some Problems and a Bibliography', *English Literature in Transition (1880–1920*, 5/1 (1962), 6–26 at 9.

27. Gillen, *H. H. Munro*, 47.

28. First seen in the US in 'Extricating Young Gussie', *Saturday Evening Post* (18 September 1915) and in Britain in *Strand* (January 1916). The story was collected in *The Man with Two Left Feet and Other Stories* (London: Methuen, 1917), 25–54.

29. Referred to by Will Self as 'screaming queenies', introduction, Saki, *The Unrest Cure*, p. xvi.

30. John Batchelor, *The Edwardian Novelists* (London: Duckworth, 1982).

31. E. F. Benson, *The Babe, BA: Being the Uneventful History of a Gentleman at the University of Cambridge* (London: G. P. Putnam's Sons, 1897), 30.

32. See e.g. Benson, *Babe*, 305.

33. Ibid. 30.

34. The *OED* defines a fusee or fuzee as a light musket or fire-lock. Here it might possibly be a misprint for fuse.

35. Oscar Wilde, *The Picture of Dorian Gray*, ed. David Crystal and Derek Strange (Harmondsworth, Penguin, 1992), 30.

36. Oscar Wilde, *A Woman of No Importance*, ed. Ian Small (London: A &C Black; New York: W. W. Norton, 1993), 65.

CHAPTER 7

1. Quoted in the introduction.

2. This story, 'Sredni Vashtar', is discussed in more detail elsewhere.

3. Nancy Mitford's Linda Radlett makes a similar distinction. She describes the garden of her mother-in-law, Lady Kroesig, an example of all she finds worst in bourgeois suburban taste, as a 'riot of sterility'. See *The Pursuit of Love*, 91–2.

4. The story does not appear in any of the collections published in Saki's lifetime or immediately afterwards, nor in the Penguin *Complete Saki*, but it was reprinted with a short commentary in James R. Thrane, 'Two New Stories by "Saki" with an Introduction', *Modern Fiction Studies*, 19/2 (Summer, 1973), 139–51 (the other story was 'A Sacrifice to Necessity') and in Langguth, 287–92.

5. Gillen, *H. H. Munro*, 102.

6. Grahame's writing was not always whimsical. *The Golden Age* (1895) and *Dream Days* (1898) could have provided Saki with a model for representing the impervious egocentricity of children.

7. Gillen, *H. H. Munro*, 83.

8. Kenneth Grahame, *The Wind in the Willows* (New York, 1917), 151–7.

9. Rudyard Kipling, *Puck of Pook's Hill* (1906), p. x (Kipling's italics).

10. Batchelor, *Edwardian Novelists*, 10.

11. Ibid.

12. Spears, *Satiric Art*, 51–2.

13. The Reverend Harry Jones, *East and West London* (London, 1875), 130.

14. Ibid. 129–30.

15. Drake considers the ways in which Saki characters deprecate the important and exult the trivial in his 'The Sauce for the Asparagus', *The Saturday Book*, 63.

16. See *English Literature in Transition*, 9 (1966), 33–7.

17. Philip Stevick, 'Saki's Beasts', ibid. 37.

18. *The Ruling Passion: British Colonial Allegory and The Paradox of Homosexual Desire* (Durham, NC Duke University Press, 1995), 213.

19. The dandies are not truly like either Dionysus or his worshippers, since they neither generate nor experience a sublimation of self in communal identity—far from it.

20. Drake, 'Saki: Some Problems and a Bibliography', 9.

21. Ellen Moers, *Dandies from Brummell to Beerbohm* (New York: Viking, 1960), 294.

22. Joseph S. Salemi, 'An Asp Lurking in an Apple-Charlotte: Animal Violence in Saki's The Chronicles of Clovis', *Studies in Short Fiction*, 26/4 (Fall 1989), 429.

23. Robert Drake, 'Saki's Ironic Stories', *Texas Studies in Literature and Language*, 5/3 (Autumn 1963), 285–6.

24. See Drake, 'Saki's Ironic Stories', 374–80.

25. Drake, 'Sauce for the Asparagus', *Saturday Book*, 63.

26. Ibid. 70.

27. For a reprint of the original version, see *Saki Short Stories 2*, 83–90.

28. Drake, 'Saki's Ironic Stories', 386–7.

29. 'The Almanack' was published in the *Morning Post* on 17 July 1913 but not collected in *Toys* or *Square Egg*. It is reprinted in Haining, *Saki Stories 2*, 78–83, hereafter *Stories 2*.

30. Drake, 'Saki: Some Problems and a Bibliography', 10.

31. Brian Gibson, 'Saki's Dependent Dissidence: Exploring "The East Wing"', *English Language Notes* 42/3 (March 2005), 40.

32. V. S. Pritchett, 'The Performing Lynx', *New Statesman* (5 January 1957), 18.

33. Ibid. 18.

34. V. S. Pritchett, 'Saki', *New Statesman* (1 November 1963), 614.

35. *The Complete Short Stories of 'Saki' (H. H. Munro)* (London, Bodley Head, 1948), 713–18. Before publication of Gibson's article, the story was also reprinted in pamphlet form in Saki, *'John Bull's Christmas Tree' and 'The East Wing'*, ed. Adam Newell (London: The Sangrail Press, 2001), 6–14.

36. Gibson, 'Saki's Dependent Dissidence', 40.

37. Ibid. 41.

38. John Daniel Stahl, 'Saki's Enfant Terrible in "The Open Window"', *Language Quarterly*, 15/3–4 (Spring–Summer 1977), 6.

39. See Janet Overmyer, 'Turn Down an Empty Glass', *Texas Quarterly*, 3 (Autumn 1961), 170.

40. *Bystander* (31 July 1912), 230.

41. James Elroy Flecker, 'The Golden Journey to Samarkand', *The Golden Journey to Samarkand* (London, 1913), 5–6.

42. Ibid. 7.

CHAPTER 8

1. *Times Literary Supplement* (1 August 2003), 13.

2. 'Saki', *Bodleian*, III/33 (December 1911), 330–1.

3. Also in the Middle Temple at the time, in Library Chambers, 2 Plowden Building, was a Scottish barrister, John Buchan.

4. Hector Munro, *Mrs Elmsley* (London: Constable, 1911), 55.

5. Introduction to the novels, *The Complete Novels and Plays of Saki* (London: The Bodley Head, 1933), 3.

6. See J. M. Barrie, 'Peter Pan in Kensington Gardens', section of *The Little White Bird* (London: Hodder & Stoughton, 1902), repr. as Peter Pan in Kensington Gardens (London: Hodder & Stoughton, 1906); *Peter Pan: The Boy Who Would Not Grow Up* (play) (London, 1904; play script published London: Hodder & Stoughton, 1928), and *Peter and Wendy* (later *Peter Pan*) (London: Hodder & Stoughton, 1911).

7. For the argument about the public school system producing the *puer aeternus*, see Jeffrey Richards, 'Passing the Love of Women: Manly Love and Victorian Society', in J. A. Mangan and James Walvin (eds.), *Manliness and Morality: Middle-Class Masculinity in Britain and America 1800–1940* (Manchester: Manchester University Press, 1987), 92–122.

8. Maryann McGuire, *Milton's Puritan Masque* (Athens, Ga.: University of Georgia Press, 1983), 82.

9. David Trotter, *The English Novel in History: 1895–1920* (London: Routledge, 1993).

10. Ibid. 57.

11. See Bristow, *Empire Boys*, 216.

12. George James Spears, *The Satire of Saki: A Study of the Satiric Art of Hector H. Munro* (New York: Exposition, 1963), 58.

13. Spears, *Satiric Art*, 80.

14. Gillen, *H. H. Munro*, 95.

15. Evelyn Waugh, introduction, Saki, *The Unbearable Bassington* (London, 1947), p. v.

16. Ibid. v–vi.

17. Ibid. viii.

18. Trotter, *English Novel in History*, 57.

19. Described in Ch. 4.

20. Jonathan Rutherford, *Forever England: Reflections on Race, Masculinity and Empire* (London: Lawrence & Wishart, 1997), p. x.

21. Waugh, introduction, *Bassington*, p. v.

22. Ibid. viii.

CHAPTER 9

1. John Lane, 42.2, The Harry Ransom Humanities Research Center, University of Texas, Austin.

2. Coward, introduction, *Penguin Complete Saki*, p. xiii.

3. Ibid. xi.

4. Ibid. xii.

5. Ibid. xiii.

6. Anticipated by H. G. Wells, *The War in the Air* and *The World Set Free*.

7. Lorene M. Birden, 'Saki's "A Matter of Sentiment" ', *Explicator* 56/4 (Summer 1998), 201–4.

8. In the *Westminster Gazette* 37/5631 (3 June 1911); repr. in *The Chronicles of Clovis* the following year.

9. Birden, 'A Matter of Sentiment', 202.

10. Of July 1870 to May 1871.

11. Birden, 'A Matter of Sentiment', 201.

12. Ibid. 202.

13. Ibid. 202–3.

14. Ibid. 204.

15. For some reason, whitebait and reproach seem to be associated in Saki's mind. See 'Reginald at the Carlton', *Reginald*, 65.

16. Lane, *Ruling* Passion, 218–19.

17. Baring, Introduction, *Complete Novels and Plays*, 4.

18. Leland, *Johnnykin*, 160–1. Discussed in Ch. 1.

19. See Bristow, *Empire Boys*, 181–7.

20. See his piece on military-style dress in the *Morning Post* of 29 August 1905; repr. Munro, 78–9.

21. A story told as both a play and a film after Saki's lifetime.

22. See Robert Baden-Powell, *Scouting for Boys*, first published fortnightly in six pamphlets and subsequent reissued in book form (London: Windsor House, 1908).

23. Michael Rosenthal, *The Character Factory: Baden Powell and the Origins of the Boy Scout Movement* (London: Collins, 1986), 60 (Bristow's note).

24. Bristow, *Empire Boys*, 175.

25. See Ch. 2, above.

26. Spears, *Satiric Art*, 87–8.

27. E. V. Lucas collection, The Harry Ransom Humanities Research Center, University of Texas at Austin.

CHAPTER 10

1. G. K. Chesterton, introduction, *The Toys of Peace and Other Papers*, Uniform Edition (London: The Bodley Head, 1926), p. xii.

2. This is a mistake or misprint, unless Spikesman means the afternoon and evening of 1 August, leading to the early hours of 2 August, which was a Sunday.

3. Saki illustrates the consequences of teaching the rules of German grammar in 'Tobermory', *Clovis*, 29–44, in which an elephant tramples to death someone allegedly trying to teach it irregular German verbs.

4. Ethel Munro gives January 1915, but adds that he only had a few days' leave, and the letter to Charlie quoted by Langguth is dated 13 February 1915.

5. Later in the possession of Felicia Munro's younger sister, Juniper, who became Mrs P. A. G. Bryan, and shown to Langguth in the late 1970s.

6. 'Saki', *Bodleian*, III 33 (December 1911), 350.

7. Dornford Yates, *Lower than Vermin* (London: Ward Lock, 1950), p. iii.

8. J. M. Greenslade MM, 'The Beginning', in Major Christopher Stone DSO MC, *A History of the 22nd (Service) Battalion Royal Fusiliers* (Kensington) (privately printed for the Old Comrades Association of the Battalion, 1923); repr. (Uckfield: The Naval and Military Press, 2000), 64.

9. Ibid. 40.

10. 'Death of Mr H. H. Munro. Lance-Sergeant "Saki"', obituary, *Morning Post* (25 November 1916), 4.

SELECT BIBLIOGRAPHY

WORKS BY SAKI

'Dogged', *St Paul's Magazine* (18 February 1899).

The Athenaeum, 3779 (31 March 1900), 398. Letter signed 'H. H. Munro'.

The Athenaeum, 3781 (14 April 1900), 466. Letter headed 'The Religion of the Slavs', signed 'H. H. Munro'.

The Rise of the Russian Empire. London: Grant Richards, 1900.

John Bull's Christmas Tree', in *'The House' Annual*. London: Gale & Polden, 1902.

The Westminster Alice. London: The Westminster Gazette, 1902.

Reginald. London: Methuen, 1904.

Morning Post (15, 17 January, 5 June 1906). Writing as foreign correspondent.

Reginald in Russia. London: Methuen, 1910.

The Chronicles of Clovis. London: John Lane, The Bodley Head, 1911.

The Bodleian: A Journal of Books at the Bodley Head, III/3 (December 1911), 330–1. Interview.

The Unbearable Bassington. London: John Lane, The Bodley Head, 1912.

'The Holy War', *Morning Post* (5 May 1913).

'A Sacrifice to Necessity', *Morning Post* (15 October 1913).

When William Came: A Story of London under the Hohenzollerns. London: John Lane, The Bodley Head, 1913.

Beasts and Super-Beasts. London: John Lane, The Bodley Head, 1914.

'The East Wing', in *Lucas' Annual*. New York: Macmillan, 1914.

The Morning Post (25 November 1916), 4. Obituary.

The Westminster Gazette (24 November 1916), 5. Obituary.

The Toys of Peace and Other Papers. London: John Lane, The Bodley Head, 1919.

The Square Egg and Other Sketches. London: John Lane, The Bodley Head, 1924.

Reginald and *Reginald in Russia*, Uniform Edition. London: John Lane, The Bodley Head, 1926.

The Chronicles of Clovis, Uniform Edition. London: John Lane, The Bodley Head, 1926.

Beasts and Super-Beasts, Uniform Edition. London: John Lane, The Bodley Head, 1926.

When William Came: A Story of London Under the Hohenzollerns, Uniform Edition. London: John Lane, The Bodley Head, 1926.

The Toys of Peace and Other Papers, Uniform Edition. London: John Lane, The Bodley Head, 1926.

The Short Stories of Saki. Uniform Edition. London: John Lane, Bodley Head, 1930.

The Complete Novels and Plays of Saki, Uniform Edition. London: John Lane, Bodley Head, 1933.

The Miracle Merchant, in Alice Gerstenberg (ed.), *One-Act Plays for Stage and Study*. New York: Samuel French, 1934.

The Unbearable Bassington, Uniform Edition. London: John Lane, The Bodley Head, 1947.

The Bodley Head Saki, selected and introduced by J. W. Lambert. London: The Bodley Head, 1963.

Miss Pell is Missing. London: Samuel French, 1963. Adaptation by Leonard Gershe of Saki's work.

'The Holy War' and 'A Sacrifice to Necessity'; repr. in James R. Thrane, 'Two New Stories by "Saki" (H. H. Munro)', *Modern Fiction Studies*, 19/2 (Summer 1973).

The Complete Saki. Harmondsworth: Penguin, 1982.

Saki Short Stories 2, Everyman Library, selected and introduced by Peter Haining. London: Dent, 1983.

'John Bull's Christmas' and 'The East Wing', selected and introduced by Adam Newell. London: The Sangrail Press, 2001.

OTHER WORKS CITED

Alderman, Geoffrey, *The Jewish Community in British Politics*. Oxford: Clarendon, 1983.

Allen, Walter, *The Short Story in English*. Oxford: Clarendon, 1981.

Anon., 'Extract of a letter from a Gentleman to his friend at Calcutta, dated on board the Ship Shaw Ardasier, off Saumur Island, Dec 23 1792', *The Gentleman's Magazine*, July 1793, 671.

_____ Letter printed in *The Scots Magazine*, July 1793, 360.

Anstey, F., *The Long Retrospect*. London: Oxford University Press, 1936.

Baden-Powell, Robert, *Scouting for Boys: A Handbook for Instruction in Good Citizenship* (1908); repr. ed. Elleke Boehmer. Oxford: Oxford University Press, 2004.

Balfour, The Right Hon. Arthur James, MP, *Decadence: Henry Sidwick Memorial Lecture*. Cambridge: Cambridge University Press, 1908.

Ballantyne, R. M., *Coral Island* (1858); repr. London: Bloomsbury, 1994.

Baring, Maurice, introduction. *The Unbearable Bassington, The Complete Novels and Plays of Saki* (H. H. Munro). London: The Bodley Head, 1933, 3–19.

Barrie, J. M., 'Peter Pan in Kensington Gardens', *The Little White Bird* (London, 1902).

——— *Peter Pan: The Boy Who Would Not Grow Up* (London, 1904).

——— *Peter and Wendy* (later *Peter Pan*) (London, 1911); repr. London: Hamlyn, 1989.

Batchelor, John, *The Edwardian Novelists*. London: Duckworth, 1982.

Beerbohm, Max, *Zuleika Dobson* (1911); repr. New Haven: Yale University Press, 1985.

Benson, E. F., *The Babe, BA: Being the Uneventful History of a Gentleman at the University of Cambridge*. London: G. P. Putnam's Sons, 1897.

Birden, Lorene M., 'Saki's "A Matter of Sentiment"', *Explicator*, 56/4 (Summer 1998), 201–4.

Blackwood, Algernon, *The Empty House and Other Ghost Stories* (1906); repr. London: Edward Nash, 1930.

Braddon, Mary Elizabeth, *Lady Audley's Secret* (1862); repr. Oxford: Oxford University Press, 1998.

Bristow, Joseph, *Empire Boys: Adventures in a Man's World*, Reading Popular Fiction Series. London: Harper Collins, 1991.

Buchan, John, *The Thirty-Nine Steps* (1915); repr. London: Chatto & Windus, 1985.

Burnet, Frances Hodgson, *The Head of the House of Coome*. London: Heineman, 1922.

——— *Robin*. London: Heineman, 1922.

Carey, Tim, *Mountjoy: The Story of a Prison*. Wilton, Cork: Collins, 2000.

Carroll, Lewis, *Alice's Adventures in Wonderland* (1865); *Through the Looking Glass, and What Alice Found There* (1871); *The Annotated Alice*, ed. Martin Gardner. Harmondsworth: Penguin, rev. edn. 2001.

Charnwood, Lord, introduction, *Complete Novels and Plays of Saki*. London: The Bodley Head, 1933.

Cheikin, Miriam Quen, 'Practical Jokes as a Clue to Comedy', *English Literature in Transition*, 21 (1978), 121–33.

Chesterton, G. K., introduction, *The Toys of Peace and Other Papers*. London: The Bodley Head, 1926.

Childers, Robert Erskine, *The Riddle of the Sands* (1903); repr. London: Dent, 1970.

Collins, Wilkie, *The Woman in White* (1859–60); repr. Oxford: Oxford University Press, 1980.

Coward, Noel, introduction (1967), *The Complete Saki*. Harmondsworth: Penguin, 1982.

Darwin, Charles, *On the Origin of Species by Means of Natural Selection* (1859); repr. London: Faber & Faber, 1979.

Drake, Robert, 'The Sauce for the Asparagus: A Reappraisal of Saki', in John Hadfield (ed.), *The Saturday Book* 20. London: Hutchinson, 1960, 61–73.

―― 'Some Problems and a Bibliography', *English Literature in Transition 1880–1920*, 5/1 (1962), 6–26.

―― 'Saki's Ironic Stories', *Texas Studies in Literature and Language*, 5/3 (Autumn 1963), 374–88.

Easthope, Antony, *Englishness and National Culture*. London: Routledge, 1999.

Empson, William, *Some Versions of Pastoral*. London: Chatto & Windus, 1935.

Evelyn Waugh, introduction, Saki, *The Unbearable Bassington*. London: The Bodley Head, 1947.

Farrar, Revd Frederick William, *Eric, Or Little By Little: A Tale of Roslyn School*. Edinburgh: Adam & Charles Black, 1858.

Firbank, Ronald, *Odette: A Fairy Tale for Weary People* (1905); *Vainglory* (1915); *Inclinations* (1916); *Valmouth: A Romantic Novel* (1919) in *The Complete Ronald Firbank*. London: Gerald Duckworth, 1961.

Flecker, James Elroy, 'The Golden Journey to Samarkand', *The Golden Journey to Samarkand*. London: Max Goschen, 1913.

Fogle, Richard Harter, 'Saki and Wodehouse', in Joseph M. Flora (ed.), *The English Short Story, 1880–1945: A Critical History*. Boston: Twayne, 1985, 83–111.

Garnett, Edward, 'Early Russian History', *The Bookman* (August 1900), 155.

Gerber, H. E., 'H. H. Munro (Saki)', *English Literature in Transition 1880–1920*, 11 (1968), 54–5.

Gervais, David, *Literary Englands: Versions of 'Englishness' in Modern Writing*. Cambridge: Cambridge University Press, 1993.

Gibson, Brian, 'Saki's Dependent Dissidence: Exploring "The West Wing"', *English Language Notes*, 42/3 (March, 2005), 39–52.

Giles, Judy, and Middleton, Tim (eds.), *Writing Englishness 1900 to 1950: An Introductory Sourcebook on National Identity*. London: Routledge, 1995.

Gillen, Charles H., *H. H. Munro (Saki)*. New York: Twayne, 1969.

Grahame, Kenneth, *The Golden Age* (1895); *Dream Days* (1898); repr. in *The Golden Age* and *Dream Days*. London: The Bodley Head, 1962.

Greene, Graham, Letter to the *Spectator* (20 June 1952), 811.

Greenstein, Tony, 'Zionism's Attitude to Anti-Semitism', *Return* (London, March 1989), <http://www.codoh.com/zionweb/ziondark/zionsym1.html>, accessed 17 April 2007.

Hadfield, John (ed.), *The Saturday Book* 20. London: Hutchinson, 1960.

Hawkin, Martin, *When Adolf Came*. London: 1943.

Henty, G. A., *Friends Though Divided: A Tale of the Civil War* (1883); repr. London: Griffith Farren Browne, 1900.

Hindle, Wilfred, *The Morning Post 1772–1937: Portrait of a Newspaper*. London: Routledge, 1937.

Hoare, Philip, *Oscar Wilde's Last Stand: Decadence, Conspiracy, and the Most Outrageous Trial of the Century*. New York: Arcade, 1997.

James, M. R., *Ghost Stories of an Antiquary*. London: Edward Arnold, 1904.

Jones, Revd Harry, *East and West London*. London: Smith & Elder, 1875.

Kipling, Rudyard, *Puck of Pook's Hill*. London: Macmillan, 1906.

Lambert, J. W., introduction, *The Bodley Head Saki*. London: Bodley Head, 1963.

—— and Ratcliffe, Michael, *The Bodley Head 1887–1987*. London: The Bodley Head, 1987.

Lane, Christopher, 'The Unrest Cure According to Lawrence, Saki, and Lewis', *Modernism/Modernity*, 11/4 (November 2004), 769–96.

Lane, Christopher, *Ruling Passion: British Colonial Allegory and the Paradox of Homosexual Desire*. Durham, NC: Duke University Press, 1995.

Langguth, A. J., *Saki: A Life of Hector Hugh Munro*, with six stories never before collected. London: Hamish Hamilton; New York: Simon & Schuster, 1981.

Lawrence, D. H., *England, My England* (1915); repr. London: Dodo, 2005.

Le Queux, The *Invasion of 1910: With a Full Account of the Siege of London*. London: Eveleigh Nash, 1906.

Leland, Charles G., *Johnnykin and the Goblin*. London: Macmillan, 1877.

McGuire, Maryann, *Milton's Puritan Masque*. Athens, Ga.: University of Georgia Press, 1983. Mais, S. P. B., *Books and their Writers*. New York: Dodd Mead, 1920.

—— 'The Humour of Saki', ibid.

May, J. Lewis, *John Lane and the Nineties*. London: John Lane, The Bodley Head, 1936.

Milne, A. A., introduction, *The Chronicles of Clovis*, Uniform Edition. London: The Bodley Head, 1926.

—— *The Wind in the Willows* (1917); repr. Oxford: Oxford University Press, 1983.

Milroy, Sean, *Memories of Mountjoy*. Dublin: Maunsell, 1917.

Mitford, Nancy, *Love in a Cold Climate*. London: Hamish Hamilton, 1949; repr. Harmondsworth: Penguin, 1995.

—— *Don't Tell Alfred*. London: Hamish Hamilton, 1960; repr. Harmondsworth, Penguin, 1980.

—— *The Pursuit of Love*. London: Hamish Hamilton, 1945; repr. Harmondsworth: Penguin, 1994.

Moers, Ellen, *The Dandy: Brummell to Beerbohm*. New York: Viking, 1960.

Morley, Christopher, introduction, *The Complete Short Stories of Saki*. London: John Lane, The Bodley Head, 1930.

Mortimer, Armine Kotin, 'Second Stories', in Susan Lohafer and Jo Ellyn Clarey (eds.), *Short Story Theory at a Crossroads*. Baton Rouge: Louisiana State University Press, 1989, 277–300.

Munro, Ethel M., 'Biography of Saki', *The Square Egg*. London: John Lane, The Bodley Head, 1924, 3–120.

—— Letter to the *Spectator* (13 June 1952), 780.

—— Letter to the *Spectator* (27 June 1952), 856.

Nevinson, H. W., introduction, *Beasts and Super-Beasts*. London: The Bodley Head, 1926.

—— *More Changes, More Chances*. London: Nisbet, 1925.

Onions, Oliver, *Widdershins* (1911); repr. London: Penguin, 1939.

Orczy, Baroness E., *The Scarlet Pimpernel* (1905); repr. London: Hodder & Stoughton, 1950.

Overmyer, Janet, 'Turn Down an Empty Glass', *Texas Quarterly*, 3 (Autumn 1964).

Pritchett, V. S., 'The Performing Lynx', *New Statesman* (5 January 1957), 18–19.

—— 'Saki', *New Statesman* (1 November 1963), 614–15.

Raby, Peter, 'A Weekend in the Country: Coward, Wilde and Saki', in John Kaplan and Sheila Stowell (eds.), *Look Back in Pleasure: Noël Coward Reconsidered*. London: Methuen, 2000.

Reynolds, Rothay, 'A Memoir of H. H. Munro', in Saki, *The Toys of Peace*. London: John Lane, The Bodley Head, 1919.

Richards, Jeffrey, 'Passing the Love of Women: Manly Love and Victorian Society', in J. A. Mangan and James Walvin (eds.), *Manliness and Morality: Middle-Class Masculinity in Britain and America 1800–1940*. Manchester: Manchester University Press, 1987, 92–122.

Rutherford, Jonathan, *Forever England: Reflections on Race, Masculinity and Empire*. London: Lawrence & Wishart, 1997.

Salemi, Joseph S., 'An Asp Lurking in an Apple-Charlotte: Animal Violence in Saki's *The Chronicles of Clovis*', *Studies in Short Fiction*, 26/4 (Fall 1989), 423–30.

Self, Will, introduction, *The Unrest Cure and Other Beastly Stories*. London: Prion, 2001.

Shaw, Valerie, *The Short Story: A Critical Introduction*. Harlow: Longman, 1983.

Sinfield, Alan, *Cultural Politics—Queer Reading*. London: Routledge, 1994.

Spears, George James, *The Satire of Saki: A Study of the Satiric Art of H. H. Munro*. New York: Exposition, 1963.

Spender, J. A., foreword, Saki, *The Westminster Alice, Complete Novels and Plays of Saki*. London: The Bodley Head, 1933.

Squire, J. C., introduction, *The Complete Novels and Plays of Saki*. London: The Bodley Head, 1933.

Stahl, John Daniel, 'Saki's Enfant Terrible in "The Open Window"', *Language Quarterly*, 15/3–4 (Spring–Summer 1977), 5–8.

Stephens, James, *The Crock of Gold*. London: Macmillan, 1912.

Stern, Simon, 'Saki's Attitude', *GLQ: A Journal of Lesbian and Gay Studies*, 1/3 (1994), 275–98.

Stevenson, Robert Louis, *Treasure Island*. Harmondsworth: Penguin, 1994.

Stevick, Philip, 'Saki's Beasts', *English Literature in Transition*, 9 (1966), 33–7.

Stone, Christopher, *From Vimy Bridge to the Rhine: The Great War Letters of Christopher Stone*, eds. G.D. Sheffield and G.I.S. Inglis. Marlborough: Crowood, 1989.

Summers, Montague, *The Galanty Show*. London: Cecil Woolf, 1980.

Symonds, John Addington 'Our Life in the Swiss Highlands', *The Fortnightly Review* (July 1878), 74–87.

Taylor, Anthony, 'London Bombs and Alien Panics', *Chartist* (November 2005), <http://www.chartist.org.uk/articles/econsoc/novo5taylor.htm>, accessed 17 April 2007.

Thrane, James R., 'Two New Stories by "Saki" (H. H. Munro)', *Modern Fiction Studies*, 19/2 (Summer 1973), 139–51.

Tindall, William York, *Forces in British Literature: 1885–1946*. New York: Knopf, 1947.

Toye, Francis, *For What We Have Received*. London: Heinemann, 1950.

Travers, Ben, *Vale of Laughter: An Autobiography*. London: Geoffrey Bles, 1957.

—— *A-Sitting on a Gate*. London: W. H. Allen, 1978.

Trotter, David, *The English Novel in History: 1895–1920*. London: Routledge, 1993.

Walpole, Hugh, preface, Saki, *Reginald* and *Reginald in Russia*. London: The Bodley Head, 1926.

Waugh, Evelyn, *A Handful of Dust*. London: Chapman & Hall, 1934.

Wilde, Oscar, *Lady Windermere's Fan; Salomé; A Woman of no Importance; An Ideal Husband; The Importance of Being Earnest*, ed. Peter Raby. Oxford: Oxford University Press, 1995.

—— *The Picture of Dorian Gray*; repr. Oxford: Oxford University Press, 1981.

Wilson, Keith M., *A Study in the History and Politics of* The Morning Post *1905–1926*. Lewiston, NY, Edwin Mellen, 1990.

Wodehouse, P. G., *The Little Nugget*. London: Methuen, 1913.

—— *The Man with Two Left Feet and Other Stories*. London: Barrie & Jenkyns, 1917.

—— *The Swoop! Or How Clarence Saved England: A Tale of the Great Invasion*. London: Alston Rivers, 1909.

Yates, Dornford, *Lower than Vermin*. London: Ward Lock, 1950.

INDEX